HANSON

True Faith and Allegiance

True Faith and Allegiance

The Burden of Military Ethics

JAMES H. TONER

THE UNIVERSITY PRESS OF KENTUCKY

Scholarly publisher for the Commonwealth,
serving Bellarmine College, Berea College, Centre
College of Kentucky, Eastern Kentucky University,
The Filson Club, Georgetown College, Kentucky
Historical Society, Kentucky State University,
Morehead State University, Murray State University,
Northern Kentucky University, Transylvania University,
University of Kentucky, University of Louisville,
and Western Kentucky University.

Editorial and Sales Offices: Lexington, Kentucky 40508-4008

Toner, James Hugh, 1946-
    True faith and allegiance : the burden of military ethics / James
H. Toner.
        p.   cm.
    Includes bibliographical references and index.
    ISBN 0-8131-1881-6 (alk. paper) :
    1. Military ethics.   2. Civil-military relations—United States.
I. Title.
U22.T65   1995
174'.9355—dc20   94-18472

To James Blaise Toner

The Lord bless you and keep you!
The Lord let his face shine upon you, and be gracious to you!
The Lord look upon you kindly and give you peace!
(Numbers 6:24-26)

I (full name) do solemnly swear that I will support and defend the Constitution of the United States against all enemies, foreign and domestic; that I will bear true faith and allegiance to the same; and that I will obey the orders of the President of the United States and the orders of the officers appointed over me, according to regulations and the Uniform Code of Military Justice. So help me God.

—Enlisted Oath of Office

I (full name) do solemnly swear that I will support and defend the Constitution of the United States against all enemies, foreign and domestic; that I will bear true faith and allegiance to the same, and that I take this obligation freely, without any mental reservation or purpose of evasion; and that I will well and faithfully discharge the duties of the office on which I am about to enter. So help me God.

—Officers' Oath of Office

Contents

Preface

As a political theorist, I have long been interested in international politics, national security studies, American government, political philosophy, ethics, theology, history, and literature. One field, I have found, comprises all of them: military ethics.

The term is not easy to define; in fact, my principal task in this book is to glue together "military" and "ethics." Such a task is impossible for pacifists because for them the military can hardly be ethical. It is equally impossible for bellecists, to whom war is the great adventure in which "all is fair." I address the book not to these extremes but to those who hate the things and thoughts of war but accept its necessity when the alternatives are greater evils.

Having taught military ethics to soldiers, to students at a military college, and to senior officers, I strongly believe that military ethics is a fascinating and vital field. Ethics itself is fascinating because it raises the timeless questions and inveigles us into the Great Conversation about what it means to be human and about which values ennoble us. It is vital because it deals with the greatest issues: life and death, honor and shame, courage and cowardice, virtue and vice. And the military must deal virtuously with one of the greatest vices: killing human beings.

My goal, then, is to help unite understanding of the military profession with the general field of ethics, for this book proceeds not only from the belief that soldiers *can* be moral, but from the conviction that soldiers *must* be moral.

On the practical level, this book attempts also to serve as a sourcebook for students and others interested in the congeries of topics and ideas subsumed under the heading "military ethics." The notes, bibliography, index, and most of Chapter 8 have been developed as guides to a substantial amount of material dealing with the field. Relevant articles, books, and films are referred to throughout so that, in addition to my views, the reader will have many other sources to consult.

Readers of the book will very rapidly note how much indebted I am to scores of thinkers who have preceded me. I have read, listened to, and talked with such scholars as Malham Wakin and Kenneth Wenker of the U.S. Air Force Academy, Anthony Hartle of the U.S. Military Academy, and Nicholas Fotion of Emory University. Guenter Lewy, formerly of the University of Massachusetts, William V. O'Brien of Georgetown, and Michael Walzer of Princeton are among those whom I met some years ago at a summer institute sponsored by the National Endowment for the Humanities; that experience changed much of the focus of my academic work and led to this book, among others.

I would never have been able to think through some of the problems in this book, let alone write it, without the advice, encouragement, collegiality, and friendship of many people at the Air War College of Air University at Maxwell Air Force Base in Montgomery, Alabama (one of five senior service schools, along with the National War College and the Industrial College of the Armed Forces, both in Washington, D.C.; the Army War College at Carlisle Barracks, Pennsylvania; and the Naval War College at Newport, Rhode Island). The Air War College—with its annual class of 250 lieutenant colonels and colonels from all the U.S. armed services, civilians selected from various government agencies, and forty or so international officers—has offered me teaching and research challenges and the constancy of purpose I only dreamed of before. Much as I miss teaching undergraduates, I thank Air University for the opportunities that institution has given me.

Scholars and friends encountered here include Grant Hammond (from Rhodes College), Bob Wendzel (from the University of Maine), Dave Sorenson (from Denison University), and Bob Jordan (from the University of New Orleans). They have come to the Air War College from all over the country to share their teaching and research interests. I have intellectually exploited them without mercy, seeking their advice and picking their brains. I am particularly grateful to Michael Boll (from San Jose State University), a man of vast learning and a great sense of humor who critically read my manuscript and offered wise counsel.

I wish I could hold any or all of these scholars responsible for my errors of fact or misjudgment, but I am solely responsible for the content of this book. It includes some very controversial statements, and my convictions are not always shared by the scholars whose names appear above. As grateful as I am to these friends and colleagues, I must state that the opinions in this book are mine alone.

Numerous officers at the Air War College, too, have helped me form my judgments about matters of military ethics. I particularly appreciate and deeply respect the views of Col. Bill Phillips, USAF (Ret.) and Col. Larry Carter, USAF. I could name scores of other officers with whom I have had occasion to talk at great length, but Colonel Phillips and Colonel Carter deserve special mention. If it is all right for a civilian to offer a salute, those two men just got mine.

This book does not, of course, carry the endorsement or express the official views of the United States government, the Air Force, Air University, or the Air War College.

I am very grateful to the staff of the University Press of Kentucky and to the two anonymous reviewers for their comments and criticisms. One was especially generous in providing advice, and I regret that I cannot acknowledge him or her by name.

Finally, I thank my family for all it has endured as their husband and father "grew up." Becky has been transplanted from Massachusetts to Georgia to Germany to Virginia to Indiana to Vermont to Alabama, each time making a home for us—sometimes under difficult circumstances. Little did we think, when we were married in Monson, Massachusetts, in 1969, that our best home in every way would be in Montgomery, Alabama. Without Becky, my lovely lady, there would be no book, no position at the Air War College, and very little of anything else that brings joy and meaning to my life.

As I write these words my mind often wanders to my son Chris, a U.S. Army lieutenant serving with the Second Infantry Division in Korea. My son Pat, in Panama with the U.S. Army National Guard as I write, has long been an avid reader and one who does not supinely accept the judgments of his philosophically importunate father. This book, I hope, will be grist for our talks, much too rare, but better every time. To my son Jamey, a high school junior who displays a remarkable talent for writing and debate, I dedicate the book as a token of my confidence in him.

If we are to make sense of our lives, we need to work. Genuine work—bringing order out of chaos—is, in a way, what ethics is all about. I think every major decision made is, at root, an ethical judgment. I know enough of myself to recognize that I still have much work to do in writing about ethics and in practicing better what I preach. I am reminded of the last sentence in Chapter 32 of *Moby-Dick*: "This whole book is but a draught—nay, but the draught of a draught. Oh, Time, Strength, Cash, and Patience!" Given modest amounts of those four desiderata—with a dash of increased wisdom—I hope to work again in this vineyard and to live, to think, to write, and to teach (how closely related they are!) better every time.

Introduction

The principal foundations of all states are good laws
and good arms; and there cannot be good laws where
there are not good arms.
—Machiavelli, *The Prince* (1513)

This book must overcome two main obstacles. The first is created by those, often connected with the far left of the political spectrum, who argue that military people have already renounced ethics by donning uniforms. The second is created by those, often connected with the far right of the political spectrum, who argue that military people should not be accountable to usual ethical standards because "all's fair in love and war." This book proceeds in the firm conviction that ethics in the military is possible, desirable, and necessary. It is probably best, at the outset, to describe first the vexations and then the values that shape and inform it.

I am disturbed by writers, such as George Bernard Shaw (1856-1950), who imperiously dismiss military professionalism. In 1909 Shaw wrote: "There can no longer be any question of the fact that military service produces moral imbecility." There *are* moral imbeciles in the military—as there are everywhere—but I do not believe that military service necessarily and invariably produces them.

I am troubled by American academic institutions that offer courses in "ethics" without, in many cases, having any reasonable moral standards (or sometimes even scholastic standards) themselves. For the last thirty years, however, the military has been a target of opportunity on many American campuses. These same institutions used to be able to dismiss faculty members for moral turpitude. As Irving Kristol points out, "Our universities don't know what moral turpitude is. But they are very busy devising courses in ethics, for themselves and everyone else. What can they be teaching in such courses? Well, they can teach why and how it is that an educated person should find it presumptuous to claim to know what moral turpitude is. Which is what they do. . . . [Academic ethics] is no longer committed to moral instruction or moral elevation. It is proudly 'value-free'—i.e., committed to radical, rationalist and supposedly scientific skepticism."[1]

There seems to be great difficulty in conducting discussions about ethics in the "academic" climate to be found on many campuses today. One no longer has principles, only biases. Ideas about duty are often regarded as old-fashioned; conversations seem to be exclusively about rights. Concepts derived from religious traditions are often dismissed as the property of cranks, even where astrological horoscopes and objects of the occult appear acceptable.

I am irritated by the sometimes very difficult prose of ethics textbooks. Most people seem to have a pretty fair sense of what is right and wrong, but the language of instruction seems to confuse, rather than to clarify, issues—perhaps because the content of many courses in ethics suggests that those courses themselves have no clear idea of right or wrong.[2]

I am upset by the American national attitude toward questions of ethics. The Wall Street Journal of 8 September 1987 front-paged this short news summary item: "Ethics are nice, but they can be a handicap, some [business] executives declare." And the media, Irving Kristol has pointed out, "refuse to go beyond the most sketchy and primitive codes of professional behavior, lest this impinge on their rights, as they perceive them, under the First Amendment."[3] It would be funny, if it weren't so sad, to see the media and business accusing each other of sleazy practices (in one instance, business correctly won when NBC admitted it had rigged the crash-and-burn scene of a General Motors truck).[4]

Finally, I am vexed by the explosion of materials on ethics, very few of which seem concerned with inculcating virtue or with elevating the lives of the students to whom they are addressed. One writer asserts that "schools are increasingly becoming emergency rooms of the emotions, devoted not only to developing minds but also to repairing hearts," perhaps because Americans are less inclined today to value sexual fidelity, lifelong marriage, and parenthood as worthwhile goals.[5] About fifteen years ago philosopher Alasdair MacIntyre pointed out that moral argument in the United States had been so corrupted that Americans could no longer reasonably say to one another, "You should do this or that" and then discuss the issue; instead, we would have to say, "I feel as though you should do this or that." MacIntyre talked about the moral *emotivism* that had arisen in the absence of moral conviction and generally recognized ethical standards. The concepts of virtue and duty, he said, had "gone away."

But there is also room for optimism in *True Faith and Allegiance*. Almost a quarter-century ago the British soldier-scholar Sir John Hackett, speaking at the U.S. Air Force Academy, said in part: "The major service of the military institution to the community of men it serves may well lie neither within the political sphere nor the functional. It could easily lie within the moral. The military institution is a mirror of its parent society, reflecting strengths and weaknesses. It can also be a well from which to draw refreshment for a body politic in need of it. . . . the highest service of the military to the state may well lie in the moral sphere."[6]

At Arlington National Cemetery, there is an inscription: "Not for fame or reward, not for place or rank, not lured by ambition or goaded by necessity, but in simple obedience to duty as they understood it, these men suffered all, sacrificed all, dared all, and died."[7] On a recent trip to Washington, D.C., I had my first chance to see the "Wall." A memorial to the thousands who died in the service of their country in Vietnam, the Wall is fittingly close to the Lincoln Memorial. How can anyone look at such a memorial, or the rows of crosses at Arlington, without at least momentarily thinking of duty, honor, and sacrifice? In a way, it was of this that Hackett had spoken: the military code and spirit can—and, I think, must—serve as "a well" from which our ethically beleaguered society may draw moral refreshment.

This is a profound irony: because the military's premier responsibility lies in killing or in preparing to kill designated enemies of the country, the well would appear to be "poisoned." But even Thomas Merton, noted for his pacifism, said that "where non-violent resistance is impossible, then violent resistance must be used rather than passive acquiescence. . . . Merely passive acquiescence in evil is in no sense to be dignified by the name of non-violence. It is a travesty of Christian meekness. It is purely and simply the sin of cowardice."[8]

The "true faith and allegiance" of the military ethic[9] rests on these three pillars of moral philosophy: first, recognition that evil exists and should be resisted, by force if necessary; second, acknowledgment of human duty, obligation, and responsibility; third, appreciation of virtue and of the attempt to inculcate it by word and deed.

An Army officer recently wrote: "We [in the military] must decide on and publish a definition of ethics that everyone can understand."[10] I think what Lt. Col. Douglas Martz meant was a definition that people would *accept*. That is no small order. The coincidence of what I term the pillars of "true faith and allegiance" (knowing that evil exists, understanding duty, and proselytizing for virtue) are the elements of moral philosophy which is another—probably better—term for ethics.

Military ethics is the study of honorable and shameful conduct in the armed services. The Arlington inscription testifies to honor; the names on the Wall testify to honor; what is in the mind and heart and soul of the military professional testifies to honor. But we study as well the reality of shame, defined by one dictionary as "the painful feeling arising from the consciousness of [having done] something dishonorable or improper." The subtitle of this book—"The Burden of Military Ethics"—reflects the recognition that professional soldiers bear the burden not only of past glories to emulate but also of past blunders of earlier soldiers, which they can resolve not to repeat but can never wholly eradicate. Against a backdrop of violence, they must adhere to the highest standards of personal and professional integrity, even as they pursue a life's work often little appreciated or understood by the civilians to and for whom the soldier is responsible.[11] There will always be ethical tension in the military because its primary purpose is *armed* service—occasionally carried on in circumstances seemingly hostile to the very idea of virtue.

Nevertheless, the professional military is one element of our American society that can help us to resurrect the American eagle; there are others that maintain the ancient ideals of wisdom, courage, temperance, and justice. Some American colleges and universities hold to high standards of academic achievement and of honorable personal conduct, still preserving the idea that education means character formation. Many scholars and writers still fight the good fight, not yet surrendering to the moral nihilism around them.[12] Many churches and synagogues hold true to their faith. In August 1993 hundreds of thousands of young people converged on Denver for the Pope's visit (some called it "Popestock" in opposition to the countercultural Woodstock of a previous generation) in a remarkable outpouring of spirituality and ecumenicism. If the 1990s have had David Koresh, they have also still had Mother Teresa. If there is much around us that is vicious, there is also much that is virtuous. Ethics can help us distinguish between them.

Many of the writers and teachers and soldiers and ministers quoted in this book would hold steadfast to the idea that the honorable person is one who tries throughout life to know and to do the virtuous thing. The man of honor, if he be entirely honest with himself, will admit to failure—perhaps even to grievous failure—but because he is inviolably fixed on true faith and allegiance to a sense of obligation outside his own skin, he returns to the paths of integrity. Character, in the end, is not about never failing; it is about never quitting in the task of finally knowing the right and consistently doing it.

On Memorial Day in 1884, Judge Oliver Wendell Holmes (1841-1935), speaking in Keene, N.H., said: "The generation that carried on the [civil] war has been set apart by its experience. Through our great good fortune, in our youth our hearts were touched with fire. It was given to us to learn at the outset that life is a profound and passionate thing. While we were permitted to scorn nothing but indifference, and do not pretend to undervalue the worldly rewards of ambition, we have seen with our own eyes, beyond and above the gold fields, the snowy heights of honor, and it is for us to bear the report to those who come after us."[13] One hundred years after his speech, we Americans have greater need than ever to listen to reports of the snowy heights of honor. I have tried to assemble some of them here. At one time, moral philosophy was the parent of military ethics. It may well be that now the relationship has been reversed and that the wellsprings of military ethics can help restore the health and usefulness of moral philosophy.

True Faith and Allegiance is intended to serve as both sourcebook and textbook. It is written, I hope, so that the sometimes obscure language of ethics can be seen clearly in its application to the profession of arms. The first of its eight chapters defines "military ethics" and examines the question of whether it is a contradiction in terms. The second explores the relationship between civilian and military sectors in the United States. The third argues that military training must be tough and realistic; the fourth argues, however, that military *education* must have place of honor over military *training*. The fifth examines idea of character and the place of codes of conduct. The sixth raises some of the cases and controversies often prominently in the news. The seventh studies the *profession* of arms and recapitulates the book's major points about the armed services. The concluding chapter contains recommendations for the further study of military ethics.[14]

Many of the topics discussed here are controversial. I have not hesitated to express my own opinions, but, hard as it is for me to imagine, I may be wrong at some points. Students should therefore read the book actively and critically, arguing mentally and developing their logic about where and why and when I am right or wrong.[15] Only in this way can we strive for consensus.

1. Military Ethics
Is There Any Such Thing?

Men who take up arms against one another in public
war do not cease on this account to be moral beings,
responsible to one another and to God.
— General Orders No. 100 (the Lieber Code),
24 April 1863

At a garden party not long ago I was introduced to a British
Royal Air Force group captain. When our host identified me as
a professor of military ethics, the group captain smiled and
asked the question I knew was coming: "What is military ethics?" I was prepared for that: "It's the study of honorable and
shameful conduct in the armed services," I responded. I was
not prepared for his response: "You can't very well teach such
things to the military, now can you!" Teaching philosophy to
undergraduates was fine, he said, but real soldiers who knew
the real world would find "military ethics" a contradiction in
terms.

Because it was a party, we soon went off to neutral corners,
but I hope to respond to that challenge here. Is military ethics a
contradiction in terms? Is it sensible to teach ethics to college
students but not to professional soldiers?[1] Is ethics[2] a nice,
warm, fuzzy subject for discussion in classes or around a roar-
ing fire but not relevant at all in the real world? In other words,
am I wasting my time writing this?

I hope not. In fact, I know not. If military ethics is an irrelevant exercise, why did we conduct war crimes tribunals after
World War II? Why is there a Code of Conduct for members of
the armed forces, and articles in the Uniform Code of Military
Justice—the legal code of service members—about "conduct
unbecoming"? Why do we tell our soldiers to search, silence,
segregate (by rank), safeguard, and speed to the rear all prison-

ers of war? Why not just torture and kill them? Why are lying, cheating, and stealing so strictly prohibited in the military? Why do we still talk about "officers and gentlemen"?

Let's begin at the beginning—with the concept of ethics itself.

Ethics: A Definition

Justice Potter Stewart of the U.S. Supreme Court once participated in a case involving pornography, and a key element of that case involved the definition of the term. Justice Stewart found that he could not adequately define *pornography*, "but I know it when I see it."[3] To define key terms is a customary procedure because it is a sound one. The problem with "ethics" and our words for many important concepts is that no one is able, entirely satisfactorily, to define them. My desk dictionary defines "love," for example as "a profoundly tender, passionate affection." Yet there are people well into their mature years who deeply regret having said "I love you": they made a mistake; they mistook infatuation for love. That the word is ambiguous, however, hardly means that *love* does not exist. "Justice" is a concept equally hard to define. "Rightfulness or lawfulness, as of a claim," my dictionary says. But equating *justice* with *legality* is not entirely satisfactory, is it? What is legal may not always be just, and something that is just may not always be legal (as Harper Lee's novel *To Kill a Mockingbird* helps to illustrate). Nazi Germany had plenty of laws but little justice.

Vitally important terms such as *love, justice, honor, integrity* are as hard to define as other terms (*table, hypotenuse, home run*) are easy. The more important a word is, the more difficult is its definition. If, for instance, we say that God cannot do something, can't we say that because God is thus not omnipotent, he must not be perfect and, lacking perfection, must not be God? Well, can God make a rock so big that he can't lift it? If we answer no, we are saying that he can't do something. Because he can't do something, it follows that he can't do everything. Because he can't do everything, he is not omnipotent and therefore is not perfect, and therefore is not God.[4] The problem with this, of course, is that the idea of God cannot be compacted into convenient language.

In the same way, *ethics* is too large to be disposed of with a simple definition, yet I must try to capture its meaning. Knowing it when we see it is not enough, for ethics is a matter of the mind, as well as of the heart (in much the same way that religious believers accept God both with reason and with faith). Ethics involves study and theory and academic discipline. As one scholar put it, "*Ethics is the critical study of standards for judging the rightness or wrongness of conduct.*"[5] But it is also about *doing* what is right. People must both know what ethics is and be capable of "doing ethics." Albert Schweitzer's definition may help: "In a general sense, ethics is the name we give to our concern for good behavior. We feel an obligation to consider not only our own personal well-being, but also that of others and of human society as whole."[6]

One important question at this juncture is whether there is a difference between *ethics* and *morality*. In the strictest sense, "ethics" refers to theory, and "morality" to behavior. But if we made this a strict distinction, we couldn't discuss "ethical conduct" (because that is behavior) or "moral attitude" (because that is theoretical).[7] To be sure, precision in language and in meaning can be vital (imagine a patrol leader in combat telling a subordinate to "take care of" a prisoner; the slightest change in voice modulation can change the meaning of that order). But in this book, unless precise distinctions are necessary, I use *ethical* and *moral* interchangeably. Remembering that we are concerned about both thought and action, we can cite the following definition of ethics as especially useful: "the study of good and evil, of right and wrong, of duty and obligation in human conduct, and of reasoning and choice about them."[8]

The Problem of Cultural Relativism

In Shirley Jackson's powerful short story "The Lottery," a society annually selects a family from which one member will be chosen, by a second lottery, to be stoned to death in order to propitiate nature. By custom, others in the family join in to kill the lottery "winner." Since it has always been done that way, is it all right to continue the practice? What gives one the right to challenge the customs of any other society? Isn't it all relative? If cannibalism is acceptable in one society, do people of another society have the right to question or challenge it? What gives missionaries the right to proselytize, to win converts to their faith, in parts of the world that espouse a different faith? In going to teach all nations, aren't they saying, in essence, "We know best, and we're coming to teach you heathens and pagans real truth"? In short, are there any standards that transcend the feelings and norms of the group? Or are all standards relative?

One textbook says that ethics is "a pattern or norm or code of conduct actually adopted by a group of people"; ethics, therefore, is "the business of sociology, anthropology, and history, [for] these disciplines have shown beyond question that there is a great diversity among the ethical codes that have existed and do exist today."[9] But if the adoption of a certain practice (as in "The Lottery") is equal to ethical approval of it, then ethics amounts to no more than custom. Ethics is thus tautological, or needlessly repetitive: to find out what is right conduct, we need only ask what is ordinary conduct. What *is* done therefore *should* be done. When we describe what society does, we prescribe what it ought to do.

I believe, however, that some concepts transcend the patterns or norms or codes of conduct actually adopted by a given group of people. We have noted that what is legal is not always just, and how can people judge whether a law is just unless they have an idea of justice itself? Ethics is ordinarily deductive, proceeding from a general understanding to a particular instance. For example, examine the chair you are sitting on. Is it a "good" chair? How do you know? You compare it with other chairs. You compare it with the idea of "chair" in the abstract. You devise a series of questions based on the qualities of a "good chair" (can it support my weight? is it comfortable?) and apply those questions to your chair. That is the task of ethics: to compare what is done here with what is done elsewhere; to analyze what is done here with the idea of what ought to be done in the "good society"; to prepare a checklist of questions by which to evaluate local practices against universal ideals. Ethics is *prescriptive* or *normative* as well as *descriptive* or *empirical*. Ethics concerns itself

both with what is done and with what ought to be done. Therefore, we conclude that the society in which the lottery is conducted is a corrupted society.

Let's suppose that you know a young man named Joe. Joe
uses heroin. You know what heroin does to its addicts, so you
try to convert Joe away from its use. Joe asks you if you have
ever used heroin, and you tell him no. "Then don't knock it if
you haven't tried it," he says. (You manage to restrain your urge
to ask him his opinion of death.) You persist, telling Joe that he
will surely hurt or kill himself by using poison. He tells you to
have fun your way; he will have fun his. Is his use of heroin
ethical? Who are you to judge his practices? to impose your
views upon him? to preach to him? The simple answer is that
you do know better than Joe. His use of heroin is unethical; it is
also illegal. You are being a good person, a good citizen—and a
good friend as well.

What if almost "everyone" used heroin? It would then be
customary. Suppose its sale were legalized. Would its use be
ethical? I would argue no, because even if it became customary
and legal, the use of heroin would be nonetheless—according
to universal medical standards—an evil. It destroys. It enslaves.
It kills. Customs and legal systems approving the use of heroin
would thus be unjust and unethical.

If a given society establishes certain customs for the wearing
of clothes, or the consumption of food, or the observation of
certain rules of etiquette, we should in most cases respectfully
observe them. "When in Rome, do as the Romans do" does
make good sense—unless their lotteries are about stoning people to death. Your negative reaction to that custom is a product
of ethical reflection on universal norms and comparisons. Joe's
use of heroin and the practice of sacrificing to idols are wrong—
and unethical.

Occasionally, one meets the objection that this is a value
judgment, and that scholarship should refrain from passing
judgment on any values. Ethical studies must indeed be open to
discussion and debate, but ethics should not suffer from paraly-
sis by analysis; there are times and places to say, "This is wrong.
This is evil. This is unethical. It must be changed." The task of
ethics is to give us a sense of those universals according to

which we can judge, and of those comparative ideas that allow us a general, well-formed perception permitting valid value judgment. Ethics, finally, studies the critical idea of *obligation*. The ethical person has a sense of duty and routinely attempts to live up to that sense. The importance of all this to *military* ethics will become clear as we proceed.

The Problem of Social Decay

Which came first, the chicken or the egg? Which comes first, good people making good education or good education making good people? In Frederick County, Virginia, the superintendent of public schools recently issued a memorandum informing teachers and administrators that Christmas would no longer be referred to by that name but instead be called the "winter holiday"; Christmas parties were to be called "holiday parties." One newspaper columnist responded: "Children as young as kindergarten must be now sensitized to AIDS and gay and lesbian lifestyles. But apparently the words 'Christmas' and 'Easter' are regarded as a more clear and present danger."[10] This relatively minor problem over Christmas in Virginia merely suggests a much larger problem: the decay of American education. Whether the decline of American education is a product of social dissolution or social dissolution is a product of educational decadence, I will leave to you to determine. Either way, there is overwhelming evidence, as Thomas Sowell (among others) has recently written, of serious and substantial problems in American education, now reaching into undergraduate colleges around the United States. Problems, from what Sowell identifies as "new racism" (by which he refers in particular to gross favoritism and discrimination in favor of minorities), to ideological double standards ("political correctness") and "brainwashing," to diminishing academic expectations and munificent athletic programs—all these difficulties plague many U.S. college campuses.[11]

If the link is strong between good education and good people, the quality of education in the United States today bodes ill for society. Consider the quality of education to which, to date, you have been exposed. Were the teachers highly competent, enthusiastic, organized, and fair? Were the standards rigorous and demanding, requiring substantial but reasonable work loads? Or was there emphasis on maintaining order and discipline, on keeping knives and guns out of the schools, on social conditioning programs: driver education, race relations, sex education, "family services," and so on? One scholar has compared

> what classroom teachers identified as the greatest threats to the educational process in 1940 and today. First on the list in 1940 was talking out of turn; today it is drug abuse. The number-two concern in 1940 was chewing gum; today it is alcohol abuse. Number three in 1940 was making noise; number three today is pregnancy. The fourth most pressing problem in 1940 was running in the halls; today it is suicide. Fifth, sixth, and seventh on the list in 1940 were getting out of line, wearing improper clothing, and not putting paper in the wastebasket; today, they are rape, robbery, and assault.[12]

This is not the forum in which to engage in a lengthy examination of contemporary American education; it is enough, at present, to recognize the problems that plague our schools and colleges. We have the prospect of ethical barbarism hard upon us. Alan Wolfe says that "Modern people need to care about the fate of strangers, yet do not know how to treat their loved ones. Moral rules seem to evaporate the more they are needed. The paradox of modernity is that the more people depend on one another owing to an ever-widening circle of obligations, the fewer are the agreed-upon guidelines for organizing moral rules that can account for those obligations."[13]

We have all read that too many American students know far too little. Shockingly large numbers, for example, can't find the United States on a map of the world, or distinguish World Wars I and II, or identify Stalin or Churchill. A survey conducted in 1989 discovered that only one-quarter of interviewed college seniors could distinguish between the ideas of Karl Marx and the ideas expressed in the U.S. Constitution.[14]

E.D. Hirsch, in his book *Cultural Literacy*, develops a list of about 5,000 things that people in a literate society ought to know in common. His thesis is that unless there is shared knowledge, communication becomes virtually impossible, and societies will break apart.[15] But American institutions, under the banner of "multiculturalism," are offering courses—even majors—in various and disparate "studies" that essentially deny the unity of knowledge and the shared social and cultural realities that result in a truly *United* States. Arthur Schlesinger, Jr., recently wrote a book deploring multicultural studies entitled *The Disuniting of America*.[16] As William Kilpatrick points out, some multiculturalists "insist that no common culture is possible."[17]

Yet there *is* a common culture of sorts, one that spawns "knowledge" and "ethics" of sorts. James Twitchell's *Carnival Culture* lists the twenty-five best-selling books of the 1980s in the United States (authors Tom Clancy, Danielle Steel, and Stephen King wrote ten of the top thirteen novels selling one million or more copies) and the major blockbusters in films (including *Beverly Hills Cop* I and II, *Three Men and a Baby*, and *Rambo: First Blood, Part II*). The subtitle of his book is "The Trashing of Taste in America."[18] But these are not merely aesthetic complaints. The amount of violence on television is mind boggling, and the average American *preschooler* watches more than twenty-seven hours of television per week; violence on TV is having measurably injurious effects on children.[19] Increased TV viewing correlates with other problems as well. In 1960, American households watched an average 5:06 hours per day of television; by 1992, the figure was 7:04. In 1960, average SAT scores were 975; in 1992, the average was 899. In 1960, 5.3 percent of total births were to unwed mothers; the figure in 1990 was 28 percent. Youth suicides in 1960 were 3.6 per 1,000 (ages fifteen to twenty-four); in 1990, the figure was 11.3 per 1,000. In 1960, there were 16.1 violent crimes per 10,000 people in the United States; by 1991, the figure had grown to 75.8.[20]

Of course, this kind of objection can be carried too far. Reading *Clear and Present Danger*, the top-selling novel of the 1980s, after all, is not such a bad thing; watching Captain Picard and Commander Data on TV is hardly sinister; and seeing *E.T.*, or *Star Wars*, or *Back to the Future* will not unglue the morals of young Americans. As recreation, such things are not so bad, but if they are the basic source of Americans' knowledge and ethical education, our society is in trouble. And it gets worse.

Movie critic Michael Medved, writing on what he calls "Hollywood's poison factory," says:

> Take a look, for example, at the [1991] Oscars. Five very fine actors were nominated for best actor of the year. Three of them portrayed murderous psychos: Robert De Niro in *Cape Fear*, Warren Beatty in *Bugsy*, and Anthony Hopkins in *The Silence of the Lambs* (this last a delightful family film about two serial killers—one eats and the other skins his victims). A fourth actor, Robin Williams, was nominated for playing a delusional homeless psycho in *The Fisher King*. The most wholesome character was Nick Nolte's, a good old fashioned manic-depressive-suicidal neurotic in *The Prince of Tides*.

Medved goes on to discuss Hollywood's "anti-religious bias" and to ask, "Did you ever notice how few movies there are about happily married people?" What can we do about the prevalence of such films as *Sleeping with the Enemy*, *Mortal Thoughts*, *Thelma and Louise*, *She-Devil*, *Kiss before Dying*, *Total Recall*, and *Deceived*? Medved says, "We can clamor for movies that don't portray marriage as a living hell, that recognize the spiritual side of man's nature, that glorify the blessings in life that we enjoy as Americans and the people who make sacrifices to ensure that others will be able to enjoy them."[21]

If the schools are in turmoil and if our picture of the family is drawn from the films Medved refers to, the very idea of ethics is impossible. As Alan Wolfe tells us, the tight-knit family and local community that once taught us moral rules of interdependence are withering away.[22] Thomas Sowell argues that "All societies which have survived have had some particular set of values, some canons of right and wrong. To banish right and wrong is to attempt something which no society has achieved—survival without shared values. Different societies also have different ideas of what kinds of food to eat, but that does not mean that food is something arbitrary that we can do without."[23] We seem to be losing the very idea of common purpose, of civic virtue, of common destiny that unites us as a people.[24] "If well-educated managers, experts, political leaders, and elected offi-

cials seem to lack an adequate public philosophy to help them
assess facts and determine goals," say one group of writers, "it
is hardly surprising that ordinary citizens are often baffled by
what they see."[25]

Developing Values

How can we expect people to know and to do good when all
around them is moral chaos? To some extent, the answer is provided by the fictional character of Sam Damon in the military
novel *Once an Eagle*. Damon tells his son Donny: "Accept what
you are and go on from there. You can't change the circumstances
of your birth and condition—it's unprofitable to torture yourself
with too much speculation as to why you've been placed in existence at a given point in time. . . . That's the whole challenge of
life—to act with honor and hope and generosity, no matter what
you've drawn. You can't help when or what you've drawn. You
can't help when or what you were born, you may not be able to
help how you die; but you can—and you should—try to pass the
days between as a good man."[26] To act with honor and to live as
a good man or woman are noble, if circular, goals. They are
circular because to be *good* and to act with "honor" demand
definition—and we are back at the chapter's beginning. How
can we hope even to define these terms, given the moral mud-
dle of our schools, our books, our movies? To resurrect the
American eagle demands that we have the ethical knowledge of
how to effect that resurrection and then the ethical courage—
and grace—to do so.

Let us examine four sources of ethics. Ethics comes, in part,
from *customs*. For example, "My society generally disapproves
of killing; therefore, I won't kill." In part, ethics comes from
rules, such as "Thou shalt not kill."[27] Ethics derives as well from
our *goals* or our appraisal of probable *outcomes*: "I wish to stay
out of jail; if I kill, I may well wind up in jail; therefore, I won't
kill."[28] Further, ethics may derive from our *circumstances* or situations: "In circumstances of military combat, my life and the
lives of others in my platoon are at risk; therefore I may fire my
weapon at the enemy with intent to kill."[29] It is important to
note that ethical conduct normally is based upon a wise blend-

ing of customs, rules, outcomes, and circumstances. Blindly following the dictates of one source alone can lead to trouble.

William Graham Sumner (1840-1910), a cultural anthropologist, argued that it is mores, or customs, that make an action right or wrong. The correct act is one that conforms to the customs of the agent's society; if the act violates those customs, it is wrong.[30] But the notion that ethics comes from social norms *alone* carries us back to "The Lottery"! The late Catholic theologian Fulton J. Sheen said that "conscience cannot come to us from the rulings of society; otherwise it would never reprove us when society approves us, nor console us when society condemns."[31] Clearly, however, the society of which we are a part—particularly our voluntary association with religions, fraternities, circles of friends, civic organizations, and the like—influences and affects us greatly. That is not always bad.

Rules are critical, for the centuries have taught us things we often anneal into rules. But the question is whether any rules can be considered absolute. "Thou shalt not steal" appears absolute, and it is reinforced by the utilitarian or outcome-based ethics which suggests that, generally, there is advantage in *not* stealing. Yet suppose you and your family are starving, and you have the chance to steal a loaf of bread from a wealthy merchant. You know stealing is wrong and you are afraid of being caught, but the benefits in this case (temporary relief from hunger for your family) seem to outweigh the liabilities. Do such circumstances "justify" theft?

Is anything absolute and binding? Even the rule "do good and avoid evil" is subject to interpretation.[32] Doing good depends upon knowledge and education—upon *right reason*. The word *conscience* actually means "with knowledge." Consider this case. You promise a friend that you will meet him for lunch at noon—and promises are binding. On the way there, you find a man lying in the street. You know CPR and set about reviving him. You know that doing so will make you late, but who could fail to see the injustice in abandoning a sick man to get to lunch on time? In choosing to aid the stricken man, are you deliberately defaulting on your promise? Do you abandon the very idea of truth-telling? Of course not. Duties can conflict, and the stronger obligation in this case is to aid the ill man.[33] That is not an endorsement of utilitarian ethics or of situation ethics, for no effort is made, or intended, to deny or disparage the absolute of promise-keeping.

Suppose you are a Polish Catholic in 1939. After Germany invades your country a Jewish person, understandably desperate to avoid the Nazi persecutions, requests shelter in your basement, and you comply. A few days later a German officer knocks on your door, asking if you are harboring any Jews. Knowing that telling a lie is wrong, do you say, "Yes, I am hiding a Jew downstairs"? Of course lying is wrong; in this case, however, the absolute of truth-telling is *served* by a direct lie. By telling this lie, you do not renounce truth itself; you do not set a pattern for the future (unless the Nazi returns); you do not choose deception over honesty. This is not "situation ethics," which holds that no absolutes exist and that everything is relative to the situation. Rather, it is recognition that universal obligations do exist and are binding, but also that evil abides in human affairs and that the tragedy of human life compels us occasionally to choose among competing demands.[34]

"Reasoning and choice" are critical to the study of ethics. If the American eagle is to be resurrected and if America is to experience a moral wake-up call, our reasoning must be logical and our choices wise. The sound teaching of good leadership is essential to restoring a national sense of purpose and of rebuilding the American ethical compass. The difference between faithful leaders and fraudulent ones rests in their character, defined by Lewis Sorley as "the commitment to an admirable set of values, and the courage to manifest those values in one's life, no matter the cost in terms of personal success or popularity."[35] But character is not developed from pulp novels and witless movies. The character of children and cadets and students is developed by loving parents, by competent teachers, and by concerned priests, ministers, and rabbis. It is developed by homes and schools and churches where virtuous conduct is modeled, as well as insisted upon. It is developed, too, by loving spouses and by wise friends.

Sam Damon, whom I quoted above, is a figure from good literature. James B. Stockdale is a figure from real life who spent eight years as a prisoner of war in Vietnam. Stockdale's answer to the question of how character is developed is this: "My formula for attacking this problem [of how to develop character] . . . is the assignment of enough hard-core philosophy (the Book of Job, the Socratic dialogues of Plato, some of Aristotle's Nichomachean Ethics, Epictetus' Enchiridion, enough of Immanuel Kant to understand his concept of duty) and the reading of enough high-quality ultimate situation literature (Feodor Dostoyevsky's *House of the Dead*, Albert Camus's *Plague*, Joseph Conrad's *Typhoon*, and Herman Melville's *Billy Budd*) as to deter self-pity when in extremis."[36] Had Lt. William Calley, Jr., been well read in Stockdale's classics, one can imagine that the massacre at My Lai during the Vietnam War might never have happened. But Calley had not the education—hence not the character—to deal with the terrible problems confronting him and his Army platoon. When he ordered the slaughter at My Lai, he showed us, in a terrible way, that good ethics and good education are the two sides of the same coin. The way to resurrect the American eagle is to revivify American education. But of the list of readings proposed by Stockdale, how many are commonly read in American colleges—let alone high schools—today?

On Officers and Character

Thus we arrive at an understanding of both the particular subject of military ethics and the larger parent field of ethics itself. Ethics is the study of virtue. But study is not enough. We need both the grace of understanding and the willpower of enlightened action; one must not only *know* what is ethical but also *do* what is ethical. Similarly, the soldier must not only *know* what he ought to do; he or she must also *do* it. But life is hard, even cruel (as Stockdale can tell us). Sometimes we are not sure what the proper thing to do is. Sometimes we know the right thing but lack the virtue to carry it out. Therein lies the burden suggested by the subtitle of this book. There can be severe physical or mental pain in our failure to know what is right or our failure to do what is right.[37] Even doing the right thing can be painful for us. (Consider the case of a West Point cadet who turns in a friend for cheating.)

Most of us struggle to know the right and then to do it.

There, then, is the property of *character*: one has character who struggles (perhaps not always successfully) to do what should be done. Military officers—and noncommissioned officers (sergeants)—owe obligation, not just to their own well-formed conscience, but to their command, to their service, to their country. The test of officers' true faith and allegiance lies always in attempting as best they can to know the right thing to do and then to do it to the best of their ability. In October 1970, General Sir John Hackett spoke at the U.S. Air Force Academy. In his address, he made a number of telling points, including this one: "A man can be selfish, cowardly, disloyal, false, fleeting, perjured, and morally corrupt in a wide variety of other ways and still be outstandingly good in pursuits in which other imperatives bear than those upon the fighting man. He can be a superb creative artist, for example, or a scientist in the very top flight, and still be a very bad man. What the bad man cannot be is a good sailor, or soldier, or airman. Military institutions thus form a repository of moral resource that should always be a source of strength within the state."[38] Hackett's point that one can perhaps be an effective scientist while having a defective character but that one cannot be a good soldier while having a defective character is at the heart of this book—and at the heart of military ethics.

While it is true that, in the heat of combat, evil persons who kill the enemy can, for that short time, be considered "good soldiers," their corruption and venality disqualify them from being good soldiers for the 99 percent of the time they otherwise spend in the armed service of their country. Not all good people are always good soldiers; but bad people are almost always bad soldiers.

To understand military ethics, therefore, we must understand both the nature of ethics itself and its peculiar application in the context of the armed forces. I think the definition of military ethics I provided that night to the RAF officer (*the study of honorable and shameful conduct in the armed services*) is sensible. We must know both what is honorable *and* what is shameful. This book cannot and should not determine for each reader and in every case the precise nature of either honor or shame. But the book will be successful if its readers are stimulated or provoked to greater thought about honor and shame in civil and military life. The next chapter deals with the important prepositional phrase "in the armed services."

Conclusions

As moral philosophy, ethics is about trying to separate right from wrong, honor from shame, virtue from vice. It is the studied search for wisdom and an inquiry into what we ought to do. It also entails the obligation of acting wisely and resolutely upon the judgments we make. Ethics derives from custom, from rules (deontology), from goals (teleology), and from circumstances (situationalism). A mature, settled sense of ethics understands and incorporates all sources in wise decision-making.

Achieving a mature sense of ethics requires character, which is developed by rigorous education and fixed by virtuous habit. We are, as Aristotle once tried to tell us, the product of our practices. Without serious, substantial education we will not have the conscience ("with-knowledge") necessary to act as we ought. Military personnel must be capable of reflection about the nature of virtue and its implications for action. They must distinguish in word and deed between killing as a function of legitimate military necessity and the murder of innocents; they must separate the application of lawful military power from wanton, frenzied destruction.

2. The U.S. Military
Sovereign or Subordinate?

> In its proper manifestation the jealousy between civil
> and military spirits is a healthy symptom.
> —Alfred Thayer Mahan (1903)

In Robert Heinlein's remarkable novel *Starship Troopers*, a student is asked to explain the difference between a soldier and a civilian. Drawing upon his course text, the student responds: "The difference . . . lies in the field of civic virtue. A soldier accepts personal responsibility for the safety of the body politic of which he is a member, defending it, if need be, with his life. The civilian does not."[1]

Aristotle argued that in order to understand something, one had to inquire into its functions: What, after all, was it supposed to do? To understand the United States military, one has to ask the same question. What is the United States military supposed to do?

Military Tasks

The preeminent military task, and what separates it from all other occupations, is that soldiers are routinely prepared *to kill*. Even policemen, who must also often deal with violence, do not routinely train to kill. One can argue, of course, using the Army as an example, that there are combat support and combat service support branches in addition to the combat arms (such as infantry and artillery). But every soldier undergoes initial entry training known as BCT (basic combat training), and every soldier has to be qualified in BRM (basic rifle marksmanship). Every soldier, in short, is an infantryman. If U.S. Army positions are overrun in the heat of combat, enemy forces do not pause to investigate a soldier's MOS (military occupational specialty).

Contending that every soldier is a "trained killer" brings on self-conscious chuckles among young soldiers and invites scorn from critics. For many years the U.S. military itself has downplayed this most basic fact of its existence: its purpose is to kill national enemies of the United States. Soldiers are, or are supposed to be, masters of the arts of violence. That is why they are paid. But the thought of killing is unsettling, as it should be, to decent and rational people. Military ethics is a burden precisely because the profession of arms is centrally concerned with killing but must also be a paragon of virtue, able always to distinguish the honorable from the shameful—one of the reasons military ethics must study examples both of integrity and of corruption.

An army or a navy or an air force is thus not primarily about job training—or building roads, or delivering mail, or milking cows. There are many other organizations and agencies to do those things. But only the military is called upon, in time of war, to risk life and limb to protect the nation's safety. When soldiers are not actually killing, they should be training to kill. The president of Boston University, John Silber, explains this concept succinctly:

> I was once asked by a friend to recommend his son for the U.S. Naval Academy. I asked in response, "Does your son want to be a professional killer?" And he said, "Well, no, of course not. He wants to be a peacemaker." I replied, "Well, then, tell him to enter a seminary."
>
> A person not prepared to use his skill, knowledge, techniques, and all the weapons at his disposal for the purpose of killing on behalf of the United States of America when ordered to do so has no business in the military. That is the military's ultimate business.[2]

In addition to killing and preparing to kill, the soldier has two other principal duties, rarely discussed—and probably never discussed by recruiters. Some soldiers die; when they are not dying, they must be preparing to die. From time immemorial, young men (and now young women) have joined armies the world over in time of national peril. Only very occasionally are these youths forced to consider their mortality. (As we grow older, we attend funerals more frequently, an all too constant reminder of our own approaching end.) It is difficult enough— and a good thing too,—to convert decent young people into soldiers prepared to kill; it is practically impossible for them to think of themselves as the objects of others' military actions.

Everyone who has been a soldier in time of war has witnessed friends go off to battle questioning, in most cases, only their enemies' mortality rather than their own. Few American soldiers who went to Vietnam were persuaded of their own imminent deaths, although 58,000 Americans perished in that war. A reading of the "Code of Conduct for Members of the Armed Forces of the United States" puts the matter squarely, however: "I am an American, fighting in the forces which guard my country and our way of life. I am prepared to give my life in their defense" (Article I). Still, a corollary of that article might be (there is, of course, no such language): "I am an American, fighting in the forces which guard my country and our way of life. I am prepared to kill in their defense."

During the Korean War (1950-53) the U.S. Army, fighting under the banner of the United Nations, kept North Korean and Chinese Communist prisoners of war (POWs) in a camp on Koje Island off the southern coast of the Korean peninsula. In order to gain a propaganda triumph, the POWs planned to capture the commanding general of the compound and then to trade him back to U.S. forces after extorting a statement to the effect that Americans routinely tortured North Korean and Chinese prisoners. Such a statement, however false, could be used to advantage by the Communists in the negotiations then under way at Panmunjom. Brig. Gen. Francis Dodd, the hapless Koje commander, was taken hostage by the POWs. His successor, Brig. Gen. Charles Colson, afraid for the life of his friend and fellow officer, delivered a note to the Communists essentially admitting to torture practices on the island. Dodd was released.

The general officer then in charge of the United Nations Command in Korea, Gen. Matthew B. Ridgway, U.S.A., later observed:

While I could sympathize with the desire . . . to save a friend's life, I felt that Dodd, like every other professional soldier, had accepted the risk of violent death when he chose his profession. A great many men had already given their lives to back up our government's refusal to confess uncommitted offenses to the Communists or to compromise our stand on repatriation. In wartime a general's life is no more precious than the life of a common soldier. Each is asked to risk his life every day to protect the safety, the freedom, and the honor of his country. If, in order to save an officer's life, we abandoned the cause for which enlisted men had died, we would be guilty of betraying the men whose lives had been placed in our care.[3]

In early 1968 the U.S.S. *Pueblo*, in international waters off the coast of Korea, was ordered by North Korean vessels to "heave to." The *Pueblo* was a floating listening post with highly sensitive electronic eavesdropping devices on board. When its skipper, Commander Lloyd "Pete" Bucher, U.S.N., became convinced that the North Koreans intended to seize his vessel and its highly classified cargo, he stalled as best he could to allow his sailors time to smash equipment and shred documents. But before they had finished, the North Koreans became impatient and fired on the *Pueblo*, killing one crewman. Bucher surrendered his ship, as one of his officers read the Code of Conduct to crew members over the loudspeaker system.[4]

Once the North Koreans had ordered Bucher to surrender, however, his mission had changed, from one of listening to Korean broadcasts to protecting the classified data and machinery on board. For Commander Bucher and the crew of the *Pueblo*, the time had come to risk life and limb to buy more time to protect those materials. "Buying more time," in this case, would have meant heading for the open seas, no doubt taking enemy fire, and preparing to repel boarders—a drill routinely practiced by Navy crews on ships of such size. It would have meant more American deaths. Confronted with the terrible choice between saving the lives of his crew and accomplishing his new mission of document destruction, Bucher chose the former. He proved to be a heroic leader in captivity. About a year after being taken prisoner (and having suffered a terrible ordeal in North Korea), Bucher and his crew were released after the United States signed another false propaganda statement.[5] The *Pueblo* is still in Korea today.

If your friend were going to be killed by his captors, would you sign an obviously phony statement to effect his release? If your crew were going to pay with their lives while you stalled for the time essential to your mission, would you decide to surrender? I believe that any decent *civilian* would have chosen as Colson and Bucher did. I also believe, with Ridgway, that Colson was wrong. By the same token a U.S. Navy board of inquiry considered punishing Bucher but chose not to in recognition of his exemplary leadership and courage while a prisoner.[6]

Note that questions of military ethics—honorable and shameful conduct—are rarely crystal clear. The second article of the Code of Conduct says, "I will never surrender of my own free will. If in command, I will never surrender the members of my command while they still have the means to resist." Did the *Pueblo* have the means, such as flight or fight?[7] Frequently, the problems of military ethics are far easier to resolve in the comfort of a classroom than on the battlefield or high seas.

Military commanders are supposed to accomplish their mission *and* look out for their people. This is a vital concept requiring more analysis, but at this point it is enough to ask: in times of peril, when getting the mission done means getting members of your command killed, which comes first, mission or people? (By the way, beware the fallacy of the false dichotomy! Usually, when something is X *or* Y, with no other possibility offered, you are dealing with a "stacked deck.") We will return to this quandary.

The Loyalty Dilemma

Aside from the "mission vs. people" problem, there is a perhaps equally burdensome problem that professional soldiers must face. What I call the "loyalty dilemma" can be so perplexing that it is rarely examined. Simply put, the loyalty dilemma poses two difficulties. Soldiers pledge obedience to constitutional precepts—but whose interpretation of them? And soldiers are responsible to superior authority—but not always.

The officer's oath is a short, solemn statement: "I [full name], having been appointed a [rank] in the United States [military service], do solemnly swear that I will support and defend the Constitution of the United States against all enemies, foreign and domestic, that I will bear true faith and allegiance to the same; that I take this obligation freely, without purpose of evasion, and that I will well and faithfully discharge the duties of the office upon which I am about to enter, so help me God."[8]

In 1951, General of the Army Douglas MacArthur was relieved of command in the Far East after a series of disagreements with President Harry Truman (making clear, in my view, Truman's plain responsibility to take action). The immediate cause was a letter MacArthur had written to Massachusetts Congressman Joe Martin, clearly indicating that the general disagreed, in significant ways, with the president's policies for prosecuting the war in Korea.

MacArthur never questioned Truman's *right* to relieve him, only Truman's judgment (or lack of it) in firing him. After his return to the United States, the general said (among many other things): "I find in existence a new and heretofore unknown and dangerous concept that the members of our armed forces owe primary allegiance or loyalty to those who temporarily exercise the authority of the Executive Branch of the Government rather than to the country and its Constitution which they swore to defend. No proposition could be more dangerous."[9] MacArthur was arguing that allegiance to the person of the president and to temporary political policies should not command primary military loyalty. German officers during the Hitler era, for example, were required to swear an oath of personal fealty to Hitler. Should American officers swear an oath of loyalty to President Clinton? Though Truman, of course, was arguing for no such thing,[10] is there not a strong case to be made in behalf of the general's position?

Sir John Hackett, however, contends that "MacArthur's insistence upon his right as an individual to determine for himself the legitimacy of the executive's position, no less than his claim of the right of a military commander to modify national policies, can never be seen in any way other than completely out of order."[11] Wasn't MacArthur, then, contending that his chief loyalty should be to *his own version* of the Constitution? Having concluded that Truman's policies were mistaken or defective, MacArthur had the responsibility—or so he claimed—of correcting or at least refusing to follow those policies.

Therein lies the dilemma. Of course, no commander's loyalty to the temporary occupant of the White House should be supreme; presidents can be wrong. But MacArthur was not thus empowered to choose for himself what to do and whom to obey. Quietly and discreetly, through the chain of command, to make known his reservations; manfully to insist that his position be heard; finally, to resign in protest if he could not, in true faith and allegiance, carry out his orders—these were his options, of Constitution and of conscience. But MacArthur had no right to challenge frontally the authority of his commander in chief.

At the same time, *total* obedience is not owed by any soldier to any politician (or even to a commanding officer). Though soldiers are not free to substitute their own version of the Constitution for the political decisions made by democratically elected officials, neither are soldiers free, in good conscience, merely to accept unthinkingly the military and geopolitical decisions of their superiors. The doctrine of *respondeat superior* ("Let my boss answer because I was just following orders, so I'm 'off the hook'"), which we will explore later, was struck down by the war crimes trials after World War II. Even generals are not free simply to say, "I was just following orders."

Obedience to personal constitutional interpretation will not do. Total obedience to political leaders will not do, either. "True faith and allegiance," then, depend upon well-formed conscience. The danger in the notion, heard even during the Gulf War of 1991, that once wars start the politicians should get out of the way was once realistically assessed this way, *by a soldier*, General Ridgway: "The persistent contention by some of our own private citizens as well as military men that wars, once started, should be shaped and conducted solely by the military indicates that, improbable as it now may seem, and incompatible as it is with our whole way of life, military dominance over our affairs 'could happen here.'"[12] MacArthur was certainly not planning a coup d'état. But the late Samuel Eliot Morison, a distinguished American historian, said of MacArthur: "He never crossed the Rubicon, to be sure, but his horse's front hoofs were in the water."[13] Forty years after MacArthur's insistence that it was up to him to read the Constitution his way, another officer—this time a Marine lieutenant colonel—would make a very similar claim.

Twenty years after MacArthur was relieved, there was a spectacular (in the sense of "spectacle") military trial involving Lt. William L. Calley, Jr., accused (and subsequently convicted) of the murders of unarmed and unresisting inhabitants of the Vietnamese village of My Lai. Calley argued that he was merely following the orders of his chain of command in slaughtering the men, women, and children of that rural hamlet; he was simply doing his duty. An improbable mix of Americans on the left of the political spectrum (arguing that Calley was just a scapegoat for a rotten capitalist system) and on the right (insisting that Calley was just a clean-cut American hero with a silver bar on his shoulder) seemed to agree that Calley should be released. After Calley's conviction, President Nixon personally intervened to lessen his sentence. An anguished Capt. Aubrey Daniel III, Calley's prosecutor, protested Nixon's action, saying that he was "shocked and dismayed at the reaction of many people across the nation . . . [who] undoubtedly viewed . . . Calley's conviction simply as the conviction of an American officer for killing the enemy. Others . . . have seized upon the conviction as a means of protesting the war in Vietnam." He added, "For this nation to condone the acts of Lieutenant Calley is to make us no better than our enemies and make any pleas by this nation for the humane treatment of our own prisoners meaningless."[14]

In response to Calley's argument that he was merely following orders and killing enemies, one of the members of the jury said that there has to be a "higher law" to which soldiers must be responsible: "There are some things that a man of common understanding and common sense would know are wrong."[15] We return once more to the bedrock notion of military ethics that there are some things so shameful that we can understand them without much effort and that there are also certain "rules" that have come down from the centuries which help us distinguish between honor and shame. Mass murders committed against unarmed and unresisting men, women, and children cannot be explained away by invoking the defense of *respondeat superior* or by claiming that those slaughtered were enemies. There is a higher loyalty, available to reasonable human beings.

The "Semper Fidelis" Corollary

Forty years after MacArthur's arguments that his first loyalty would be to his reading of the Constitution and of the national interest and not to the temporary occupant of the White House, another military officer, Marine Lt. Col. Oliver North, wrote, "I never saw myself as being above the law, nor did I ever intend to do anything illegal." [16] But Congress had passed laws in 1982 and 1984, the Boland Amendments, which had forbidden American aid to the Contras, who were fighting to topple the Sandinista regime in Nicaragua. A number of people in the Reagan administration—apparently including CIA Director William Casey—believed that continued aid should be given to the Contras. North conducted covert operations from the National Security Council with the approval of Vice Admiral John Poindexter, U.S.N., the assistant to the president for national security affairs. American arms were shipped to Iran, funds from which were diverted to the Contras. As one group of analysts explained, "Although this involvement of North and Poindexter was an isolated incident, their influence on U.S. policy toward Iran and the contras was so extensive that at least one senator argued that 'in effect there was a junta within the government of the United States.'" [17]

North later admitted that, in testimony before the Congress, he had lied under oath. "Congress is to blame," he said, "because of the fickle, vacillating, unpredictable, on-again, off-again policy" toward the Contras.[18] North claimed, "Until Congress resumed its funding for the Contras, we fulfilled the mission assigned by the President: to keep the [Contra] resistance alive." He argued that the Boland amendments were not meant to abandon the Contras. North was eventually acquitted of nine counts but found guilty of three; including helping to obstruct Congress and tampering with documents.[19] His loyalty had been to his conception of the national interest. Forty years before North's book *Under Fire* appeared in 1991, General Mac-Arthur had determined that the government's policies were mistaken. In the American system of government, national policies are not dictated by generals—or by lieutenant colonels. Yet after MacArthur's relief from command in 1951, during Calley's trial in 1971, and again during North's trial, there was public outpouring of sympathy for these military men—*for very different reasons and for three very different officers and human beings*. But the lesson is that the American public, viewing the military as a model of patriotism (and often for good and substantial reason), is sometimes unable to sort out quickly the emotional facts bearing upon seemingly difficult cases. The American public—with the exception of a radical leftist fringe—retains strong loyalty to its soldiers, sailors, airmen and women, and marines (if not always to the U.S. Army, Navy, Air Force, and Marine Corps).

The military's task is always to return that loyalty to the American public by being "always faithful" to the legitimate orders it receives. The difficult case of Marine guards at the U.S. embassy in Moscow from 1985 to 1986, who allegedly were recruited as spies after sexual encounters with Soviet women, illustrates the problem. The charges were that these Marines—as well as numerous other spies (such as Jonathan Jay Pollard and the Walker family)—had lost their ethical compasses. How could that happen? Former CIA analyst George Carver, Jr., had it exactly right: "The real problem is that we're feeling, as a country, the corrosive effects of 20 years and more of situational ethics. We've lost the sense of 'off-limits'—that there are things you simply don't do, principles that aren't subject to analysis by deconstructionists at the Harvard Law School. One of them is that you don't betray your country."[20]

If loyalty is to "me first," the timeless notion of obligation disappears. As military sociologist Charles Moskos said about the Marine spy scandal, "There's no real institutional center, either in the military, or in the country, telling people what's right and wrong, and enforcing it."[21] If there is no sense of obligation, there is no sense of honor and shame; without a sense of honor and shame, the idea of treason disappears. All that matters then is loyalty to self.

By naming this problem the "Semper Fidelis corollary" to the loyalty dilemma, I do not mean for a moment to malign the Marine Corps, whose well-known and highly honored motto that is. The question is, who receives the highest loyalty? An old Marine saying is that a Marine on guard duty has no friends— or lovers. The wisdom of that adage was apparently forgotten in Moscow a few years ago.

The "Boss Is Always Right" Corollary

If the president of the United States is not always right, then we can safely assume that your boss—even your professor—is not always right. Loyalty to one's boss is a prized and worthy thing. But it can become an evil and a danger, as Kermit Johnson put it, "when a genuine, wholesome loyalty to the boss degenerates into covering up for him, hiding things from him, or not differing from him when he is wrong."[22] Johnson paraphrases Gen. David M. Shoup, a former Marine Corps commandant (1960-63) who said that he didn't want a "yes man" on his staff because all he could give back to the general was what he already knew.[23]

We use unpleasant words such as *obsequious, servile, sycophantic, fawning, groveling* to describe this attitude of subordinates toward superiors. Granted, no person of sense wants to court problems with a boss. If loyalty means anything, however, it is something well beyond self-serving behavior or craven cowering. The boss deserves better, and a mature and upright boss will not only want honesty but demand it. On the other hand, there may be times when a subordinate's attitude can be spiteful and malicious. As an obsequious demeanor cannot be tolerated, neither can a rancorous one. For example, at a banquet in the Netherlands on 24 May 1993, Air Force Maj. Gen. Harold N. Campbell referred to President Clinton as "dope smoking," "skirt chasing," and "draft dodging." He was soon fined $7,000, reprimanded, and retired. Air Force Chief of Staff Gen. M.A. McPeak said of the Campbell incident, "This is not a trivial matter," because the chain of command "has to be almost pollution free. It runs from the President all the way down to the corporal who pulls the trigger."[24] Campbell had violated Article 88 of the Uniform Code of Military Justice, which forbids "contemptuous words against the President" and other governmental officers. For his public denunciations of the commander in chief, Campbell could have faced a court-martial.

"Loyalty" was defined early in the twentieth century as "the willing and practical and thoroughgoing devotion of a person to a cause."[25] The cause to which one is devoted clearly should be one beyond the limits of one's own skin—and a certain amount of reason is always called for. Loyalty is one manifestation of integrity, and integrity involves neither timidity nor stupidity. Sidney Axinn, for example, tells the story of Hachiko, the loyal dog, who used to walk with his master to the train station every day and came back to meet him in the evening. In 1925 the master died while away from home, and Hachiko, subsisting on handouts, waited at the station for ten years for his master. After the loyal dog died, a statue was erected to him.[26] Such extreme "faith and allegiance," given by a human, would be regarded as a symptom of mental illness, not as loyalty.

Loyalty to constitutional principles, loyalty to a government, loyalty to a service, loyalty to a boss—all these depend for their beginning and their end upon a well-formed conscience. Without that conscience, "true faith and allegiance"—that is, genuine loyalty—is not possible. But there will always be great anxiety—*anguish* may not be too strong a word—in forming, or dissolving, the bonds of loyalty.

"I Pledge Allegiance . . ."

The bonding of men and women in a loyal confraternity of commissioned violence leads to a sense of fellowship that, in the words of philosopher Manuel Davenport, "is almost inherently anti-civilian" and that "has an addictive effect upon the normally intoxicating influences of possessing the ultimate powers of destruction."[27] MacArthur and North, for very different reasons, objected to allowing the president or the Congress to make policy. Yet, as Professor Davenport points out, "duty to client [that is, our country] must take priority over duty to the profession, and in this nation we recognize this by the principle of civilian control of the military."[28] No stronger principle of American civil-military relations exists than this: In the United States, the professional military is wholly subsidiary to the civilians elected to high office in our republic.[29] Despite fiction and fantasy, there is no real prospect of a military takeover in this country.[30] (If anything, the greater danger for the past thirty years is the civilianization of the military arm.)

To understand civil-military relations in the United States, one has to develop a clear picture of the basic organizational concept behind the U.S. government. Dissenting in the case of *Myers v. United States* (1926), Justice Louis Brandeis wrote that "the doctrine of the *separation of powers* [emphasis added] was adopted by the Convention of 1787, not to promote efficiency but to preclude the exercise of arbitrary power. The purpose was, not to avoid friction, but, by means of the inevitable friction incident to the distribution of the governmental powers among three departments, to save the people from autocracy."[31] The division of political power—*horizontally* among the executive, legislative, and judicial branches; *vertically* between the national government and the individual states—deliberately complicated the processes of decision-making in the United States in order to thwart tyranny. Since 1787, the system has worked.

A basic question for soldiers has always been, which branch receives my first loyalty? According to the Constitution, Congress (legislative branch) has the responsibility of declaring war,[32] of raising armies (that is, imposing a draft or conscription), of maintaining a navy, and of establishing rules for military regulation (Article I, section 8). But the president is commander in chief of all armed forces (Article II, section 2). As Army Gen. J. Lawton Collins once said, "As a military man my Commander in Chief is the President of the United States. My loyalty is therefore to him."[33] But General Ridgway, a brave soldier who rarely complained about the enemy, did complain that, when he was Army chief of staff, the executive branch pushed him hard to tell Congress its position: "The pressure brought upon me to make my military judgment conform to the views of higher authority was sometimes subtly, sometimes crudely, applied."[34] And during the Gulf War of 1991, Air Force Chief of Staff Gen. Michael Dugan was summarily fired by Secretary of Defense Dick Cheney after Dugan made some observations clearly out of step with Bush administration policies.[35] In fact, Dugan was the first chief of staff to be fired since Admiral Louis Denfield was fired by the Truman administration in 1949, and the highest-ranking officer to be fired since MacArthur. So the relationships between the highest ranking officers of the U.S. military and the executive branch are not—nor should they be—entirely settled and secure.

The president of the United States as the chief executive is constitutionally responsible for "tak[ing] care that the laws be faithfully executed" (Article II, section 3) and is sworn to "preserve, protect, and defend the Constitution of the United States" (Article II, section 1). That means that the president is not free to devise policy wholly independent of congressional wishes. As long ago as 1956, one scholar said that "if Congress is to have the information from which debate flows and policy is resolved, the military must be allowed, and indeed encouraged, to speak freely."[36]

Civilian control of the military does not mean that there will be no tension between a fundamentally liberal American society and a basically conservative American military.[37] Samuel Huntington, for instance, has discussed two general approaches to the civilian control of the military in the United States. The first is "subjective control," by which he means an increase of civilian control to the point even of virtually civilianizing the military. "Objective control," by contrast, recognizes the particular expertise and professionalism of the military.[38] In essence, civilian control of the military is built upon two pillars. First, civilians determine the ends of the government, particularly in the area of national security policy; the military is limited to discussions about the *means* to achieve those ends. Second, the civilian leadership decides where the lines are drawn between ends and means, between civilian and military responsibilities.[39]

In the United States, the president, the secretary of defense, the secretaries of the army, navy, air force, and transportation (in the case of the Coast Guard) are civilians, whereas the chiefs of the uniformed services are professional military officers. This can lead to confrontation and controversy of course.[40] But there is not a single episode in twentieth-century American history of any American soldier challenging the *principle* of civilian control.[41] (There are, however, plenty of examples of soldiers challenging particular applications of that principle.) In an effort not only to reduce interservice rivalry,[42] but to strengthen the Joint Chiefs of Staff, Congress in 1986 passed the Defense Reorganization (Goldwater-Nichols) Act of 1986. The new law substantially increased the power of the chairman of the Joint Chiefs, who was established as the "principal military advisor to the President, the National Security Council, and the Secretary of Defense." There have been few challenges to the wisdom of that law.[43]

The American military thus works for our elected and appointed civilian leaders. The principle of civilian control is sacrosanct, whatever the occasional bewilderment owing to the concept of separation of powers. Constitutionally, the Supreme Court in the United States (the judicial branch) has the responsibility of judging the meaning of the Constitution. Although the courts generally play a small role in civil-military affairs, one thought runs like a red thread through the fabric of American civil-military relations: the subordinate sovereignty of the U.S. military.

If there is anxiety about ethics in the military, there is a similar kind of tension about politics in the military. The courts have generally supported "objective control of the military," contending, in essence, that the U.S. military, though of course subordinate to the civil authority, nonetheless, retains its own character and its own unique tasks. Two examples from 1974 will do. The Supreme Court, speaking through Justice Lewis Powell and citing precedents, contended:

> The military is "a specialized society separate from civilian society" with "laws and traditions of its own [developed] during its long history." *Parker v. Levy*, 417 U.S., at 743. Moreover, "it is the primary business of armies and navies to fight or be ready to fight wars should the occasion arise." *Toth v. Quarles*, 350 U.S. 11, 17 (1955). To prepare for and perform its vital role, the military must insist upon a

respect for duty and a discipline without counterpart in civilian life. The laws and traditions governing that discipline have a long history; but they are founded on unique military exigencies as powerful now as in the past. Their contemporary vitality repeatedly has been recognized by Congress.[44]

And Justice William Rehnquist, now Chief Justice, put it this way:

This [Supreme] Court has long recognized that the military is, by necessity, a specialized society separate from civilian society . . .

While the members of the military are not excluded from the protection granted by the First Amendment, the different character of the military community and of the military mission requires a different application of those protections. The fundamental necessity for obedience, and the consequent necessity for imposition of discipline, may render permissible within the military that which would be constitutionally impermissible outside it.[45]

The military's unique duties thus endow it with distinctive obligations and with a kind of "sovereign subordination" to the civilian government of which it is a distinctive part. Almost forty years ago, Huntington asked, "Is it possible to deny that the military values—loyalty, duty, restraint, dedication—are the ones America needs most today?"[46] A thesis of this book is that it is *not* possible to deny the need in our society today for those values, that we might resurrect the eagle.

Conclusions

The principal task of the military is to maintain true faith and allegiance to the republic by preparing to kill or die in its defense. While that statement appears to be severe, the central purpose of the military is to be an *armed force*.

This special purpose can lead to the "Loyalty Dilemma": soldiers' responsibility to be true to friends but not to the point of betraying professional duty; to be devoted to their chain of command and immediate superiors but not to the point of behaving obsequiously or illegally; to be faithful to the Constitution but not to the point of confusing their own political goals with those of elected leaders. Military recognition of the supremacy of constituted civilian authority is a chief principle of U.S. civil-military relations; civilian control of the military should always be coupled with a respect for the unique character of the armed services.

3. Military Training
Inculcating Fidelity to Purpose

> All a soldier needs to know is how to shoot and salute.
> —Attributed to John J. Pershing (1860-1948)

"To inculcate," explains one dictionary, means "to teach persistently and earnestly." Teaching may mean educating, or it may mean training. The two are often mistakenly equated, but knowing the critical—even vital—difference between the two is central to the themes presented in this book.

At its best, education has to do with examining and instilling values. A taxonomy of "levels of learning" popular some years ago (and still, somewhat curiously, employed at some military schools today) lists knowing, comprehending, applying, analyzing, synthesizing, and evaluation as the steps on the ladder of learning. Students of ethics might well respond that true knowledge is an understanding of the Good—of what ought to be—and that such contrived divisions may only divert serious students from pursuing the ends of genuine education. Genuine education, as argued in Chapter 1, consists of courses of study that help us first to distinguish between the honorable and the shameful and then resolutely to act upon those distinctions.[1] That education can for the most part be thought of in terms of *people*: their history, their culture, their relationships. Training, by contrast, involves instruction in using *things*: how to fly an airplane, how to throw a curve ball, how to change an oil filter, how to plant a garden, how to play the piano.

The distinction between training and education can easily be blurred. A high school student working in a store can be taught how to stock things on shelves and simultaneously be taught how to be courteous to customers. But the basic point is simple: education concerns values; training concerns skills. Education normally involves some training (for example, in how to use a library or a word processor); training normally involves some education (for example, "Here's how one fires an M-16 rifle; don't shoot it at friends"). Education without training in some basic skills may appear useless, but training without an understanding of values can be dangerous.

Consider a company of recruits who have just graduated from Marine Corps boot camp. They have a number of skills, many of them combat skills. But suppose they have had *no ethical education at all*—at home, in school, in church, or in boot camp. Are these new Marines likely to be a force for good or for ill? Training must be complemented by education if that training is to prove good for the student, cadet, or trainee—as well as for the parent organization and for society.

Military Training: Preventing Atrocity

In Chapter 1 you met the argument that "ethics is concerned with character, which is developed by rigorous education and fixed by virtuous habit. We are, as Aristotle once tried to tell us, the product of our practices." In Chapter 2 you met the argument that "the principal tasks of the military are to maintain true faith and allegiance to the republic by preparing to kill or die. While that statement appears to be severe, the central purpose of the military is to be an *armed force*." Military training is primarily concerned with converting civilians into soldiers who will serve their country with true faith and allegiance and, at the same time, be prepared to kill and die for it.

Military training that does not foster soldierly competence is a failure; but military training that does not also inspire soldierly values is a hazard to all concerned with it. Military training grows directly from the exigencies and needs of the armed forces. If the primary purpose of the armed forces is to fight and kill, then military training must endow soldiers with the abilities to fight well. As one writer has pointed out, "The nature of the military profession, and the responsibilities of the profession to the society it serves, are such as to elevate professional competence to the level of an ethical imperative."[2] In fact, philosopher Malham Wakin has correctly noted that professional competence may well be considered a moral obligation:

> Within the context of the professional ethic, it appears the line between incompetence and immorality is a very thin line, perhaps most obviously so in the military profession. It is obvious that an incompetent physician may, in a lifetime of practicing bad medicine, harm many of his patients, perhaps even cause some deaths. It is also disheartening to contemplate the damage that an incompetent junior high school teacher may do to developing young minds. But the incompetent military leader may bring about needless loss of life and indeed, at the extreme, may have at his fingertips the ability to destroy humanity as we know it.[3]

Speaking at West Point a few years ago, Fred Downs, a former Army infantry officer (who lost most of one arm to a land mine in Vietnam) told the cadets: "Your job is to kill the enemy and take ground!" He argued that if he were in charge of training combat officers, he would give a class called "The Dark Side of Command," which would concern killing and dying. Downs reported that at the conclusion of his lecture a high-ranking officer reproved him, saying, "Here at West Point we do not call it 'killing the enemy.' We call it 'servicing the target.'"[4] Two years later, Rick Atkinson's moving book about the West Point class of 1966 cited a number of West Pointers who echoed Downs's criticism of such sidestepping.[5]

Of course, military training and service must always deal with the fact that the perfect unit does not exist. Officers should realize that fact from the outset, says Downs: "They [officers] need to know that within their [unit] there will be people who gamble, drink, take drugs, sleep with prostitutes, get into fights, are racists, deal in the black market, defy authority, connive, malinger, are stupid, have mental illness, are major felons, rapists and killers, are petty criminals, have violent tempers, have a propensity to be undisciplined, are of low character, are defiant or just plain hard to get along with."[6] More selective recruiting and higher training standards will weed out some but not all undesirables. But military training cannot be planned or conducted by ethicists or other intellectuals who, despite (or perhaps because of) their good intentions, have no realistic understanding of military life and challenges. When malcontents like those described by Downs are accepted into and graduated from basic training or boot camp, we confront disaster.

Some might be prepared to say that the problems encountered by Downs were peculiar to the U.S. Army fighting in Vietnam, particularly from 1969 to 1973. That is not the case, as I have written elsewhere.[7] A glance at today's newspapers and magazines suggests that criminals among those supposed to be soldiers seem to be ubiquitous. "Perhaps there is a special corner in hell," *Time* magazine said in 1993, "reserved for soldiers who fire their weapons indiscriminately into a crowd of unarmed civilians."[8] The article was discussing the fifty-five people killed and scores injured when Indian soldiers conducted a massacre in Kashmir. The same issue recounted a military takeover in Haiti, the murder of Bosnia's deputy prime minister by Serb troops as he sat in a U.N. armored car, the deaths of about twenty-one Somalis in shootouts against the background of anarchy and mass starvation as "Operation Restore Hope" continued, and impending disaster in Russia.

Downs would understand another news report indicating that "elite" units of Serbian troops "have evidently made rape a gesture of group solidarity. A man who refuses to join the others in rape is regarded as a traitor to the unit, and to his Serbian blood. Sometimes, that impulse to bond with the male group becomes a kind of perverse inflaming energy inciting to rape." The report continues: "And sometimes, young men in war may commit rape in order to please their elders, their officers, and win a sort of father-to-son approval. The rape is proof of commitment to the unit's fierceness. A young man willing to do hideous things has subordinated his individual conscience in order to fuse with the uncompromising purposes of the group. A man seals his allegiance in atrocity."[9] It may very well be that the Serbian soldiers discussed here are "good" soldiers—that is, technically and tactically competent—but they bring disgrace and dishonor to the profession of arms. Their *training*, by including no genuine *education*, was hopelessly inadequate to the task of soldiering. Officers and soldiers not morally competent are not militarily competent. General Pershing (in this chapter's epigraph) was terribly wrong. Those in uniform who know no more of their ostensible profession than shooting and saluting are atrocities waiting to happen, whether in Serbia or My Lai.

On Military Incompetence

According to Norman Dixon, military incompetence is a product of complex interactions among three things: professionalized violence (by which he means "militarism," defined and discussed below), the nature of military organizations (which he sees as often fostering the ends of militarism), and the personalities of many of those attracted to a military career. Much of Dixon's work is debatable, and he sometimes begs the question by assuming the truth in matters where he is purportedly trying to determine the truth. Still, there is much in Dixon worthy of analysis. His main point is that we are mistaken in assuming that military incompetence is mere stupidity, although that can certainly be part of the problem. Training and education, to some extent, can overcome the problems Dixon outlines in a list of factors and common errors that in his view form a pattern of military incompetence among officers:

1. A serious wastage of human resources and failure to observe one of the first principles of war—economy of force.

2. A fundamental conservatism and devotion to tradition, with an inability to profit from past experience (owing in part to a refusal to admit past mistakes). This also involves a failure to use, or a tendency to misuse, available technology.

3. A tendency to reject or ignore information which is unpalatable or which conflicts with preconceptions.

4. A tendency to underestimate the enemy and to overestimate the capabilities of one's own side.

5. Indecisiveness and a tendency to abdicate from the role of decision-maker.

6. An obstinate persistence in a given task despite strong contrary evidence.

7. A failure to exploit a situation gained a a tendency to "pull punches" rather than push home an attack.

8. A failure to make adequate reconnaissance.

9. A predilection for frontal assaults, often against the enemy's strongest point.

10. A belief in brute force rather than the clever ruse.

11. A failure to make use of surprise or deception.

12. An undue readiness to find scapegoats for military set-backs.

13. A suppression or distortion of news from the front, usually rationalized as necessary for morale or security.

14. A belief in mystical forces, such as fate or bad luck.[10]

Although many of these items raise questions of high-level military strategy and thus transcend the boundaries of this book, two points must be made here. First, to quarrel with many of Dixon's criticisms as being too general or even contradictory (for example, MacArthur's 1950 triumph at Inchon was achieved despite very strong and reasonable opposition from other U.S. planners) is a mind-sharpening exercise. Second, Dixon's list does emphasize a vital fact: "Rank has its privileges" is an old military saying and a true one, but more important, rank has extraordinary responsibilities. To command is to exercise moral as well as military authority. Incompetence means moral failure.

For our purposes here, military incompetence in an officer may be understood as *mental, military, or moral lack of qualification to command*. A commander who is stupid, inept, or corrupt cannot and should not control the lives of troops—or the destiny of the country. This notion is contained in the aphorism that a commissioned leader is both "an officer and a gentleman."[11] Of course, as Stephen Covey points out in a recent book, "Most people equate trustworthiness with character alone. Character *is* vital, but it is also insufficient. For example, would you trust a surgeon to perform a critical operation who is honest in his bill-ing practices, but who has not kept up on advances in his field and is professionally obsolete?"[12] But a critical part of competence, I argue, is knowing what to be, in addition to knowing what to do—and both must be taught.

William Kilpatrick says it well: "None of us want to go to untrained doctors, or fly with untrained pilots, or have untrained soldiers protect our country, but for some reason we have come to believe that one can be a good person without any training in goodness. We have succumbed to a myth that claims that morality comes naturally, or at most, with the help of a little reasoning. . . . [But] the 'natural' thing to do in most situations is to take the easy way out. The most perfectly rational plan of action is to always put yourself first."[13] Taking the easy way out, always putting oneself first—these sound very much like a synopsis of Dixon's points, do they not? "The easy way" and "me first" are exactly what military ethics is not. Good training and education cannot wholly eliminate military incompetence, but together they can at least help to ensure that those who don the American uniform are mentally, militarily, and morally deserving of membership in the profession of arms.

Authenticity in Training

The term *atrocity*, "something shockingly bad," is most often applied to torture and massacre, but it can apply as well to misjudgment. Good military judgment is the meeting of preparation with chance: if the preparation is thorough, and the right circumstances present themselves, soldiers will do what they can and what they should. But to fail to prepare is to prepare to fail. Brutal, dehumanizing training—such as forming military bonds on the basis of shared rapes—is unconscionable, of course. But so is permissive, indulgent training which, to be blunt, accepts and passes the stupid, the immature, the lazy, or the inept—whether commissioned or enlisted.[14]

Though officers do bear the principal burden for their troops' actions,[15] there is little validity in the remark of Alexander Hamilton (1755-1804), "Let officers be men of sense and sentiment; and the nearer the soldiers approach to machines, perhaps the better."[16] Soldiers must be prepared to disobey illegal orders.

The old *respondeat superior* defense, as previously pointed out, does not release any soldier, officer or enlisted, from responsibility for his or her actions.[17] Thus we reach the dilemma of training: Civilians must be "broken" into the military mold; they are no longer "behind the plow." They must learn to follow orders *yet retain sufficient autonomy to refuse illegal orders* (more about this in Chapter 4). How is such balance to be achieved?

Soft training endangers new soldiers and the units to which they are posted after basic training or boot camp. In Robert Heinlein's classic novel about the military of the future, one soldier says of his training that "no trooper ever climbed into a capsule for a combat drop unless he was prepared for it—fit, resolute, disciplined and skilled. If he is not, it's not fair to the Federation, it's certainly not fair to his teammates, and worst of all it's not fair to *him*."[18] But Heinlein was a novelist, not a historian. The American record is not so clean. While there have certainly been multiple instances of brutality in American military training,[19] there have also been reports of training so easy that everyone slides through. Such training kills. It does not kill the enemy; it kills the very troops it is supposed to help protect.

Not even the best training can do it all, of course. The mind of the American student or soldier is no *tabula rasa*; it has already been written upon, indelibly, by the society from which he or she emerges. With respect to the devotion and discipline of both scholarship and military professionalism, colleges and military posts are powerless to make Spartans of Sybarites. Indeed, whatever the nationality in question, human "material" is malleable only to a certain point, whether by scholarly professors or by military martinets. To understand American soldiers and their training, one has to understand the society that bred them. Gen. Mark Clark put it this way: "A woman once wrote me that she hoped I would make a man of her son, who had just entered the Army, that I would develop his character. I replied to her that I would do my best, that I was sure his military service would help him, but that she should realize that we would have him for eighteen months and she had had him home for eighteen years. I added that the job of developing character in our youth was primarily the responsibility of the home, the churches and the schools."[20]

In 1950, as the Korean War began, one colonel made the remark that American soldiers of the late 1940s had "been nursed and coddled, told to drive safely, to buy War Bonds, to avoid VD, to write a letter home to mother, when somebody ought to have been telling them how to clear a machine gun when it jams. They've had to learn in combat [in Korea], in a matter of days, the basic things they should have known before they ever faced an enemy. And some of them don't learn fast enough."[21] One of the reasons that American soldiers were "nursed and coddled" in their training is that realistic combat training entails injuries— and even deaths—likely to prove unacceptable to the American public. Gen. James A. Van Fleet once observed that although the tendency to ensure perfectly safe training is surely understandable and commendable, it may at the same time defeat its purpose by costing lives in combat. He illustrated his point by telling how Americans in training are not permitted to hug their artillery's curtain of fire as they advance on an "enemy" position because it often costs casualties from "friendly" fire during the advance, even though the technique saves lives in the subsequent assault. The outcome is that, in combat, U.S. troops have to learn this tactic "on the job," resulting in much higher casualties than if they had been so trained. But, said the late General Van Fleet, "American public opinion would never allow it."[22]

Following World War II the U.S. Army became far less disciplined—at public demand.[23] There seemed to be little danger of war and thus no point in insisting on the kind of tough and realistic training that recruits had undergone during the war. The recruits of 1945-50 had not enlisted (or been drafted) to fight Hitler and Tojo. They had enlisted for any of a number of reasons: to see the world, to acquire some technical training for later jobs, to get away from home, to impress girlfriends. T.R. Fehrenbach explained the problem succinctly: "The new breed of American regular . . . not liking the service, had insisted, with public support, that the Army be made as much like civilian life and home as possible. Discipline had galled them, and their congressmen had seen to it that it did not become too onerous. They had grown fat."[24] This post-World War II Army, said Fehrenbach, "represented exactly the kind of pampered, undisciplined, egalitarian army their society had long desired and had at last achieved." In the final analysis, "it was not their fault that no one had told them that the real function of an army is to fight and that a soldier's destiny—which few escape—is to suffer, and if need be, to die."[25]

It is a truism that a military force is only as good as its training. American soldiers of 1950 were unprepared, both physically and psychologically, for the savage combat they met in the Korean hills. Combat correspondent Marguerite Higgins vividly describes the first battle shock of the undisciplined American soldiers fresh from the "vanilla-ice-cream kind of world [they had] been brought up in." She reported that to steady the troops, field-grade officers were at the front line, but even they were unable to overcome the confusion and chaos that attended the first series of North Korean attacks.[26] Many soldiers had come to Korea from Japan, where the occupation duty had been easy; few, if any, demanding field exercises had been required of them. Inadequate training doomed hundreds, perhaps thousands, of American soldiers to deaths which, had they been better trained, might have been averted.

Twenty years after the Korean War ended—or, more accurately, after a truce was agreed upon—American involvement in the Vietnam War came to an end. There were, to some degree, different American troops in Vietnam. In the early part of the war the U.S. Army, by most accounts, acquitted itself well, doing the kinds of things soldiers do when they are well trained. As hostilities continued, however, the Army began to disintegrate, as numerous studies suggest.[27] By the unhappy end of that war, the Army was in chaos.[28]

Meanwhile, the all-volunteer Army came into existence. In order to attract sufficient recruits, the Army developed a slick ad campaign, virtually imploring young men and women to sign up: "Today's Army wants to join you!" A quarter-century of experience with pampered troops had come to that. *The essence of good military training consists in fidelity to purpose.* An army exists to fight and, if need be, to kill. Basic training that is developed in response to the siren song of any other calling or purpose will eventually destroy the very fabric of the Army. Weak, ineffectual training obstructs the development of military competence and is unethical; it lacks fidelity to purpose.

In volunteer armed forces (assuming multiple divisions and a reasonably prosperous national economy), tension will always exist between the demands of serious training and the need to attract enough qualified volunteers. Generally, the Marine Corps has dealt well with the problem, but the Marine Corps is a relatively small force.[29] The Army, Navy, and Air Force must never again sacrifice fidelity to purpose on the altar of public relations. Fidelity to purpose in training means that recruits encounter serious and substantial training challenges. Training that is soft— or, alternatively, training that is brutal and dehumanizing (but militarily useless)—must never again be tolerated by the U.S. military as we move into the twenty-first century.

Again, T.R. Fehrenbach put it best: "On line, most normal men are afraid, have been afraid, or will be afraid. Only when disciplined to obey orders quickly and willingly can such fear be controlled. Only when superbly trained and conditioned against the shattering experience of war, only knowing almost from rote what to do, can men carry out their tasks come what may. And knowing that they are disciplined, trained, and conditioned brings pride to men—pride in their own toughness, their own ability; and this pride will hold them true when all else fails."[30]

A Training Philosophy

One could object that the tail is wagging the dog, that most American soldiers will never be in a combat situation. But the concept of fidelity to purpose reminds us that the task of the U.S. military is to prepare for war, as well as to wage it. Indeed, the Roman axiom *Si vis pacem, para bellum* (If you would have peace, prepare for war) suggests that the stronger and better prepared one's forces are, the less probable is conflict. That phrase is, of course, too glib, but the idea that, if a country is to have an army, it should be well trained, is plain. Edmund Burke (1729-97) once said, "An armed, disciplined body is, in its essence, dangerous to liberty. Undisciplined, it is ruinous to society." Thus both for reasons of deterrence of aggression and for reasons of simple law and order,[31] the military should be well trained and highly disciplined.

One could also object to tough training on the basis that certain skills in the Army, Navy, and Air Force are not "military." Why should cooks, clerk-typists, drivers, and even high-level technicians need to learn drill and weapons handling? Fehrenbach answers: "One of the persistent myths of American arms . . . is that technicians somehow are not and should not be soldiers. But when a man dons the uniform, whether he wears crossed muskets, the wheel, or the caduceus, events are apt to prove the falseness of that belief. For any man who wears his country's uniform, of whatever service, should be prepared to suffer, and if need be, to fight."[32]

If that argument is correct, the basic military training conducted by all the services should be the same, irrespective of military service or branch of enlistment. If bullets start flying, they do not seek out only Army Rangers or Marines; *every* person in uniform should be able to perform basic soldierly skills—or the person should be discharged as unfit to wear the uniform.

I believe the time has come for "jointness": the basic military training of enlisted personnel in all the armed forces—Army, Navy, Air Force, Marine Corps, and Coast Guard—should be consolidated and run by a central training command. The principle of fidelity to purpose suggests that all recruits should undergo substantial and serious joint training in common.[33]

No recruit, of course, would be accepted unless he or she could meet reasonable educational, fitness, medical, and personal standards. Having passed those tests, the recruit would be ready for initial military orientation (IMO), which would include

- physical fitness training; medical and dental checkups
- military socialization; understanding the military life
- drill and ceremony
- general military customs and courtesies
- military law
- basic character guidance and ethics[34]
- methods of self-protection and unit readiness for biological and chemical warfare
- first aid, including CPR
- continuing education in reading, writing, and mathematics

- basic firearms training
- map reading
- swimming certification

IMO would be conducted by selected Army, Navy, Air Force, and Marine drill sergeants and drill instructors who would come from a new branch of military service, the combined education and training command.[35] The IMO uniform would be non-service-specific fatigues, but cadre would wear the uniform of their service. IMO graduates would have to meet reasonable medical/dental, educational, fitness, and military achievement standards in order to join their service of choice after IMO. At the time of graduation from IMO, the recruit should be ready for advanced military training (AMT) in his service of choice. In short IMO would serve as an apprenticeship, during which time the recruit would essentially compete for a position in the U.S. military. Anyone entering the U.S. armed services as an enlisted member would have to be a graduate of IMO, after which he or she would be permitted the honor of official entrance into the U.S. military. AMT, conducted by each service (with different completion times), would emphasize advanced skills unique to that service:

- advanced weapons skills (Army and Marines)
- advanced map reading and land navigation skills (Army and Marines)
- patrolling, fire and maneuver (Army and Marines)
- advanced drill and ceremonies (all services)
- organizational patterns of the specific service
- advanced physical fitness (all services)
- advanced swimming and lifesaving (Navy and Coast Guard)
- advanced seamanship (Navy and Coast Guard)
- military traditions and expectations of the particular service
- continued higher education (all services)
- continued character guidance and ethical instruction (all services)

After AMT, recruits would be enrolled in skill training courses for the military occupational specialty (MOS), rating, or AFSC (Air Force Specialty Code)—that is, the military job—for which they had enlisted. Having proved themselves fit to wear the

U.S. uniform by passing IMO and AMT, they would move on to specific job training—at intervals receiving refresher training in basic military skills.

The idea of IMO and AMT would be to ensure fidelity to purpose: rigorous, serious military readiness.[36] "Military tradition," one writer observed, "can be described as the sum of attitudes, customs, and symbols of military life that succeeding generations have preserved and adapted in armies over time."[37] It is time—past time—to restore that sense of tradition, high purpose, and professionalism to every man and woman in American uniform.[38]

Anger in Training

It is a mistake of the first order to confuse rigorous, tough training with savage, sadistic treatment.[39] Young American enlisted or officer candidates should never have to confront training run by self-appointed martinets unable to distinguish between physical and mental challenge—which ought to be the rule of training—and downright cruelty, which should always be intolerable. In past military training, anger too often became a substitute for courage and a mask for fear. But disciplined armies look for reason, calm, and cool-headedness in their soldiers, and especially in their leaders.[40] This is not the proper forum for a dissertation about types and techniques of military training. But in a book on military ethics, one thing in this area must be underscored. Malicious training violates the fundamental precept of military ethics: It is shameful, and no soldier should be subjected to it, just as no soldier should practice it.

Vicious training is not the military way; it is a vile form of *militarism*. That distinction is important. Alfred Vagts, in his *History of Militarism*, writes:

Every war is fought, every army is maintained in a military way and in a militaristic way. The distinction is fundamental and fateful. The military way is marked by a primary concentration of men and materials on winning specific objectives of power with the utmost efficiency, that is, with the least expenditure of blood and treasure. It is limited in scope, confined to one function, and scientific in its essential qualities. Militarism, on the other hand, presents a vast array of customs, interests, prestige, actions and thought associated with armies and wars and yet transcending true military purposes. Indeed, militarism is so constituted that it may hamper and defeat the purposes of the military way. Its influence is unlimited in scope. It may permeate all society and become dominant over all industry and arts. Rejecting the scientific character of the military way, militarism displays the qualities of caste and cult, authority and belief.[41]

Major Tim Challans of the West Point English Department, in an eloquent paper about anger in training, suggests that the use of frenzy in combat training is counterproductive: it largely defeats its purposes. The goal is to produce soldiers who can reason and think through a problem.[42] Challans speaks of a West Point soccer coach who tells his players that he is not interested in hysteria. As a baseball coach, I offer a similar analogy: no infielder ever fielded a ground ball and no outfielder ever pulled in a fly ball by screaming invectives at them. Baseball is not frenzy; it is poise and aplomb. Military training is not frenzy, either; it is careful, crafted skill development. Anger, in the sense of screaming and being screamed at to the point of temporary loss of reason, has no place in a military—as opposed to a militaristic—training environment.

The Goals of Training

A few years ago an Air Force officer named Scott Sonnenberg explained that he hates war more than most "because I've been there and I've seen the devastation and misery it can cause. I've lost several close friends and seen my comrades in arms killed before my very eyes." But Sonnenberg explains that he is no militarist, no martinet, no mercenary:

When asked what I do for a living, I find myself in a bit of a quandary. If I wish to be perfectly honest, I should probably say that I'm a hired killer, but there's more to it than that. My usual response is to say that I'm a fighter pilot, but I don't think that makes the point either. Perhaps the best answer is that I'm a highly trained, intelligent, sophisticated killer with a conscience. Would I drop bombs on or strafe innocent women and children intentionally? . . . No. First, I'm not trained to do that. Second, such actions are militarily counterproductive. . . . Finally, I'm not an animal or a robot who either instinctively or on command reacts without fully thinking about what he's doing.[43]

In a very real sense, producing Sonnenbergs is what genuine military training is all about. Imagine a teacher who respects and even loves the students but is hopelessly incompetent and ill educated. Imagine a priest who is superbly educated in theology but routinely detests his parishioners (and who knows nothing about religion). Competence and character are inseparable, as Sonnenberg implicitly testifies. As an example, who would be the better commander, the real-life Sonnenberg or the grotesque fictional character Rambo?

Training in competence and character begins in the family, as James Q. Wilson wrote recently:

A moral virtue is not the product of formal instruction or even of mental reflection. The moral virtues include courage, moderation, fidelity, and good temper. Moral virtue is the product of habituation. "Ethics" comes from the Greek word "ethos," which means habit. Aristotle described the process as follows: "We become just by doing just acts, temperate by doing temperate acts, brave by doing brave acts." Moral virtue is the same as a good character, and a good character is formed not through moral instruction or personal self-discovery but through the regular repetition of right actions. These habits are formed chiefly in the family.[44]

The family, as Gen. Mark Clark said, is indeed instrumental in forming habits and character. For soldiers, however, there must be an additional family—their comrades-in-arms (see Chapter 7). Gen. John Vessey, former chairman of the Joint Chiefs of

Staff, said in 1984: "We, the fighters, sometimes think it all belongs to us. But, when we are wounded and picked up by some obscure medic to ease our pain, then we realize that we are no more important than he is."[45] The uniform is just that—uniform; it is an outward sign of a shared value system. It says, "We serve together. We share the risks, the sorrows, the joys, the pride; we know the meaning of 'true faith and allegiance' because it is what we say and what we do."

The military of the United States is an *armed force*, and it must always maintain fidelity to purpose, being prepared to kill and die. But that awesome responsibility must always be deeply rooted in a sense of national service, not in grandeur for a given commander or the glory of a militarist's career. In combining competence with character—and thus fulfilling the point and purpose of military training—the armed forces of the United States serve their country with honor because they serve their members well. "Successful battlefield leaders," says Army officer Don Riley, "serve their soldiers by meeting their needs for security, caring leadership, teamwork, ready equipment, discipline, tough training and *more* tough training. The selfless leader serves his soldiers so he may better serve his unit and the nation."[46]

Conclusions

Military incompetence is mental, military, or moral lack of qualification. To avoid it, training that maintains fidelity to purpose is tough, realistic, and authentic. It prepares soldiers for the responsibilities of their profession. The object of training is the inculcation of skills (competence) and appropriate values (character) into the minds and hearts of beginning soldiers. The U.S. military is an armed force, prepared to wage war, and held fast to the standard of honor by the notion of selfless service to the unit and to the nation. Ultimately, military training teaches not only the trade of soldiering but the profession of arms.

4. Military Education
Analyzing Fidelity to Purpose

> I never expect a soldier to think.
> —George Bernard Shaw,
> *The Devil's Disciple* (1897)

A professional military force exists principally to fight its country's wars and, if need be, to kill its country's enemies. Military training must therefore be faithful to this fundamental purpose. Training that is brutal and dehumanizing instills neither necessary skills nor correct values; training that lacks appropriate challenge and rigor produces soldiers who cannot perform their jobs.

The tension associated with training is that soldiers must be taught both to obey legal orders without hesitation *and* to disobey illegal orders. In order to achieve that split purpose, soldiers must be both trained in skills and educated in values. Their true faith and allegiance must be more than loyalty to leaders or comrades alone, more than loyalty to mission or task accomplishment alone. Their true faith and allegiance must be loyalty to the idea of virtue itself. Without that concept there is the danger that they will follow orders without any anxiety about the justice of those orders. Such anxiety, I will argue here, is desirable.

Obedience and Disobedience

Few, if any, students of the military would argue that obedience is not absolutely necessary to the conduct of battlefield operations or to the accomplishment even of peacetime responsibilities. As Field Marshal William Slim pointed out, "The more modern war becomes, the more essential appear the basic qualities that from the beginning of history have distinguished armies from mobs. The first of these is discipline."[1] Discipline, in this sense, amounts to strict control or orderly conduct.

The historian Barbara Tuchman once explained to the Army War College why the three-word motto for the United States Military Academy, "Duty, Honor, Country," no longer adequately defines discipline: "Country is clear enough, but what is Duty in a wrong war? What is Honor when fighting is reduced to 'wasting' the living space—not to mention the lives— of a people that never did us any harm? The simple West Point answer is that Duty and Honor consist in carrying out the orders of the government. That is what the Nazis said in their defense, and we tried them for war crimes nevertheless."[2]

Air Force Academy instructor Malham Wakin and his colleagues suggest that "because orders in the military must direct people to perform naturally distasteful acts—such as working under outrageously adverse conditions or risking their lives— obedient response ratifies the military structure."[3] They make this critically important point about obedience to the "wrong" order:

> When military officers are inclined to disobey because an order is wrong, knowledge of the facts and the probable consequences of disobedience is vital. Stupidity and incompetence, though they constitute in the military—particularly the military at war—the ultimate immorality, may be compounded when an order is disobeyed. Disobedience seldom eliminates the source of stupidity; in fact, it delivers to the incompetent commander a weapon for a righteous charge against the disobedient. A subordinate must further recognize that the wrong order may be as justified as any other order, and that it usually comes from a source with superior access to certain information.[4]

In other words, those who carry out orders may very well not have the perspective that their commanders have. (It is, however, entirely possible that commanders may not have the perspective of the troops—but it is the troops whose loyalty will be questioned in the face of their recalcitrance.) As Air Force Academy philosopher Kenneth Wenker puts it, "Obedience becomes the condition which allows us to attain the moral goals of the armed forces." Wenker calls obedience "a functional impera- tive."[5] The presumption must be, then, that orders are legal and, consequently, binding upon those who receive them.

In 1991 a doctor in the Army Reserve, Capt. Yolanda Huet- Vaughn, was charged with desertion for refusing orders to de- ploy to the Gulf during operation Desert Storm. A commis- sioned officer, Huet-Vaughn contended that the war was illegal and immoral, and she refused to accept her assignment. A mili- tary judge, during her desertion trial, said the issue was simply whether she refused deployment in order to avoid hazardous duty. She was dismissed from the Army and sentenced to two and a half years in prison.[6] Was she a conscientious person, worthy of respect, or an officer-impostor, derelict in her duty? What do custom, rules, outcomes, and circumstances have to say about her case? If the Gulf War of 1991 was a just war—as I believe it was—and if she refused service in that war, is there *any* war in which Captain Huet-Vaughn would serve? And if not, why had she continued to accept the pay and benefits of a U.S. Army officer—until deployment was ordered? One must presume that orders are valid, and that soldiers and commis- sioned officers will follow them.

"It is the duty of every good officer to obey any orders given him by his commander-in-chief." (The words are Nathan Hale's, though few now remember who spoke that sentence.[7]) Samuel Huntington argued that the military man's goal is "to perfect an instrument of obedience; the uses to which that instrument is put are beyond his responsibility." He quotes with approval the lines of Shakespeare's soldier in *Henry V* who believes that the justice of the cause is more than he should "know" or "seek after," for if the king's "cause be wrong, our obedience to the King wipes the crime of it out of us."[8] The simplest way for soldiers to go about their business is always to presume that orders are right—and even, perhaps, that "wrong" orders are "right."

Yet it is part of their burden that they cannot do that, either morally or legally. As West Point professor Anthony Hartle ex- plains, "Were the president or any other superior to issue an unlawful order, military officers would be obligated . . . to disobey it." But he points out that "equating duty with obedience to orders is a common but serious failing of the officer corps."[9]

Speaking on "Crimes in the Conduct of War," Justice Robert H. Jackson (1892-1954) said on 21 November 1945, during the Nuremberg War Crimes Tribunals: "The one who has committed criminal acts may not take refuge in superior orders nor in the doctrine that his crimes were acts of states. These twin principles working together have heretofore resulted in immunity for practically everyone concerned in the really great crimes against peace and mankind. Those in lower ranks were protected against liability by the orders of their superiors. The superiors were protected because their orders were called acts of state."[10]

In 1956 the U.S. Army spoke clearly on the issue: "The fact that the law of war has been violated pursuant to an order of a superior authority, whether military or civil, does not deprive the act in question of its character of a war crime, nor does it constitute a defense in the trial of an accused individual, unless he did not know and could not reasonably have been expected to know that the act ordered was unlawful."[11] In the next paragraph, however, the Army equivocated:

> In considering the question whether a superior order constitutes a valid defense, the court shall take into consideration the fact that obedience to lawful military orders is the duty of every member of the armed forces; that the latter cannot be expected, in conditions of war discipline, to weigh scrupulously the legal merits of the orders received; that certain rules of warfare may be controversial; or that an act otherwise amounting to a war crime may be done in obedience to orders conceived as a measure of reprisal. At the same time it must be borne in mind that members of the armed forces are bound to obey only lawful orders.[12]

What, then, are soldiers to conclude? They must obey all legal orders. They must disobey all illegal orders. The burden to distinguish legal from illegal ("We admit it's tough, but . . .") is theirs, even in a combat situation ("Well, we know that's a tough place to examine such questions, but . . ."). (Of course, the situation produces anxiety only for those who worry about such matters. Misfits who accept no authority have no such problems, nor do other misfits who accept *all* authority.) The canons of ethics (Chapter 1) are not helpful: By custom, we frown upon the slaughter of innocents, which, at root, is what a war crime is. By rule and law, we forbid war crimes. From the standpoint of result or outcome, we are hard pressed to justify war crimes. And situation ethics makes little attempt to educate us beyond telling us that we should act authentically or lovingly at the time—pretty feckless advice.

In the theater of war crimes the only things that are clear are the burdens of soldiering and of military ethics. If there is any way out of this impasse, it lies in the realm of personal character. Theodore Roosevelt is alleged to have said of William Howard Taft, "He means well—weakly." Soldiers cannot mean well weakly. They must have the ability to make their judgments of conscience (what should I do?) and their judgments of choice (what will I do?) the same. The four classic cardinal virtues— wisdom, courage, temperance, and justice (or truthfulness) are not just desirables for soldiers; they are necessities—and we sum them up in the word *character*.

Case Studies

Consider these ten actual or fictional examples of the kinds of problems soldiers confront.

1 (actual). During World War II, newsman Eric Sevareid saw two American soldiers relaxing near the body of a dead German soldier. When questioned, one of the soldiers responded, "Oh, him? Son of a bitch kept lagging behind the others when we brought them in. We got tired of hurrying him up all the time." Sevareid writes, "Thus casually was deliberate murder announced by boys who a year before had taken no lives but those of squirrel or pheasant. I found that I was not shocked or indignant; I was merely a little surprised. . . . As weeks went by and this experience was repeated many times, I ceased even to be surprised."[13] But if that was the customary treatment of prisoners, didn't custom make it all right?

2 (actual). As American troops in World War II lay under

siege during the Battle of Bastogne, Lt. Col. Creighton Abrams chose to disregard instructions and instead to try a dash straight into Bastogne. Abrams's commander was considered "weak"; if asked for a change in plans, he was thought unlikely to approve. So Abrams disobeyed orders and drove on—with fortunate results.[14] General Patton once observed that not many commanders have had the moral courage to do the right thing in the face of wrong orders. Since the results were good, didn't Abrams do the right thing? (He did end up as a four-star general and chief of staff.)

3 (actual). In World War II, a U.S. Army private approached an American lieutenant: "Lieutenant, sir, pardon me. I can't find my officer. We've got some [German] civilians in a house back there. What shall we do with them, sir?" The officer responded, "If you can spare a guard, send them back. If you can't, why, shoot 'em in the back. That's what we always did in my outfit. Don't take no nonsense from 'em." The private saluted and trotted off, perhaps to commit mass murder.[15] Was the private justified, by custom or by legal order, in shooting the civilians?

4 (actual). Three German soldiers were captured, and one of them refused to provide his name, rank, and serial number (as required by the Geneva Convention of 1929). The American battalion commander, angered, slapped the noncooperative prisoner, who then spat at the U.S. officer. Furious, the commander ordered the execution of the prisoners. Told of the impending executions, a U.S. platoon leader named Lieutenant Buxton walked away from his platoon and confronted the battalion commander, who was having the prisoners dig their own graves. He had "a heated discussion" with his commander about values; he learned later that the prisoners were not executed.[16] Was the lieutenant out of order in questioning his superior? Was he literally out of place in leaving his platoon? Was that desertion? Did the lieutenant set a good precedent?

5 (actual). After following the laws of his country ("Shoot to kill") rather than his conscience, East German border guard Ingo Heinrich was convicted of manslaughter for killing a man trying to flee to West Berlin in February 1989. Said his judge: "Not everything that is legal is right." But what is a crime now

in Germany was a soldier's duty in *East* Germany. Was Heinrich a scapegoat? He was, after all, a mere soldier at the end of a long chain of responsibility. It is understandable that some of those on trial "may view themselves as scapegoats, sacrificed to expiate the guilt of a whole society that was never taught about . . . higher moral authority."[17] Should one be tried ex post facto for something that was not a crime when it was committed? Wasn't Heinrich just doing his duty?

6 (actual). U.S. Army officers say that as tanks equipped with plows drove through Iraqi trenches in the 1991 Gulf War, enemy soldiers were trapped under tons of sand. One colonel reported seeing arms protruding helplessly from the sandy graves: "For all I know, we could have buried thousands." Suffocating in trenches is a grisly way to die. Yet a Pentagon spokesman asserted that the operation did not violate international rules of engagement: "There is no nice way to kill somebody in war," he said.[18] Should that colonel have refused to carry on with his operation? Did the Golden Rule suggest that because he wouldn't like to be buried alive, he should not have done that to others?

7 (fictional). In the novel *Once an Eagle*, the hero, an Army officer named Sam Damon, refuses to follow a training order that contravenes a standard safety procedure, citing the hazard to his men. When Damon's reservations prove to be correct, the training officer backs away from filing charges against him.[19] But doesn't realistic training sometimes require imperiling the troops? Who makes the judgment about which risks are acceptable and which unacceptable? If the trainees or cadets set the limits, what would become of demanding training? Should airborne, ranger, and other high-challenge training be abandoned? If not, what prevents training officers from going too far?

8 (actual). In Vietnam, one Army lieutenant, a platoon leader, was ordered by his commander to continue a sweep, despite the fact that his unit had already been ambushed on the same trail and some of his men killed. The lieutenant believed that the mission was unjustified and did not want to risk more lives. When the order was repeated, he recognized that "he was facing a classic conflict of a leader's dual obligations: Should he execute the mission or preserve the troops?" The choice: "I'm not going any further, he thought. I'm not going to get another

man killed. The mission was unjustified; it was an objective in the mind of a man who had never been in combat. [The lieutenant] was willing to take the consequences of refusing a direct order."[20] Was he right? Did he know more than his commander? Did he set a good example to his troops? Should he have been court-martialed for a combat refusal? Is this the *Pueblo* (see Chapter 2) all over again—on the ground?

9 (fictional). In the movie *Memphis Belle*, a U.S. aircraft is on a bombing mission over Germany. Heavy fire from the ground is endangering the lives of the crew. Cloud cover obscures the military target, and intelligence has informed the captain that near the target are a number of schools, hospitals, and churches. Some of the crew, knowing that they are over the general target area, want to drop their bomb load and escape the heavy flak. The captain decides to make another pass, desperately hoping that the cloud cover will move away and they will be able to drop their ordnance on the proper target. They make another pass, the clouds disappear, and they bomb the right target, sparing German civilians. If you had been a member of the crew, would you be proud of your captain? Did he do the right thing, legally and morally? Or did he risk your life for his conscience? The "loyalty dilemma" (described in Chapter 2) can be found in politics—and in airplanes.

10 (actual). From the Netherlands comes the report of a German soldier in World War II who was a reluctant member of a firing squad ordered to shoot innocent hostages. If he did not participate, his commander said, he could join the ranks of those about to be shot. That was his choice, and he was promptly shot by the same firing squad of which, only moments earlier, he had been a member. Was that an honorable decision from a soldier's perspective? Could the German officer have tolerated the soldier's refusal to serve on the firing squad? Did the officer do the right thing? "Were it not for the revelation of nobility in mankind, which again and again appears in time of war, we could scarcely endure reading the literature of combat," observes J. Glenn Gray.[21]

In cases like these[22] our tendency may be to say, "There are no right answers or wrong answers." In fact, I think there are some very clear right and wrong answers. But I will leave those answers to your judgment and discretion. It is true that hard cases make bad law, but it is not true that merely because a set of circumstances is difficult there is no fair, just, reasonable, and honest answer. But consider: If the person on the spot in each instance like those above is wise, courageous, temperate, and truthful, is it easy (easier?) to deal with the anguish of the problem at hand? Or are the cardinal virtues pleasant irrelevancies?

Virtue and Leadership

Jeane Kirkpatrick has said: "Good men are not necessarily good leaders. Good governments are not necessarily headed by good men." She contends that a political candidate's personal life is only one factor in choosing leaders, "and not necessarily the most important one."[23]

Contrast this view with the argument of military ethicist Anthony Hartle, who believes that "persons of strong character are the ultimate resource of military organization, and they are by definition persons of integrity—individuals whose actions are consistent with their beliefs."[24] Hartle's implied definition of integrity (actions consistent with beliefs) is incomplete, but his point is critical. Unless soldiers and public officials maintain reasonably high standards of personal honor, their personal misconduct can spill over into their professional endeavors.[25] Writing in August 1765, John Adams—later our second president—said that the people "have a right, an indisputable, unalienable, indefeasible, divine right to that most dreaded and envied kind of knowledge—I mean of the characters and conduct of their rulers."[26] Adams's counsel makes good sense when higher-ranking officials in any profession choose among candidates for election to their ranks. Characters and reputation matter. "No man is fit to command another that cannot command himself," observed William Penn in *No Cross, No Crown* (1669).

Perry Smith, a former Air Force major general and now a commentator for CNN, says that "of all the qualities a leader must have, integrity is the most important."[27] In the business world, "integrity seems to have a special meaning to executives," two students of top executives point out. "The word does not refer to simple honesty, but embodies a consistency and predictability built over time that says, 'I will do exactly what I say I will do when I say I will do it. If I change my mind, I will tell you well in advance so you will not be harmed by my actions.'"[28] The teaching profession, too, Hans Morgenthau once argued, requires "the dedication and ethos of the whole man. Of such a man, it must be expected that he be truthful not only between 9 and 10 A.M. when he teaches, but always."[29]

Perhaps the best short summary of this is that of the fictional military hero Sam Damon who says at the time of his death, "If it comes to a choice between being a good soldier and a good human being—try to be a good human being."[30] In a sentence, that is what military ethics means. People of high ability are important to any organization; people of high integrity are indispensable.

Principle, Purpose, People

Most problems in military ethics are much more prosaic problems of *ethics*, not just of military ethics. Most dilemmas in military ethics have little to do with the "adventure" and "romance" of seizing hills or conducting daring raids behind enemy lines, or performing other "Rambo-like" feats. Similarly, the favorite perplexing cases (for class discussion)—inflicting torture to get information so that one's comrades won't die in some prospective enemy ambush; shooting non-combatants in order to save other innocents; perhaps putting captured soldiers to death so that a commando operation won't be revealed—are also extremely rare. As one writer put it in a recent book, if students are given only the knottiest ethical dilemmas to deal with, they will conclude that ethics is either impossibly vague or wholly devoid of meaningful content.[31]

Many problems in the real world of military ethics deal with telling the truth to Congress,[32] filling out reports honestly,[33] or condemning sexual harassment. Very few soldiers spend even a small part of their service time in or near combat—but they do deal every day with ethical difficulties. It is all very well for new Army privates to wonder at length about the ethics of dropping atomic bombs on Japan in 1945. But one hopes that part of their military training—part of their military education—will concern the ethics of not misleading their NCOs about jobs completed, of personal conduct in a world saturated with drugs and sexually transmitted diseases, of representing their country well both at home and overseas.

Ethics classes are the places to ask questions such as whether it is ever permissible to lie (should you tell the SS officer in 1939 that there are no Jews in your basement when you are harboring a Jewish family there?) or to steal (may you rob a bakery to save your destitute family from starvation?). And ethics classes are the places to learn that, in fact, honorable men and women do not lie; they do not steal; they do not cheat; they do keep promises; they do their reasonable best to carry out their responsibilities; they try to treat others as they would like to be treated; and they attempt to set right the mistakes and omissions of their lives. Such concepts are not merely "military"; they are the stuff of integrity. And any organization or enterprise (family, church, army, corporation, university) deprived of people with such values will not and should not long endure, for it will consume itself in sheer wickedness. But where to start? Where to begin building accessible courses in ethics?

The place to start is the venerable West Point motto "Duty, Honor, Country." I say *venerable* because the motto is honorable and respectable. But it is hardly enough. Learning worthy mottoes or being exposed to honor codes cannot ensure that officers will, for example, never "lie, cheat, or steal—or tolerate those who do."

If one believes that one's first duty is to oneself, simply repeating the mantra *duty* means little if anything. Similarly, if one considers loyalty to the chain of command or the unit or the service as the highest allegiance, regarding that potentially corrupted loyalty as *honor*, the very concept of honor can ring hollow. If one exalts country before those very concepts that imbue patriotism with meaning and dignity, the ideal of *country* becomes fraudulent. A Latin phrase catches the point: *corruptio optimi pessima*—the corruption of the best is the worst. As Shakespeare put it, "Lilies that fester smell far worse than weeds" (Sonnet 94). A noble goal or mind perverted is worse than an evil goal or mind, for the original promises are betrayed and soiled.

After all is said and written, the ultimate task of education in ethics is to help soldiers or students at least to think through their ethical codes and standards (see Chapter 5) and to know what matters. If "Duty, Honor, Country" will not do, in and of itself, as a brief guide to ethics in the military, what will? The honest answer is, in a word, nothing. Taking courses in military ethics is no more a guarantee of ethical purity than, I must admit, teaching them. Knowledge of the good is not enough. (Some of us might insist upon moral courage and grace as well.) But of one thing we can be certain: Having discussed, read, and written about what one ought to do very probably increases the chances that one will do what one ought to do. Keeping physically fit, by the same token, is no guarantee of a long and healthy life, but it is a far better bet than indolence and obesity. Teaching military ethics is, then, an exercise in "consciousness-raising."

Ethics is about obligation, duty, and responsibility. Those who hold a personal and professional creed have the charge of trying to inculcate it in those to whom and for whom they are responsible. Although children may at times be fractious and ungrateful, parents are not relieved of their burden to teach their children right from wrong, according to the parents' best lights. Soldiers, similarly, must be educated about the nature of the profession they are about to enter. In a well-known science fiction novel, a teacher explains his view of why the term "juvenile delinquent" is a contradiction in terms: He argues that *duty* is an *adult* virtue: "Indeed a juvenile becomes an adult when, and only when, he acquires a knowledge of duty and embraces it as dearer than the self-love he was born with."[34] A man or woman devoid of a sense of responsibility can have no integrity, and any lessons in ethics will be worthless until that person develops the maturity to care deeply not only about others but also about the very nature of responsibility itself.

Teaching students that the trinity of military values is duty and honor and country is necessary but not sufficient: that is, soldiers must understand that theirs is a duty bounded by honor and beholden to country, but they must understand more than that. In fact, that trinity is in the wrong order. It should be honor first, then duty, and country—which I revise to *Principle, purpose, people*.

The soldier's first responsibility is to *principle*. We know since the war crimes tribunals after World War II that although obedience is essential, blindly following orders is not acceptable. Illegal orders *must* be disobeyed. But that requires knowing that principle precedes practice. The average trainee in basic training or in boot camp, quite frankly, is not interested in Kantian deontology but must nonetheless be taught, first, to obey all legal orders and, second, to disobey all illegal orders.

Military instructors must teach trainees that orders are to be presumed legal and ethical and consequently binding, yet that if an order flies directly in the face of all the soldier has learned to value, to take pride in, to believe in, then possibly the order is wrong. Would soldiers want people in their family, in their community, in their church, to watch them follow the order they received—to lie, to torture, to murder? (See the six-question guide to ethics in Chapter 7.) Would they want their soldierly peers to know what they are doing? Would those actions pass muster if understood and evaluated by responsible, respectable soldiers of yesteryear and of today? I don't suggest that soldiers would want their families to watch them in all military operations, but if those operations were publicized as conducted and later judged by a panel of professional military reviewers, would those soldiers feel comfortable and proud? Or would they feel guilt or shame or sorrow for their actions?[35] Attention to detail means attention to principle.

The second element in military ethics is the idea of *purpose*: that is "mission," "objective," "function," or "rationale." Soldiers are supposed to follow the general principle of honorable conduct, but they must conduct themselves honorably in the context of achieving their mission. The soldiers' purpose, after all, is to carry out orders; they serve the state; they are instruments of national policy. They exist for purposes beyond their own. Soldiers who elevate their personal well-being above their mission accomplishment are guilty of crass careerism, the kind of egoism that can have no proper home in the military ethic.

Not long ago, a team from Zamboanga City in the Philippines won the Little League World Series. Soon, however, authorities discovered that the team included a number of players older than the legal limit and recruited nationally, not just from the area around one city. On the baseball diamond, the Filipino team had a mission: to win. That was their purpose, and they fulfilled it. But no mature and reasonable person, knowing the facts, would applaud them. Purpose cannot ethically subvert principle. When it became known and published that they had cheated, they properly lost their tarnished title.

Finally, attention to *people* is critical. All worthy schemes of leadership and management, from those of the early Greeks to today's industrial efficiency standard known as Total Quality Management (TQM), emphasize the importance of treating people right—of being fair and honest. Soldiers, however, cannot elevate their countrymen to the highest position in the trinity of values. In the military, lives occasionally must be risked—never, of course, in a careless or negligent fashion. Without risk, many military purposes (and much military training, such as airborne training) could not be fulfilled. Sir John Hackett has written about the "clause of unlimited liability"—by which he means the idea that soldiers are signed on possibly to the death—as a reading of Article I of the Code of Conduct testifies.[36] People are not chattel to be spent at the whim of military commanders—as great leaders have known from Valley Forge to Desert Storm—but in the military, principle precedes purpose, and purpose precedes people.

That is the basic trinity of military values. Ethicists will be dismayed at how simplistic is that formula of Principle, Purpose, People, which is, of course, just a restatement of Honor, Duty, Country[men]. But it may make the point that the U.S. military treasures its people; conducts its operations with the conviction that missions can and will be carried out; and exalts, above all, belief in military operations and conduct that, if and when universally known, would bring credit upon its soldiers, its traditions, its institutions—as well as upon the country. The Uniform Code of Military Justice states that conduct unbecoming an officer or NCO is unjustifiable; so it is with the conduct of military operations.[37] The MacArthurian epigram "In war, there is no substitute for victory" is not enough; in the military profession, there is no substitute for integrity. As Air Force Chief of Staff General John D. Ryan put it twenty years ago, "Any order to compromise integrity is not a lawful order."[38]

Integrity

Integrity is a word which, like *time*, everyone can define until asked to. The *Oxford Dictionary* of 1901 defines *integrity* as "soundness of moral principle; the character of uncorrupted virtue, esp. in relation to truth and fair dealing, uprightness, honesty, sincerity." It is "soundness of moral principle" with which military education (indeed, all education) must primarily be concerned. Historically treasured principles provide criteria by which to assess actions which, although appearing virtuous or proper for a moment, may, in the light of reflection about the long-standing values of the institution, be judged wrong or even odious. Public and professional review of actions, leading to communal honor or shame, provides perspective from which to judge the case at hand.

Under the malfeasant leadership of a rifle platoon leader, a group of American soldiers is ordered to fire indiscriminately at unarmed and unresisting civilians, having been told that they are the enemy. If everyone in the platoon fires at the civilians, is the action acceptable because everyone does it? Philosophers will recognize the circular reasoning here: everyone does it, so it's "moral"; it's "moral" because everyone does it. In any case, the platoon members draw closer together, protecting one another from the possibility of being labeled "war criminal." But what of the long-standing values of the institution to which the platoon belongs? What of the ideal code of the warrior? Is there no clash here between the murderous actions of a small group and the cherished traditions of the United States Army?

In fact, *integrity*, the *Oxford Dictionary* of 1901 goes on to tell us, also means "the condition of having no part or element taken away or wanting; undivided or unbroken state; material wholeness, completeness, entirety." In mathematics, an *integer* is any positive or negative number (or zero), as opposed to a fraction. Integrity, then, is wholeness within the treasured principles of an institution. Murders committed by war criminals are clearly and reasonably not in the hallowed tradition of the institution in whose service that platoon was supposed to be. The actions of that group or platoon may have appeared proper at the moment (given the order by the lieutenant and the participation of all in the platoon), but there is not a shred of doubt that what took place was murderous. What may appear moral can be seen as completely unethical once the accurate, authentic perspective is attained. And "fraudulent morality" tears open the character and the unity of the group.

The key is, again, integrity. Is this action right—regardless of what the people in my group at the moment may think—in view of the long-term values and virtues of the larger institution whose principles I serve? Is this purpose, this practice, consistent with what the pioneers and pacesetters of this institution would say? Will this action stand the test of publicity among the leaders of the past, the present, and the future?

An officer stands before a congressional committee to offer testimony—and lies, justifying the lies in the name of his skewed perception of the national interest. But can such rationalization stand the test of long-term ethics (even if his temporary group approves his prevarications)? Would his country, his government, his church, his community, his college approve those lies? That "everybody here does it" may be true, but have the venerable and cherished traditions of his country, government, church, community, and college consistently applauded lies and cheered fraud? As Colonel Wakin explains: "When the military or any branch of the military places its own interests ahead of the nation's overall interest, we soon see elements of . . . militarism," which is "careerism writ large, and both are grounded in the ethics of self-interest."[39]

Ethics demands loyalty to and respect for more than sheer self-interest. Ethics education similarly demands that we emphasize not just the practices accepted by the group but larger questions and greater concerns. If all that matters is what one's group believes at any one time, then all that matters in ethics instruction is cultural relativism.[40] If every group determines its own standards of honor and of shame, we are then ethically powerless to assess Hitler's Germany or a street gang's thuggery. If no universal standards[41] exist for right and for wrong, might does make right; there is no profane, for there is no sacred; there are no villains, for there are no heroes; and as there is nothing worth dying for, neither is there anything worth living for. Ethics education comprehends that the liberal arts, when they are more than prostituted prizes of political correctness, teaches that men and women of integrity have existed in all creeds and colors and cultures, that character is truly universal and worthy of study and emulation.

Most ethical dilemmas confronted by most soldiers, as I have pointed out, are not the stuff of military action movies. They more often concern questions of fraud, waste, and abuse; [42] exploitation and degradation of subordinates;[43] environmental and ecological damage (the U.S. military is the nation's No. 1 polluter);[44] and the ever present challenge of truth-telling. Military ethics insists that, if necessary, we be good human beings before being good soldiers. John Silber explains it this way:

> A four-star general headed for the chairmanship of the Joint Chiefs of Staff may be asked by the commander-in-chief for his best advice on a professional issue with serious political ramifications. The general may suspect that the commander-in-chief wants advice that is contrary to the general's best professional judgment, and that to state his true opinion may lead to premature retirement. The history of Vietnam records examples of presidential importuning of just this sort. But the general should fear the dishonor of denying the commander-in-chief his best professional judgment. Morally, such a failure would be indistinguishable from abandoning one's post under fire. The soldier should be prepared not only to die for his country, but to be fired for it.[45]

When Gen. Colin Powell expressed reservations—his best professional judgment—about gays in the armed forces, one newspaper columnist named Collins took him to task for "insubordination." Retired Chairman of the Joint Chiefs Gen. John Vessey wrote back to challenge Mr. Collins, quite correctly, for failing to understand Powell's responsibilities.[46] All General Vessey really needed to do was to send the columnist a copy of the passage quoted above from Boston University President Silber. A sense of duty and a sense of loyalty mean neither timidity nor obsequiousness.

Ethical study does not inoculate people against all evil. At best, it helps them ask questions about genuinely virtuous conduct. It helps them ask not merely whether an order was given but whether it should have been given. Ethical education does not undermine proper authority; it is not seditious. Rather, ethical education helps achieve strong support for authority that is legal and moral and ethical. Actions that are in keeping with good law, consistent with traditional practice and high purpose, and compatible with honorable principle are invariably deeds of integrity.

In 1949 Douglas Southall Freeman lectured to the Naval War College on the subject of leadership. "I don't believe I'm oversimplifying it," he said, "when I say to you, know your stuff, be a man, look after your men."[47] I don't believe I am oversimplifying ethics when I write that good leaders and sound teachers put principle first and purpose second and people third. Their own careers and their own conceits are a very distant fourth. In this way, the old Fort Benning motto "Follow Me!" is given new meaning and new purpose.

Conclusions

Soldiers must disobey illegal orders, which they are best able to identify not as lawyers but as human beings who refuse to commit acts that their families, schools, churches, and communities would regard as barbarous and shameful. They must become persons of integrity, because without proper moral character talent lacks purpose, direction, and meaning; talent without honor is like a ship without a rudder. Whether or not character can be taught, there is little doubt that it can be learned. In the end, "teaching character" is best done by modeling character: that is, by teachers who display those traits and embody those principles essential to integrity.[48]

5. Military Codes
Mars and Cupid

> The superior man is intelligently, not blindly, faithful.
> —Confucius (c. 500 B.C.), *Analects* 15.36

In Roman mythology, Mars was the god of war, and Cupid was the god of love. Among the words we derive from *Mars*, of course, is *martial*. Among the words we derive from Cupid are *cupidity*, meaning strong desire, especially for wealth, and *concupiscent*, referring to strong appetites, especially lust. The tension between Mars and Cupid, dating at least to Roman times, may be particularly strong today.[1] Understood properly, the code of the warrior, with its emphasis on sacrifice, "will stand the test of any ethics or philosophies the world has ever known," said General MacArthur, because "it emphasizes the things that are right and condemns the things that are wrong."[2] The chief challenge to ethics in America—hence, to military ethics—is, in a word, cupidity: greed, excessive self-indulgence, insatiable appetite for the goods of the body.

This is not the forum to engage in a jeremiad about the imminent demise of America. The United States, of course, is not the Rome of yesteryear, and the collapse of the republic is hardly impending. It is nonetheless true, as George Roche has pointed out, that "we live in deepening shadow."[3] Historians such as Oswald Spengler and Arnold Toynbee, and more recent scholars such as Paul Kennedy, have studied in some detail the rise and fall of civilizations, particularly of Western civilization. Except for certain cults, few people expect American society to disintegrate in the next few decades. But the signs seem to be all around us that the American eagle is sick unto death. In virtually every aspect of American society there is a kind of cupidity at work, attacking the fabric of the ministry, government, education, business and commerce, the law, the entertainment industry, and the military.[4]

The chasm between Mars and Cupid can be seen clearly in one example. Professor Joseph Brennan recently published *Foundations of Moral Obligation: The Stockdale Course*.[5] The book emerged from the course in moral philosophy that Admiral James B. Stockdale pioneered at the Naval War College after his searing experiences as a prisoner of war in Vietnam. Professor Brennan went to the Naval War College to work with Stockdale in developing the course, the fruits of which are available in this volume. He writes, "To the prisoner escaped from the cave or released at last from the prison cell, the right and the good cannot be taught by precepts mounted with fine words like *values, integrity, morality*, or even *leadership*. Instead, the right and the good must be demonstrated every day in the choices that we make, the actions we take, the example we set."[6] That sentence is natural in the context of this book, and that sentiment is not out of place among military officers and at reputable military schools, such as the service academies, serious military colleges such as the Citadel and Virginia Military Institute, and the war colleges in Montgomery, Newport, Carlisle, and Washington. But the chasm between Mars and Cupid is evidenced by the fact that Brennan's sentence would ring hollow in many areas of American life. Not only would few leaders want to read his book; few leaders *could* read his book. Unless there are exemplars of virtue—as well as readings in virtue—the teaching and the inculcation of moral philosophy will become a lost art.[7]

The Corrosion of Virtue

Modern "progressive" education and ethics bereft of standards both owe their existence to the triumph of Enlightenment values, once succinctly explained by Carl Becker: "The essential articles of the religion of the Enlightenment may be stated thus: (1) man is not natively depraved; (2) the end of life is life itself, the good life on earth instead of the beatific life after death; (3) man is capable, guided solely by the light of reason and experience, of perfecting the good life on earth; (4) the first and essential condition of the good life on earth is the freeing of men's minds from the bonds of ignorance and superstition, and their bodies from the arbitrary oppression of the constituted social authorities."[8]

The idea that there is truly such a thing as "evil" seems, to many, a medieval notion entirely out of place in the modern world. Our understanding of evil extends to little more than the horror films (frequently amounting to celebrations of atrocity and brutality) burdening the shelves of rent-a-movie businesses. The *real* horror (such as that addressed by Mary Shelley [1797-1851] in *Frankenstein*) that humans relish dominating and exploiting other humans is rarely addressed.[9] The study of real evil, after all, requires a theological and philosophical effort and erudition rarely, if ever, found in modern film. When we restrict evil to the movie screen, or attribute its causes entirely to chemical imbalances in the brain, to poverty, to junk food consumption, to excessive or inadequate government, we essentially explain away atrocity.[10] But, the medieval philosophers told us, evil is not "out there"; it is "in here"—that is, in us—and to deal with it daily requires wisdom, courage, temperance, and justice. Those cardinal virtues seem, to some, as antiquated as they are unfashionable. But ethics rests squarely on the idea that virtue *and* vice exist; that they must be understood; that the former is to be exalted, the latter extinguished, insofar as we are able, with our own reason ennobled by grace.[11] The final triumph of evil will be universal denial of its existence (save as "entertainment" in the movies).[12]

The very idea of virtue insists that there are things worthy of "true faith and allegiance" as well as things unworthy of such devotion. Cupidity insists that only life itself merits loyalty and, more immediately, that only I merit my own loyalty. Ideas such as sin, religion, faith, obligation to first principles, and duties to comrades and country seem old-fashioned if not downright silly.[13] Although the modern emphasis on reason and science is desirable, one must ask whether science contains all that humankind needs—or does science itself require the direction imparted by moral purpose in order to deal with ultimate problems of life and death? Valuable as it is, science—as distinguished from the ethics of science—seeks to be value-free; it raises no questions about responsibilities.

When the idea of obligation to one's comrades and community is eliminated, the only hero then will be Ayn Rand's ultimate individual, who proclaims his ego to be his god. The ultimate triumph of the libertarian idea will be the abolition of heroism— unless a "hero" is redefined to mean one enslaved to cupidity itself. Russell Kirk put the matter well: "What binds society together? The libertarians reply that the cement of society (so far as they will endure any binding at all) is self-interest, closely joined to the nexus of cash payment. But the conservatives declare that society is a community of souls, joining the dead, the living, and those yet unborn; and that it coheres through what Aristotle called friendship and Christians call love of neighbor." [14]

Modern life is characterized by so much bewilderment about right and wrong that some people insist there are no questions of right and wrong, of honor and shame, of virtue and vice. Because there are no universal standards from which to judge, we are told, there is not way of determining the "Ought" from the "Is." Alasdair MacIntyre labels this view "emotivism," which he defines as "the doctrine that all evaluative judgments and more specifically all moral judgments are *nothing but* expressions of preference, expressions of attitude or feeling, insofar as they are moral or evaluative in character." [15] Cupidity, the disease of the American eagle, has two main symptoms: nihilism (the belief that there is no purpose in existence and the rejection of traditional morality) and solipsism (the belief that the self is all that matters and is real). If there is no purpose to life and if there is no meaning except what pleases me, ethics has no function; it is a shallow, pedantic exercise, and its conclusions must be mere emotivism. There may well be "rights" under the banner of emotivism, for each individual will insist on his or her privileges and prerogatives. But the final triumph of solipsism will come when the idea of "right" and of duty is blotted out as archaic and absurd.

There is, as Hannah Arendt has pointed out, no authority left to us, for "authority has vanished from the modern world." She explains that "since we can no longer fall back upon authentic and undisputable experiences common to all, the very term has become clouded by controversy and confusion." Finally, she contends that authority implies "an obedience in which men retain their freedom."[16] But we know that authority, in one sense of the term, has certainly not vanished; the policeman who stops us for speeding is an authority. But that is not the sense in which the term is used philosophically. One dictionary suggests that *authority* means "the power to judge, act, or command." In precisely that sense, the modern world lacks those reference points upon which there is moral consensus, obedience to which confirms and fulfills our liberties.

Obedience to certain nutritional laws, for example, does not enslave us but increases our prospects for health. Obedience to certain physiological laws—such as the need for adequate exercise or sleep—likewise improves or preserves our health. No one will call us slaves because we do what nature clearly intends us to do as healthy humans. Yet numerous people would object that it is little better than silly to insist that moral laws too can sustain and guide us. It is in the existence of moral law, however, so often disputed these days, that virtue, a sense of community and of duty, and the noble notion of heroism find unity. Hans Morgenthau explains:

> It is one of the great paradoxes of civilized existence that . . . [human life] is not self-contained but requires for its fulfillment transcendent orientations. The moral law provides one of them. . . . human existence . . . cannot find its meaning within itself but must receive it from a transcendent source. . . .
>
> You are still in all likelihood closer to your birth than to your death, yet in the measure that your life approaches its natural limits you will become aware of the truth of that observation. For when you look back on your life in judgment, you will remember it, and you will want it to be remembered, for its connection with the things that transcend it. And if you ask yourself why you remember and study the lives and deeds of great men, why you call them great in the first place, you will find that they were oriented in extraordinary ways and to an unusual degree towards the things that transcend their own existence.[17]

The Ominous and the Occult

Why should a book on military ethics concern itself with such matters as transcendent moral law? The reason is pressing: the American military, as suggested in Chapter 2, is separate from but nonetheless a part of a larger parent society. Eventually, cupidity and crass narcissism in that larger society will seep into and destroy the ethics of the smaller body. The ethical beacon light of Mars, emphasizing Principle, Purpose, People (Honor, Duty, and Country), must light the path for society to follow or, as time passes, the beacon light itself will burn out. American society is not dead, but it is diseased, and time is not on our side. Autism is a psychological term meaning a state of mind characterized by daydreaming, hallucinations, and disregard of external reality. *The eagle's disease is moral autism.* And the autistic cannot distinguish right from wrong; ethics does not exist in their world.

But humanity cries out for some god, and Americans are no exception. Consequently, we are in the midst of a supposedly pious wave known as the New Age movement. A hybrid mix of spiritual, political, and social forces, it counts perhaps 10 percent of Americans as followers. In this movement, there are no absolutes; humanity itself is divine; contact with the dead is not only possible but frequent; and psychic experiences are common.[18] More than half a century ago, J. Elliot Ross (1884-1946) pointed out that "man's curiosity is unlimited, and designing persons have always been able to play upon it in various ways."

> P.T. Barnum said that the American people wanted to be fooled, and what he said of Americans is true quite generally of the human race. Men have been willing to believe in all sorts of false and foolish ways of forecasting the future, from reading signs in the flight of birds to inspecting the viscera of persons especially sacrificed for this purpose, from the oracles of pagan Greece down to our own gypsies and spiritists.[19]

The "superstition" which many Enlightenment thinkers—notably Voltaire—wished to destroy was Christianity; we witness now the resurgence of a real superstition which is increasingly part of the American social ethos. As Robert Maginnis quite correctly points out, "The Army faces a value crisis because many influential American institutions communicate ideas that are often contrary to the critical Army values."[20] That is, in fact, something of an understatement. The American military ethic[21] cannot long endure in the face of the emotivism and the occultism saturating American society. For military professionals to discuss honor and shame, to preach the ideals of duty and obligation, and to teach moral philosophy to those imbued with the New Age ethic is to sermonize about chastity in a bordello.

George Will had it exactly right in his observation that "never before in the nation's experience have the values and expectations in society been more at variance with the values and expectations indispensable to a military environment."[22] "The fact of the matter is that those who serve the nation in a military capacity no longer can assume any dominant moral consensus in the United States," writes Professor Donald A. Zoll, who believes that the lack of ethical homogeneity may be tolerable in the country as a whole but that "ethical incongruities are simply not feasible in a military establishment."[23]

The Restoration of Virtue

A strong, healthy arm on a body otherwise diseased will not long endure. Despite the end of the Cold War and giddy talk about the end of history, we recognize that problems are all around us. Cecil Crabb once pointed out that "Americans have found it difficult to accept *partial solutions* to age-old problems disturbing the peace and security of the international community." We are slow to learn, he says, that "few problems in human affairs are ever 'solved' in a final sense. They are ameliorated, softened, mitigated, made endurable, adjusted to, outlived—but seldom eliminated."[24] Acknowledgment that we are not God, that progress in critical moral issues is neither inevitable nor even likely, that the existence of cupidity suggests the importance of safeguards of power abuse both nationally and internationally[25]—the recognition (that is, knowledge again) of these verities will do a great deal to restore our sense of perspective about people and politics.

A good place to begin thinking about both politics and ethics is Lord Acton's apothegm "Power tends to corrupt and absolute power corrupts absolutely." Ethics and politics are rooted in human nature—its power, its peril, its potential—and "no process has been discovered," Stephen Bailey has written, "by which promotion to a position of public responsibility will do away with man's interest in his own welfare, his partialities, race, and prejudices. Yet most books on government neglect these conditions; hence their unreality and futility."[26]

And yet, Bailey's brilliant essay continues, "man's feet may wallow in the bog of self-interest but his eyes and ears are strangely attuned to calls from the mountaintop. As moral philosophy has insistently claimed, there is a fundamental moral distinction between the propositions 'I want this because it serves my interest,' and 'I want this because it is right.'" No one ever framed ethical questions more concisely than this: "Man's self-respect is in large part determined by his capacity to make himself and others believe that self is an inadequate referent for decisional morality. This capacity of man to transcend, to sublimate, and to transform narrowly vested compulsions is at the heart of all civilized morality."[27] Reflection on the truth that ethical relativism leads inevitably to nihilism can do a great deal to restore serious examination of the idea of moral and natural law.

Colonel Wakin of the Air Force Academy has suggested that the military virtues (subordination of the self to the good of the nation and to that of one's unit; courage, obedience, loyalty, and integrity) are, in fact, virtues in any human society; in the military, these virtues are "functional imperatives."[28] Rights, we must learn all over again, flow from duties done; personal and political liberty results from obedience to the moral law, not from its denial or annihilation.

Our society continues to have a desperate need for heroes, not to worship but to emulate. The notion of a hero as one who is successful in achieving multiple sexual conquests, in accumulating vast wealth, or in engaging in Rambo-like exploits will lead to our total spiritual impoverishment. The choice of hero reveals a great deal about the one who chooses. (Try, for example, to name five contemporary, genuine heroes.) Gilgamesh, Achilles, Beowulf, Sir Gawain, Roland—compile your own list of classic heroes—must replace the Sybarites too many of us seem to adore today. Our present heroes should be our parents and grandparents, teachers and priests, and other honest and industrious people around us. But until we recover the meaning of "hero" (see Chapter 8), and until our entertainment industry develops a sense of social responsibility, we may be calling "hero" people whom we should pity rather than praise.

Finally—in addition to recovering our sense that evil exists and that cupidity is a fact of personal and political life; that obligation to our community should be as important to us as it was to Socrates;[29] that real heroes can and do exist—we need to restore our respect for authority. Students learn in college English classes—or used to—that writers footnote papers so that readers, if interested, can check on the sources used. If I quote the college baseball coach as my authority on a short story by Flannery O'Connor, someone might well suggest that there are other, better authorities. If we differ as to the date of American entry into World War I, we might agree to accept, say, the *Encyclopedia Americana* as a common and authoritative reference on which to rely for the correct date.

There are two basic kinds of authority, directive and assertoric. A person who has directive authority can give orders that others are bound to follow. The person who has assertoric authority can speak from recognized expertise to some area in which he or she can offer instruction and guidance that others have reason to follow.[30] How do we find leaders whose directive *and* assertoric authority we can trust?

Good leaders are the products of a serious, substantial system—as are good soldiers. Good education helps to produce virtuous and competent leaders; weak education helps to produce vicious and incompetent leaders. The connecting point between good ethics and good politics is good education in the very same way that serious, challenging military training and education are the source of leaders whose character inspires the reasoned obedience that, we have seen, is the core of true faith and allegiance. Military ethics, properly understood, can present a moral wake-up call to America. Military ethics, properly taught, reminds us that there are things worth knowing and doing. Military ethics, properly lived, informs us that soldiers and civilians alike lead lives of honor to the extent that concern for principle and purpose and people animates them. Military ethics tells us that integrity can be taught well by word but better by deed. We so much need that clarion call of the ancient spirit code!

Moral Leadership

Moral leaders serve as role models to subordinates, peers, and superiors. Aside from keeping their own affairs in order, they will not tolerate serious failings in others who share their profession. They build trust in themselves, even though they will admit errors.[31] Moral leaders frequently subordinate their personal goals to those of the organization.[32]

Without moral leaders there cannot be any military ethics, which demands reasoned choice among competing alternatives. Military institutions form their leaders as surely as leaders built the institutions that "shape character by assigning responsibility, demanding accountability, and providing the standards in terms of which each person recognizes the excellence of his or her achievements."[33] The leader produces and is produced by institutions. As one group of scholars put it: "We are not self-created atoms manipulating or being manipulated by objective institutions. We form institutions and they form us every time we engage in a conversation that matters, and certainly every time we act as parent or child, student or teacher, citizen or official, in each case calling on models and metaphors for the rightness or wrongness of action. They are the substantial forms through which we understand our own identity and the identity of others as we seek cooperatively to achieve a decent society."[34]

Good customs matter in ethics and in politics. The company we keep, the counsels of our society, and the social conventions and rituals we accept and practice help to form us, as do the dogmas that inform our actions. Although the word *dogma* is often misunderstood, Russell Kirk argues persuasively that it is critically important to moral leadership: "A dogma is not a value-preference [or mere emotivism]. A dogma is a firm conviction, received on authority. No one but an ass would die that his value-preference might endure; while dogmatic belief sustains saints and heroes."[35]

Good laws and rules matter in ethics and in politics. Moral leaders are virtuous both during and after duty hours. As Justice John Marshall Harlan (1899-1971) put it in a 1969 Supreme Court case: "The soldier who acts the part of Mr. Hyde while on leave is, at best, a precarious Dr. Jekyll when back on duty."[36] Kenneth Wenker has emphasized that American military leaders, when confronted with ethical conflict, must choose "on the side of basic American values rather than on the side of expedience or mere reflex to orders."[37]

Good outcomes, consequences, and goals matter in ethics and in politics. It matters, too, about the situations in which leaders find themselves. Rick Atkinson's study of the West Point Class of 1966 recounts the experience of officers who frequently discovered after leaving the service that church, family, school— "all of the temples of authority and moral instruction—had been weakened." In the world of business the fundamental query to be asked was, will it earn a buck? In the Army there had been basic precepts to apply "in times of moral quandary." A conscientious officer could rely on a few simple questions: "Is it good for the troops? Is it good for the country? Is it honorable?"[38]

The ability to apply enduring principles to shifting circumstances matters in ethics and politics. When West Point instructor Anthony Hartle discusses moral education, he refers to "the process of learning what is acceptable behavior and recognizing that others expect such behavior."[39] Thus, knowledge of custom and dogma; of rules and laws; of probable outcomes, consequences, and goals; and of applying general principles to specific situations—this knowledge is the product of a conscience well formed by serious and substantial education.

Codes of Conduct

Such knowledge and such education may not always be available to young officers and to even younger enlistees. The military codes are "paradigm examples of sets of ready-made rules."[40] Codes differ little from dogmas, which are doctrines put forth authoritatively. Here again is Russell Kirk on *dogma*: the word "is derived from a Greek root meaning 'that which seems good.' A dogma is a settled opinion: a principle, maxim, or tenet firmly established. It is a principle or doctrine received on authority—as opposed to one based on personal (or general short-run) experience or demonstration." [41] Like dogmas, codes are encapsulations of wisdom and of virtue. They are hortatory and heuristic: that is, they exhort us to act as we should and, at their best, stimulate us to investigate and discover more about the concepts they seek to promote.

Professors Fotion and Elfstrom have explained different kinds of military codes. A *creedal* code is a statement of the fundamental, general beliefs of the profession. An *internal* code governs relationships among personnel within the organization. A *fighting* code contains rules for soldiers' behavior in combat and toward the enemy. The *prisoner's* code explains proper conduct during captivity. [42]

The advantages of codes are clear. [43] Like dogmas, they reflect the wisdom of generations; they urge us to act honorably and contain short guides to honorable action; and they capture, in brief form, much of the discerning judgment we would hope students can develop in moral philosophy courses. But they are not the perfect solution to all moral dilemmas. Reading, thinking about, and discussing the following examples will provide valuable intellectual and moral exercises.

The Honor Code of the U.S. Air Force Academy

We will not lie, steal, or cheat, nor tolerate among us anyone who does. Furthermore, I resolve to do my duty and live honorably, so help me God. [44]

A Proposed "Code of Ethics for the Armed Forces" by William Diehl

Loyalty
As an American serviceman, I will remain loyal to the Armed Forces and its fundamental role of providing service to my nation: a commitment that is much larger than any individual. I will remain loyal to my unit: a two-way commitment between those whom I lead and those who lead me.

Competence
My performance of duty will demonstrate standards of excellence for others to emulate. I have a moral requirement to maintain professional competence in my specialty.

Selfless Service
The Armed Forces is characterized by teamwork. I will subordinate my personal advancement to the training, welfare and discipline of my unit.

Commitment
I have sworn an oath to support and defend our Constitution. To this end, my dedication to the Armed Forces allows no compromise. I will accept any risk and endure any sacrifice which I would ask my subordinates to bear.

Candor
My integrity will remain unswervingly nonnegotiable. I am bound by my oath to make ethical judgments, and I will accept responsibility for them. I will never violate my integrity, and I will always be open and frank with my superiors. The oath I have sworn compels me to tell the truth, no matter how unpleasant and regardless of the potential cost to my career.

Courage
My moral convictions require that I uphold my position of special trust and responsibility. I will not execute any order that I deem to be morally wrong, nor will I allow the concealment of any act that violates the services' code of ethics.[45]

A Proposed "Soldier's Code of Ethics" by Richard Gabriel

The nature of command and military service is a moral charge that places each soldier at the center of unavoidable ethical responsibility.

A soldier's sense of ethical integrity is at the center of his effectiveness as a soldier and a leader. Violating one's ethical sense of honor is never justified even at a cost to one's career.

Every soldier holds a special position of trust and responsibility. No soldier will ever violate that trust or avoid his responsibility by any of his actions, no matter the personal cost.

In faithfully executing the lawful orders of his superiors, a soldier's loyalty is to the welfare of his men and mission. While striving to carry out his mission, he will never allow his men to be misused in any way.

A soldier will never require his men to endure hardships or suffer dangers to which he is unwilling to expose himself. Every soldier must openly share the burden of risk and sacrifice to which his fellow soldiers are exposed.

A soldier is first and foremost a leader of men. He must lead his men by example and personal actions; he must always set the standard for personal bravery, courage, and leadership.

A soldier will never execute an order he regards to be morally wrong, and he will report all such orders, policies, or actions of which he is aware to appropriate authorities.

No soldier will ever willfully conceal any act of his superiors, subordinates, or peers that violates his sense of ethics. A soldier cannot avoid ethical judgments and must assume responsibility for them.

No soldier will punish, allow the punishment of, or in any way harm or discriminate against a subordinate or peer for telling the truth about any matter.

All soldiers are responsible for the actions of their comrades in arms. The unethical and dishonorable acts of one diminish us all. The honor of the military profession and military service is maintained by the acts of its members, and these actions must always be above reproach.[46]

A Proposed Code of Ethics by Anthony Hartle

PROFESSIONAL SOLDIERS
1. Accept service to country as their watchword and defense of the Constitution of the United States of America as their calling.
2. Place their duty first. They subordinate their personal

interests to the requirements of their professional functions.

3. Conduct themselves at all times as persons of honor whose integrity, loyalty, and courage are exemplary. Such qualities are essential on the battlefield if a military organization is to function effectively.

4. Develop and maintain the highest possible level of professional knowledge and skill. To do less is to fail to meet their obligations to the country, the profession, and fellow soldiers.

5. Take full responsibility for the manner in which their orders are carried out.

6. Promote and safeguard, within the context of mission accomplishment, the welfare of their subordinates as persons, not merely as soldiers.

7. Conform strictly to the principle that subordinates the military to civilian authority. They do not involve themselves or their subordinates in domestic politics beyond the exercise of basic civil rights.

8. Adhere to the laws of war and the regulations of their service in performing their professional functions.[47]

The Navy Uniform

You wear the Navy uniform.

That means a lot to your country, your service, yourself.

It means KNOWING THE JOB.

Professional competence comes first. Without skilled men and women, the Navy cannot carry out its mission. That mission is to defend the nation at the risk of death.

It means COMMITMENT TO DUTY.

To serve for pay is good.

To serve for travel, education, and training is better.

To serve for love of country and comrades is best.

It means COMMITMENT TO LEADERSHIP.

Leadership consists of those qualities of skill and character that command respect and cause others to follow loyally and willingly. It, in turn, requires fairness, a reluctance to ask more than you yourself would give, a sense of justice.

It means HONESTY.

If you wear the Navy uniform, you don't lie; you don't cheat; you don't steal. If you lead others, those in charge are watching you and noting your example. The way you act, officer or enlisted, means "I'm saying that everybody should do this. I'm not making an exception of myself."

It means COURAGE.

You must also have courage, both moral and physical, for it is the virtue on which the exercise of all other virtues depends. You must have the courage to fight. You must have the strength of character to say "no" to what is wrong, to persevere in what is right no matter how difficult the task becomes, and, even to face pain and death in defense of the things you value and love, should honor and duty demand. Yours is not an easy commitment, but a worthy and noble one.

It means LOYALTY.

To let those over you know that they have your support. To show those in your charge you will go to bat for them, never asking them to do something you would not do yourself. Sometimes loyalties conflict. You must choose. Never mistake loyalty for doing wrong to help someone out, even if he is your superior.

It means OBEDIENCE.

Obedience requires that you carry out the lawful orders of your superiors, as we are all pledged to do, with pride and determination.

It means COMMITMENT TO THE BEST. For the Navy, for comrades, for self. We give what we have. We do what we can. We commit the highest in us to the service.

For the Navy, only the best is enough.

Always to excel.

Always to be the best.[48]

The Sailor's Creed
- I will be loyal to my country, its Constitution and laws, and to my shipmates.
- I will be honest in my personal and professional life and encourage my shipmates to do the same.

- I will, to the best of my ability, do the right thing for its own sake, and I am prepared to face pain or death in defense of my country.
- I will be a professional, wearing my uniform with pride and accepting responsibility for my actions.
- I will set excellence as my standard and always strive for ways to make me a better sailor and my crew a better crew.[49]

Code of Conduct for Members of the Armed Forces of the United States

I

I am an American, fighting in the forces which guard my country and our way of life. I am prepared to give my life in their defense.

II

I will never surrender of my own free will. If in command, I will never surrender the members of my command while they still have the means to resist.

III

If I am captured, I will continue to resist by all means available. I will make every effort to escape and aid others to escape. I will accept neither parole nor special favors from the enemy.

IV

If I become a prisoner of war, I will keep faith with my fellow prisoners. I will give no information nor take part in any action which might be harmful to my comrades. If I am senior, I will take command. If not, I will obey the lawful orders of those appointed over me and will back them up in every way.

V

When questioned, should I become a prisoner or war, I am required to give name, rank, service number, and date of birth. I will evade answering further questions to the utmost of my ability, I will make no oral or written statements disloyal to my country and its allies or harmful to their cause.

VI

I will never forget that I am an American, fighting for freedom, responsible for my actions, and dedicated to the
principles which made my country free. I will trust in my
God and in the United States of America.[50]

These actual and proposed codes of conduct provide reasonably clear summaries of many of the ethical arguments and analysis offered in this book. There is a major problem, however, with
codes. As William Stayton put it, "To the degree that one finds
moral decisions difficult and burdensome and does not want to
be troubled, any theory that promises to remove the necessity for
thought is likely to be viewed favorably."[51] Honor and shame are
not easily defined; reasoned choice among competing obligations can rarely be spelled out in advance of circumstances; a
proper ordering of custom, rule, outcome, and situation is difficult to anticipate.

Colonel Malham Wakin, certainly the foremost teacher of military ethics in the nation, offers this additional note of concern:

Codes of conduct, whether they be framed as honor codes
for service academies, moral commandments for religious
groups, prescriptions for medical or legal practitioners,
and so on, all seem subject to the same sort of narrow
interpretation which may cause distortions in our general
view of moral behavior. The immature or unsophisticated
frequently narrow their ethical sights to the behavior specifically delineated in the code so that what may have originally been intended as a minimum listing becomes treated
as an exhaustive guide for ethical action. We forget all too
easily the wisdom concerning these matters given us by
almost every moral philospher dating back as far as Socrates, Plato, or Aristotle.[52]

In short, codes serve hortatory and heuristic purposes, but
they are not—and should never be intended as—substitutes for
education in wisdom and in virtue. Codes may be thought of as
primers, as hornbooks, as shorthand—and, as such, they are
useful. There is value, for example, in teaching soldiers about

the "Five S's" as a guide to treating prisoners—search, silence, safeguard, segregate by rank, and speed them to the rear—but no one seriously suggests that the law of war with respect to the treatment of prisoners is thereby completely taught. Just as serious students do not read only review notes when the classic texts are assigned, neither do they regard a code as a substitute for learning; to do so defeats its purposes.

Mars and Cupid: An Example

A moving song (1969) made famous by Roy Clark contains these lyrics: "Yesterday when I was young, the taste of life was sweet as rain upon my tongue. . . . so many happy songs were waiting to be sung, so many wild pleasures lay in store for me, and so much pain my dazzled eyes refused to see. I ran so fast that time and youth at last ran out. I never stopped to think what life was all about. And every conversation I can now recall concerned itself with me and with nothing else at all."[53] In 1966 a remarkable popular movie asked the question "What's it all about, Alfie?" And in 1984 a deeply moving book by Viktor Frankl, *Man's Search for Meaning*, suggested that it is not power, not sexual urge, and not greed that sustain us in our darkest moments; rather, purpose and faith and conviction are what "it's all about."[54]

How striking it is to me to compare two men of whom I heard so much when I was in college. Abbie Hoffman, a perpetual protestor of yesteryear, and Col. James N. Rowe, U.S.A., for five years a prisoner of war in Vietnam and the author of the deeply moving *Five Years to Freedom*,[55] died within days of each other. Hoffman was found dead on 12 April 1989; Rowe was gunned down on 21 April. The former killed himself with alcohol and a drug overdose; the latter was ambushed and murdered in the Philippines. For much of their lives, one suspects—one hopes—they were animated by the search for truth, which led them down remarkably different paths. No doubt both men suffered from the belief that too few of their countrymen cared enough about those causes in which Rowe and Hoffman, exemplifying Mars and Cupid, found meaning and purpose.

We are all—save the few saints among us—ever on the verge of the egotism, the solipsism, the narcissism which inform us that the sun, as in Ptolemy's universe, spins around us. I contend that the core of education and of maturity—the essence of being a lady or a gentleman—consists in the painful daily recognition that our teacher must be Kepler or Copernicus or Galileo: we spin around the sun; we have our places defined by a greater power.

Plato's troglodyte was a mature man because he sought the sun and, having found it, sought heroically to tell others about it. Plato's Socrates was a mature man because, having found truth (or elements of it), he did not accept with apathy others' false knowledge; he did not suffer fools gladly.

We honor and cherish those people who die in the cause of beliefs greater than they—or at least we—are. Consider Socrates, Jesus of Nazareth, Sir Thomas More, the defenders of the Alamo: these and other heroes, sacred and secular, are bigger than life now because they were bigger than life then. They knew a purpose, a meaning, a destiny that endowed their lives with sufficient light to guide them through their days and sustain them.

The existentialist writer Albert Camus suggested that the only real philosophical question was, "Why not suicide?" Apparently, Abbie Hoffman could no longer answer that question. Can the rest of us? In a nihilistic world in which few contemporary students and few contemporary faculty would attempt a response to the assertion that "nothing is worth dying for," I suggest that there you have the very definition of cowardice. Those who can find no purpose in noble death can find no purpose in noble life: They are left rudderless on the seas of daily living. As Roy Clark put it in the lyrics quoted above, these people never stop to think what life is all about. Only when one discerns that he or she is not the sum and substance of the universe does one begin to seek an external truth—and that way lies education. Having discovered that the personal pronoun *I* must yield at one point to the plural *we* (or, the religious might well say, to the full meaning of *He*), we begin to look for truth to God, to neighbor, or to some combination of them. That way lies responsibility;

that way lies meaning; that way lies reason for getting up in the morning; that way lies the answer to Camus's question.

In classical Christianity the faithful used to pray for a happy and watchful death, rather than for a sudden and unprovided-for death. They wanted time to reflect and to set things right. But isn't that what life is all about? The unexamined life, Socrates told us, isn't worth living. Isn't that what Paul also contended at one point (1 Cor 13:12) in suggesting that "now we see through a glass, darkly. . . . And now abideth faith, hope, and charity; but the greatest of these is charity." To find the sun to light our lives; to find true north whereby to chart the seas; to find ultimate value rather than mere proximate pleasure—these are the things that endow the man or woman with enough sense and enough gumption to know when something is worth dying for *and* when something is worth living for.

Most of us would rather think about more immediately enjoyable things than truth or faith or hope or love. But genuine education calls us to the task of finding out what life really is about, lest in our old age we find ourselves deeply regretting that "every conversation I can now recall concerned itself with me and with nothing else at all."

Conclusions

The major challenges to the idea of virtue are denial of evil (and, consequently, the implausibility of preventing its expansion); celebration of individual rights (at the expense of duties); ridicule of heroism (which deprives us of models); and the abolition of authority (leading to the triumph of mere preference).

The prospects for reestablishing the concept of virtue—hence, of military ethics—rest upon recognizing evil (and being thus capable of distinguishing good); of revitalizing the idea of duty to community as a complement to the idea of personal rights; of reviving the tradition of heroes; and of once again recognizing legitimate authority.

Until moral health is restored to the American republic, military ethics can, at best, serve society as a reminder of honor, of shame, and of reasoned moral choice about obligation; at worst, ethics in the military will suffer the infection of the parent society.

Military codes of conduct alone are not enough: they can promote discussion of ethical concerns and serve as guides to right behavior, but they cannot replace learning or serve as final arbiters of wise ethical choice.

6. Active Duty
Enlisting, Serving, Resigning

> . . . nor [shall any State] deny to any person within
> its jurisdiction the equal protection of the laws.
> —U.S. Constitution, Fourteenth Amendment,
> Section 1

It is all very well in military ethics to speculate about difficult, if relatively rare, combat cases. But, as is often emphasized in this book, military ethics concerns far more than issues about "taking hills" and "mistreating prisoners." More often than not military ethics is about seemingly simpler things such as false reporting or degradation of subordinates. Military ethics demands that we be able to distinguish between honor and shame and thus be able to choose appropriately among competing obligations.

The most serious challenges we can see for military ethics as we enter the twenty-first century will lie in the area of human relations. The treatment given to all soldiers and potential soldiers is clearly an ethical concern for commanders and citizens alike. Should women be combat soldiers? Should homosexuals be fully integrated into the U.S. military? To what extent is inter-rank and intersex fraternization tolerable? Finally, under what circumstances must the man or woman of honor resign?

In this chapter, probably the most difficult in the entire text, I make an appeal to the reader: these issues are so inflammatory, so emotional, that they must be approached in as unruffled a manner as possible. Because I am convinced that ethical studies frequently demand the staking out of positions—if only to provide a starting point for discussion—I will state my own views of these provocative issues. I recognize that there are serious and legitimate competing claims to be made; it is imperative that everyone concerned understand that point. But the existence of strongly competing viewpoints does not mean that "truth lies in the middle" or that equal merit attaches to both sides. If ethics means anything, it is that we try honestly and earnestly to determine the right course and then follow it— though always remaining willing to review from time to time the wisdom of our judgment.

On Women in the Military

The presence of women is an unescapable fact of life in the military. In fiscal 1991, the figure was 11 percent of total U.S. military personnel, up from 8.9 percent only a decade earlier. In 1971, women made up less than 2 percent of the armed forces. About 1.5 million women are veterans today; about 211,000 are on active duty; and (although the exact percentage varies with retirements and promotions) about 1 percent of general officers are women.[1]

It has been a long haul for women interested in military careers. In 1901 the Army established an auxiliary organization for nurses, and in 1942 the Women's Army Auxiliary Corps, which soon dropped its auxiliary status, came into existence; it was dissolved in 1978. In 1948 Congress passed legislation limiting to 2 percent the number of women on active service; that limit ended in 1967. The first women to become generals were Anna Mae Hayes and Elizabeth Hoisington, selected in June 1970. Five years later, legislation was passed permitting women to enter the service academies.[2]

In the Army today, about 52 percent of jobs are open to women. Although no statute specifically restricts their assignment, Army policies exclude women from positions that might involve them directly in combat, defined as "engaging an enemy with individual or crew-served weapons while being exposed to direct enemy fire, a high probability of direct physical contact with the enemy, and a substantial risk of capture." Infantry, armor, and field artillery, for example, are closed to women. About 12 percent of the Army is female.

In the Marine Corps, now about 5 percent female, some 20 percent of jobs are open to women. Combat engineer, infantry, and tank units are closed to women. About 10 percent of the Navy is female, and 59 percent of Navy jobs are open to women.

Women may not serve on submarines. Finally, about 97 percent of jobs in the Air Force are open to women, who make up almost 15 percent of that service. Although the Air Force ban against women serving in combat aircraft was repealed in December 1991, women have not been assigned to fighters or bombers.[3]

Some women argue that until combat-related jobs are opened to them, they will be discriminated against, particularly in the higher echelons of military service. In fact, the question of women in the military has been particularly perplexing for those on the far left of the political spectrum. The National Organization for Women (NOW), for example, has been torn between championing "women's rights," in the form of repealing restrictions against women in combat, and the supposed danger of thereby advancing the cause of "militarism." The question is burdensome for NOW, even though it acknowledges a pacifist philosophy.[4]

The other side of the spectrum argues vigorously that women in the military undermine and compromise the code and spirit of the warrior. Among the strongest arguments—some would call them the most strident—are those of Brian Mitchell:

> Many of the most dedicated men and women see motherhood and military service as conflicting obligations. Many military men still like to think that they endure the danger and hardships of service so that mothers and children can be safe at home. Whatever they think about equal opportunity, they still find the site [sic] of a pregnant woman heading a formation of troops unsettling. Few people, civilian or military, can escape the notion that pregnancy is inconsistent with the role of the warrior, that the killing spirit and motherly love are necessarily inimical to each other, and that where the two are combined, the one is weakened and the other perverted.[5]

Although Alexander Webster finds Mitchell's assertions sometimes farfetched and unrealistic,[6] he argues that in the attempt by some women to remake the military "in accordance with their social mores and to recast the image of the male warrior into something unrecognizable," feminists subvert time-tested military values and tamper "with human nature itself."[7]

David Horowitz contends that feminism's radical wing comprises adherents of "gender feminism," which he defines as "a bastard child of Marxism. It holds that women are not women by nature, but that society has 'constructed' or created them female so that men could oppress them. . . . They deny that human biology fundamentally influences who we are." His principal point is that gender feminists have little interest in questions of national security "because they believe America is a patriarchal, sexist, racist oppressor."[8]

In January 1990, Pat Schroeder of Colorado introduced a bill in the House of Representatives directing the Secretary of the Army to establish a four-year test program to explore the implications of removing the limitations on the assignment of Army females to direct combat roles.[9] The bill was voted down, but the test may have come anyway, in the Persian Gulf. There is little question that women, as *Time* put it, "distinguished themselves" in the 1991 Gulf War.[10] Of some 35,000 women who served in the Gulf, few seemed to have the time or inclination to worry a great deal about "gender feminism." The story of Army Major Rhonda Cornum, who was captured by the Iraqis, is instructive in that regard.[11] Another Army officer, Captain Carol Barkalow, a West Point graduate, has argued persuasively that "women are competent, capable, and committed."[12] She declares that her time in command has been rewarding and effective.[13] Will Barkalow and others like her eventually fail to rise to the Army's highest ranks because they are forbidden to serve in direct combat or in a combat arm?[14] Is that reasonable? fair? ethical?

Professor Charles Moskos, America's most noted military sociologist, opposes putting women into combat roles. "Women are not little men," he argues, "and men are not just big women."[15] Pentagon studies have shown, for example, that women have only 55 percent the muscle strength and 67 percent the endurance of their male counterparts.[16] "Gender norming"— the institutionalization of a double standard whereby women are measured against other women, rather than against men— is now the rule at all the service academies.[17] But Moskos raises the question too often neglected in the debates: "Should every woman soldier be made to confront exactly the same combat liabilities as every man?" Every male soldier, regardless of his normal posting, can, if the need arises, be assigned to the combat arms. Genuine equality would mean that women would incur that same liability. As Moskos explains: "To allow both sexes to choose whether or not to go into combat would be the end of an effective military force." He is entirely correct in writing, "Honesty requires that supporters of lifting the ban on women in combat state openly that they want to put all female soldiers at the same combat risk as all male soldiers—or they don't."[18]

In the case of *Rostker v. Goldberg* (453 U.S. 57 [1981]), the Supreme Court upheld a male-only draft. If we assign women to combat, do we "overturn two centuries of settled law and military policy based on deeply held and commonly shared cultural assumptions defining how men should treat women"?[19] That was the central assumption of conservatives serving on a presidential commission that voted eight to seven, in November 1992, to continue to bar women from flying combat operations and engaging in ground combat, though it would allow them to serve aboard combat ships. But Marine Brigadier General Thomas Draude concluded, "I believe we must fill our ranks with our best, regardless of gender."[20]

The role of women in the military, I suggest, is not an easy issue to resolve. Men and women of good conscience will listen and learn—and disagree. Army Captain Barkalow and Army Major Cornum have, in my view, the best answer. Barkalow: "We have standards that we must keep. Our military readiness should never suffer."[21] And Cornum: "There is no question that the 'average' woman is not as tall, heavy, or strong as the 'average' man; we don't need a congressional committee to tell us that. . . . But at least let [women] compete. . . . just pick the best."[22] That, precisely, is the argument of recently retired Army General Evelyn Foote: "Never compromise standards. Be sure that anybody in any MOS [specialty] can do everything required in that MOS."[23]

In the American volunteer military, every job should be available to every person who meets the mental, moral, and physical requirements established for that job by the military. Every person volunteering for the military can be put at equal risk. Every person joining the military forces must understand the fundamental and enduring purpose of the military: It is not for the soldier's subsequent education, or for travel, or for adventure; it is to prepare to kill the national enemies of the United States. Women are physicians and engineers and corporate executives and lawyers in larger numbers than ever before. To the extent that any American enjoys the privileges of our society, he or she must share in the responsibilities, one of which is national service. As long as the standards of any combat specialty are in *no way* compromised, all members of the Army, Navy, Air Force, and Marine Corps should be allowed to compete for that skill training, combat-related or not.

To insist today upon segregating military skills by gender—unless there is clear reason to do so (for example, it seems wise still to foreclose routine infantry service and submarine duty to women[24]) appears to violate both laws and ethics. On the other hand, the judge of the criteria to be employed in determining professional competence in armed forces career fields must be professional military officers who will not bend to the winds of "political correctness." And their guiding star, in establishing rigorous but fair standards of moral and mental and muscular fitness, must always be the readiness of their forces to accomplish their mission.[25] As General Foote said, anyone who cannot perform his or her mission "has no place in the Army."[26] That is exactly right, legally and morally.

On 28 April 1993, Secretary of Defense Les Aspin ordered all the services to remove restrictions on women flying combat airplanes; he intended, as well, to ask Congress to repeal a law barring women from serving on many warships.[27] Other recent changes in policy are discussed in the Epilogue, below.

On Homosexuals in the Military

The notion that homosexual men are invariably effeminate, prowling about seeking young men and boys as lovers, is nonsense. The notion that those who find homosexual practices offensive are narrow-minded bigots is also nonsense. In simple point of fact, most Americans do find homosexuality (understood as sexual attraction toward members of one's own sex) to be degenerate. But ladies and gentlemen, whatever their sexual orientation, do not personally scorn, insult, or physically intimidate other human beings. Homosexuals are human beings who should be treated as such without fear of assault by word or deed. (Instances of homosexuals being beaten by gangs of heterosexuals are episodes of extreme cowardice and truly loathsome behavior). At the same time, conscientious opposition to homosexuality should not be peremptorily dismissed as a "witch hunt" or as "homophobic."[28]

When, on 19 July 1993, President Clinton announced a policy permitting gays to serve in the military if they do not engage in homosexual behavior on or off base and if they remain quiet about their sexual identity, he did not finally settle the controversy.[29] The question remains whether those who openly acknowledge their homosexuality have a right to military service.[30] Under the concept of the "equal protection of the laws," is the military ban against known homosexuals plainly wrong? Should it be lifted? Is it equivalent to the refusal of the military fully to integrate blacks until ordered to do so by the Truman administration? If women are entitled to the opportunities of full service and integration, why not homosexuals?

As John Eidsmoe points out in an extraordinarily well done paper, the Fourteenth Amendment does not prohibit all forms of discrimination—only unjust discrimination.[31] No one has a "right" to be a physician, but everyone should be permitted to compete for admission to medical school. No one has a right to be a major league baseball player. And no one has a right to military service.[32] Professional and personal standards are presumably governed by preeminent concern for the advancement of a given profession; by those standards applicants are judged, whether potential doctors, first basemen, or soldiers. And as Alan Gropman has argued, "People who enlist or who are commissioned suspend some of their civil rights." Quitting a civilian job may be a free choice, but quitting a military job is desertion. What is called a strike at a civilian plant is a mutiny on a military base or post. "The question of gays in the military, therefore, is not a civil rights issue."[33]

Discrimination against blacks was, to use the legal term, a

"suspect classification," meaning that discrimination had to survive "strict scrutiny" and be justified by "compelling state interest." Where such interest could not be shown, the classification could be regarded as contrary to the idea of "equal protection." If homosexuality is an immutable trait—like race—then to deny homosexuals the opportunity to serve openly seems wrong unless there is a compelling state interest.[34] The analogy drawn between African Americans and homosexuals, however, as General Colin Powell has pointed out repeatedly, is wrong. "Skin color," Powell says, "is a benign, non-behavioral characteristic. Sexual orientation is perhaps the most profound of human behavioral characteristics."[35] Even Mickey Kaus, who is opposed to the ban on homosexuals openly serving in the military, suggests that the military has a justification for preserving this "suspect classification": the military's judgment about the wisdom of integrating homosexuals.[36] As Justice William H. Rehnquist put it in a 1974 Supreme Court case, "The military is, by necessity, a specialized society separate from civilian society" (see Chapter 2). The military, he said, has developed laws and traditions of its own. "The differences between the military and civilian communities result from the fact that 'it is the primary business of armies and navies to fight wars should the occasion arise.'"[37]

The ban against homosexuals openly serving in the armed forces of the United States is legally and morally wrong unless there be compelling reason for its preservation. Few would quarrel with the military's ban on service by misfits, criminals, married people with more than two children under age eighteen, aliens (who can join for a time if they have green cards), non-English speakers, and certain political dissidents (such as Ku Klux Klan members).[38] Are homosexuals a "physical and psychological threat" to the military, as Navy Captain Larry Ellis, a Marine Corps chaplain, claims?[39]

Military leaders almost invariably say that lifting the ban would harm order, discipline, and esprit. A *Los Angeles Times* poll found that 74 percent of enlisted personnel opposed President Clinton's proposal to lift the ban; only 18 percent supported the change.[40] In a poll conducted by Charles Moskos and Laura Miller of Northwestern University, nearly eight in ten men and almost half the women opposed lifting the gay ban.[41] Aside from practical legal problems (twenty-two states have laws against sodomy),[42] military authorities have argued for some time that small-unit group cohesion—a critical factor in combat success—would be seriously impaired by the inclusion of open homosexuals.[43] David Hackworth is the most highly decorated living American veteran and one who, with eight purple hearts, surely knows something about combat. Says Hackworth about repealing the homosexual ban: "I cannot think of a better way to destroy fighting spirit and gut U.S. combat effectiveness."[44]

The consequences of admitting *open* homosexuals are hard to calculate. As one study has recently put it, "Once we slip the shackles of 'antiquated and legal and moral notions,' we find ourselves in the broken field of moral relativism." Would homosexual marriages be acceptable in the military? Would government quarters be authorized for homosexual couples? Would the military protect the privacy of heterosexuals from homosexuals as it now does the privacy of women from men? Would polygamy and adultery be acceptable conduct in the new morality?[45] Columnist Mike McManus asserts that for heterosexual men, "having to shower with gays is an invasion of privacy. It is as if female soldiers were forced to shower with young males."[46] And Professor Moskos writes: "Most feminists would not advocate forced intimate living between the sexes. Likewise, enlightened gay advocates should not argue for compulsory intimacy among persons of openly different sexual orientations. The military's ban on homosexuals still makes good sense."[47]

I believe there are serious and substantial reasons for maintaining the ban on open homosexuals in the military. These reasons have to do with our predominantly Judaeo-Christian culture, which generally finds homosexuality to be repugnant; with some states' laws and the Uniform Code of Military Justice, which prohibit sodomy; with the reality that Congress, at least at present, is very unlikely to agree to a complete repeal of the ban; and with the fact that the great majority of armed forces personnel find homosexual behavior offensive. All these aside, however, a fundamental truth recurs: "Homosexuality is incompatible with military service" (as a 1982 Reagan Administration directive put it). More to the point, in the best professional judgment of military officers, homosexuality is incompatible with success in battle on the ground, in the air, or on or under the seas. Any professional soldier who believes that must continue to oppose repeal of the ban.[48]

If the professional military judgment of inconsistency between homosexuality and potential combat success is correct, there is ample reason to allow continued discrimination against homosexuals in the service. "Gay Rights" pressure groups, however well intentioned they may or may not be, are clearly not military experts and are consequently unable to assess the extent to which accepting homosexuality might undermine the principal reason for the existence of the military in the first place.

Of course, the question can be asked, "As time goes on, is it likely that homosexuality will be an increasingly acceptable 'lifestyle'?" At one point, after all, segregation of blacks was an acceptable practice in many parts of the United States, and our society has at last come, quite properly, to denounce such a practice. Suppose the United States military were today to announce that, for reasons of "combat effectiveness," the policy of segregation would be reestablished at once. The American military *is* a separate society—up to a point. But such a policy would result in an entirely justified firestorm of criticism from people who recognize segregation for what it is—shameful. The American military could not now espouse such a policy; race, after all, has nothing to do with behavior, as General Powell has said. The ban against open homosexuals in the military, on the contrary, meets with strong and steady military and civilian approval. Is that bigotry? ignorance? intolerance? narrowmindedness? Or is it the product of a deeply held and highly cherished moral and religious conviction that inherently shameful and perverted behavior can be recognized and labeled for what it is—and more, that such behavior should not be legitimized by our country's armed forces? Army Capt. Mark Mensack has it exactly right: "To allow individuals who regularly and without hesitation violate moral, religious and legal standards to wear the uniform of a soldier is to tarnish the ideals of honor and respect that the uniform has come to represent."[49]

If, over time, homosexuality *were* to be generally accepted as morally agreeable behavior, could homosexuals then be admitted fully and openly to the ranks of the American military? The answer to that question has to be yes, even though moral absolutists will be troubled by it. The American military serves American society. Though its circumstances and moral understandings may differ from those of the parent society, such differences, after a point, must not be permitted, for the military is not its own master. At present, however, it seems fair to say that American social custom on the issue of homosexuality and the particular professional circumstances of the American military coincide. The banning of admitted homosexuals from the military is thus legal and moral.

On Fraternization

The basic thesis of this chapter is that military customs follow the patterns and norms of the larger society unless those civilian patterns obstruct the military mission or preclude military professionalism. At such points of obstruction the armed forces deserve—and must demand—exceptions to societal norms. Women are increasingly achieving equal treatment with men in American society, and that must be the norm in the military as well (with the probable exception of routine assignment to infantry combat units and submarines). Homosexuals, as people, receive increasingly equal treatment with heterosexuals, but homosexuality itself is viewed with disfavor in society; therefore, society—and Congress—would be unwise to demand that the professional military effectively legitimize a "lifestyle" which the great majority of Americans themselves find repugnant.

Romance, intimate friendship, and sexual attraction are a joyous part of human life. Still, romance is governed in American society by certain customs and marriage by laws. When civilians put on soldiers' uniforms, it does not mean that they cease to be human beings with all the poetical strengths and weaknesses of other mortals in this regard. Over the years the professional military has developed a series of customs and codes in an effort to clarify and regulate romantic enchantment, intimate friendship, and sexual attraction among its members. Those customs and codes fall under the heading of fraternization, or "frat," defined as *personal relationships within the military services which disrupt good order and discipline.* As explained in Chapter 5, codes and regulations serve hortatory and heuristic purposes, but for honor to take root and ultimately to flourish depends chiefly upon the character of those who teach, lead, and inspire. Much the same is true with regard to fraternization: wise and virtuous service members—men and women of discretion and decency—rarely require rules. They understand that good order and discipline may be disrupted when (1) officers date or marry enlistees, (2) senior personnel are excessively familiar with or friendly toward subordinates, or (3) favoritism—or its opposite, prejudice—is revealed in any way.

As it is unwise for officers and enlisted personnel to date, so it is unwise for senior officers to date junior officers or for senior enlisted personnel to date junior enlisted personnel. Whenever the possibility of abuse of power is present, the practicality of discouraging intimate friendship is self-evident. Although recent fraternization legal cases can be confusing, the armed forces are increasingly subscribing to an absolute: officers will not date enlisted members or in any other respect become unduly familiar. This may soon become a matter of clear law; it is at present a matter of clear professionalism. The good judgment of the old religious exhortation to "avoid the occasion of sin" should be apparent to all.

Seniors of any rank who are immoderately friendly with their juniors invite trouble. If, for example, an Army lieutenant colonel and battalion commander has four captain company commanders, one of whom he routinely addresses by his first name while referring to the others as "Captain"; if the colonel routinely has a Friday afternoon beer with one officer, to the exclusion of the others; if he and his wife entertain the captain and his wife far more than they entertain the other officers in the battalion—any of these can create a sense of fundamental unfairness. Even participation on mixed-rank sports teams can breed difficulties.

Favoritism or prejudice of any type is transparently wrong and therefore intolerable. Members of the Marine Corps used to be taught that "a Marine on guard duty has no friends." Fidelity in the military must be to principle and then purpose and then people. When a soldier extends favors to others because they are of the same race or religion, because they like the same books or sports or TV programs, because they went to the same high school or college,[50] or because their spouses are friends, that soldier is guilty of fraternization, of bad judgment, or unprofessional behavior.

In brief, wearing the uniform means that standards of professional conduct are *uniform*; that standards of professional conduct apply equally to all, without fear or favor being implied; that standards of professional conduct are rooted in high character and competence. In the military, *decency* (defined as "propriety of conduct and speech; modesty, courtesy, good taste") and *discretion* (defined as "the quality of being discreet or careful about what one says or does; prudence") are not just to be desired; they are to be demanded. And because the person who demands is the person who commands, any commander who cannot set the right example of personal and professional conduct should be relieved by his or her boss.

Fraternization is wrongful because it disrupts military order and discipline and mistreats human beings.[51] Carry fraternization to the extreme and you have the Tailhook scandal. At a Navy and Marine Corps aviators' convention (the Tailhook Convention) in Las Vegas in September 1991, drunken officers fondled and in some cases even partially stripped a number of women. It was reported that scores of male junior officers lined the corridors on one floor of the hotel and groped any woman who walked by. Fourteen women officers and twelve female civilians had their breasts, buttocks, and other bodily parts grabbed by drunken aviators. Moreover, "as appalling as the behavior itself was the reaction of more than 1,500 officers and civilians questioned about the incident," said *Time*; "a common thread running through the overwhelming majority of interviews was, 'What's the big deal?'" according to the Naval Inspector General's office.[52]

The month-long investigation of the event did not resolve the problem, leading to the resignation of the secretary of the Navy. The Navy inspector general said, "There is a sense in the tactical air community that what happened was acceptable social conduct and that the allegations concerning conduct had been blown out of proportion." During the summer of 1992 about 4,500 Navy and Marine Corps promotions were held up by Congress for fear of promoting a Tailhook offender, and John Murtha, chairman of the House Appropriations Defense Subcommittee, pegged his decision to cut 10,000 Navy headquarters jobs on what he called the Navy's "obstruction and arrogance" in the Tailhook affair.[53] Indeed, the final Tailhook report was not available until late April 1993.[54] In mid-May, after reviewing 120 cases of alleged misconduct, Vice Adm. J.P. Reason disciplined ten officers for indecent exposure.[55]

Congressional sources have estimated that the Tailhook investigation will finally cost $3 to $5 million.[56] Chief of Naval Operations Admiral Frank Kelso II ordered every sailor and officer to undergo sexual harassment training.[57] Acting Navy Secretary Sean O'Keefe admitted that the Navy has "a cultural problem which has allowed demeaning behavior and attitudes toward women to exist in the Navy."[58] *U.S. News* asked, "What's Wrong with the Navy?" and *Time* published a piece called "An Officer, Not a Gentleman."[59] Henry Mohr, a retired major general and former head of the Army Reserve, wrote that "to penalize thousands of naval officers on the chance that they may have been involved is irresponsible and counterproductive."[60] Had the entire Navy—the entire profession of arms—become a collection of drunks and derelicts?

About 180 officers were suspected of "misbehavior" during the Tailhook Convention.[61] The April 1993 Defense Department report indicated that at least 117 Navy officers could face disciplinary action because of sexual assault on ninety people at Tailhook.[62] Do those figures constitute indictment of "Navy culture," as Sean O'Keefe implied? James Webb, a former Marine and Secretary of the Navy during the Reagan administration, was incensed by the notion that O'Keefe had "the moral authority to discredit the cultural ethos of the entire Navy based on the conduct of a group of drunken aviators in a hotel suite." Webb deplored the cringing of military leaders who were "at best passive and most often downright fearful when confronted by activists who allege that their culture is inherently oppressive toward females." Webb was arguing not for protection of the guilty but for preservation of the Navy culture that senior officers seemed ready to compromise or to sacrifice upon the altar of political correctness—if, thereby, they could save their own careers. "The seemingly arcane concepts of tradition, loyalty, discipline and moral courage," Webb wrote, "have carried the services through cyclical turbulence in peace and war. Their continuance is far more important than the survival of one leader. It is the function of the military's top officers to articulate that importance to the civilian political process. And an officer who allows a weakening of these ideals in exchange for self-preservation is no leader at all."[63]

What happened at the Tailhook Convention in 1991 is an example of shameful behavior, bringing great discredit upon the Navy and Marine Corps. The officers involved deserved to be court-martialed. But the entire profession of arms hardly deserves censure and ridicule. In much the same way that some were willing to blame the whole United States Army (or, indeed, the "imperialist" United States)—for the My Lai massacre committed by Calley, some are prepared to blame the whole United States Navy (or, indeed, the "misogynist" United States) for the Tailhook crime.

As Charles Moskos put it, "You have to be a little bit crazy to fly airplanes off ships. If you get too civilized, you iron out the atavistic behavior that makes a good pilot. You can't oversocialize them because that might even drive out the best pilots."[64] Military activities are not garden parties; the military, it bears repeating, exists to kill and to prepare to kill. The bonding, the spirit, the boisterousness that are part of military culture can be good and worthy things. But carried too far—to the point of felony itself—such behavior demeans and can destroy the very institutions it is intended to serve. The bravery and high spirits necessary to fly off decks, to jump out of airplanes, or to master commando tactics in the field must never be perverted into bravado and cowardice, resulting in assaults against shocked women in hotel corridors.[65] Anyone in the military who cannot make the distinction between bravery and bravado, between attacking the enemy and assaulting women, is too stupid, too cowardly, and too immoral to wear his country's uniform.

On Resignation

"In the ten years of [the Vietnam] war," wrote Richard Gabriel, "not a single general officer resigned in protest over the policies pursued in Vietnam." Although "a substantial number of them," Gabriel contends, had "serious ethical and pragmatic objections" to the policies they had to implement, not a single general refused to do so by way of resigning.[66] Gabriel is remarkably quick to register his moral qualms with someone else's money. Resignation from the military is not retirement. Those who retire after a military career, usually of twenty or more years, are entitled to various benefits, including retirement pay. Those who resign are done with the military—no retirement pay. Although, certainly, there might be circumstances requiring resignation, it clearly constitutes an enormous financial sacrifice, that few people can make. Lloyd Matthews put the matter well:

> War is the occasion when the subject of the principled resignation is most likely to arise. This is a paradox . . . since war is the soldier's reason for being. For him to spend years readying himself for the war that finally comes, only then to turn tail because he can't resolve the moral conundrums of human conflict, is like the emergency room intern who flees the medical profession because he can't stand the sight of mangled bodies. . . . When the huns are at the gate, the nation's citizens will be rightfully resentful of soldiers who all of a sudden wax morally squeamish over the alleged brutality and incompetence that lie behind the shedding of blood.[67]

The issue of resignation raises twin dangers. On the one hand, military personnel should be warned against the danger of turning fanatical and of becoming what Matthews calls the "Moralitymonger" who "can't take a step without encountering an ethical affront." Not every issue, after all, is a moral one. "In staff meetings," as Matthews points out, "regardless of whether the problem under consideration is animal, vegetable or mineral, the Moralitymonger manages to frame it in ethical terms, thus putting the other staffers on the defensive while elevating his own soul."[68] To see "profound ethical concerns" under every rock and behind every tree is to trivialize ethics. Too often proposed as a remedy for problems in military ethics, resignation is more nearly a placebo than a panacea. Resignation is an option available to the professional soldier; but it is, and ought to be, rarely threatened and rarely employed.[69]

As we move into Chapter 7 of the book, which concerns the profession of arms, no one has better explained resignation in the context of professionalism than Col. Matthews:

> This country deserves a genuinely professional military, a group that has professed in a sacred way to the calling of arms. The country needs professionals who take their oath seriously, who commit to the long haul, who place a high premium upon faith and loyalty, who take the bitter with the sweet, who trust in the country's constitutional design. The professional soldier will distrust the advice of moral zealots hot for certainties in this our world. He will turn away from the ideologues. He will be forever mindful that he is a professional soldier, not a moral philosopher, and that his chief preoccupation must always remain the nation's security.[70]

But, on the other hand, recall that not a single general officer resigned in protest over the question of whether too little or too much applied military power was employed in Vietnam. Because the ultimate responsibility of all soldiers is first to principle above both purpose and people, there are times that simple orders must be disobeyed. How much more important it is, then, that policies and strategies can become so heinous that no man or woman of conscience can persist in their execution. The U.S. Air Force plans to change the design of its uniforms. Is this issue so important that an irritated Air Force officer should resign? But suppose that same officer discovered a pattern of lying and deception in the Air Force, approved and encouraged at the highest levels of that service. If, despite using all the channels available, the officer were unable to change that system, would he or she be justified in continuing to serve and, at least implicitly, participating in such a system?

The idea of resignation is sometimes discussed in a manner so cavalier and casual that it is essentially trivialized. Military officers refer to the idea as "falling on one's sword." Resignation is rarely a wise or even effective course of action. But there are times when the man or woman of integrity can brook no more; resignation, in such circumstances, is ethically required. We know that soldiers are not moral philosophers. But we know, too, that unless soldiers are prepared to stake out ethical positions based upon high principle, the "national security" which the military preserves could be at the cost of the honor which is at the heart of the profession of arms. The state and its security must never come before the philosophical principles that give meaning to the state and its security.

Conclusions

Women have proved themselves as military professionals. They should be permitted to compete on an equal basis with men for slots in the combat arms (except infantry and submarines). Those who meet rigorous and challenging but fair and reasonable standards set by military professionals without interference from various political interest groups should be permitted the honor of service and, if warranted, of command.

Numerous homosexuals undoubtedly have served and are serving our country in the armed forces. Flagrant homosexuality, however, is incompatible with military service because of the special character of the armed forces and because of the "way of life" our soldiers are enlisted to protect. Homosexuality is inconsistent with the deepest moral convictions of most Americans and does not, therefore, deserve recognition (with implied approval) by the professional military of the country whose people reject the culture of homosexuality.

Fraternization, understood as personal relationships within the military services that disrupt good order and discipline, is impermissible. Sexual harassment is utterly incompatible with honorable conduct. Decency and discretion are the keys to building personal and professional relationships, military or civilian.

Although resignation from the service must remain a respected alternative to continued military duty in the direst of ethical dilemmas, it is a course of action that should be very rarely threatened and very rarely seized upon as either a practical or a moral remedy for the problems of professional soldiers.

7. The Profession of Arms
The Full Measure of Devotion

> The soldier, be he friend or foe, is charged with the protection of the weak and unarmed. It is the very essence and reason for his being.
> —Douglas MacArthur, 1946, reviewing the case of a Japanese war criminal

As pointed out in the last chapter, students of military ethics must beware the simple answer and the moral zealot. Although codes and dogmas and rituals can serve well as guides to honorable conduct in trying circumstances, there are no shortcuts to morality. Ethical actions do not simply occur; they are the product of wisdom and virtue annealed into habit by good education. Although it is true that soldiers are not moral philosophers, it is not at all correct that soldiers are not moral beings. One does not have to be a restaurateur to eat, and one does not have to be a philosopher to be moral. After all, "Man doth not live by bread alone."[1]

Tragically, man also seems not to live by peace alone. As Charles de Gaulle (1890-1970) once wrote: "Hope though we may, what reason have we for thinking that passion and self-interest, the root cause of armed conflict in men and nations, will cease to operate; that anyone will willingly surrender what he has or not try to get what he wants; in short, that human nature will ever become something other than it is?"[2] "From the beginning of man's recorded history," Gen. Sir John Hackett observed, "physical force, or the threat of it, has always been freely applied to the resolution of social problems. This phenomenon seems to persist as a fundamental element in the social pattern." Hence Hackett's assertion: "The function of the profession of arms is the ordered application of force in the resolution of a social problem."[3] If we are to have military ethics, then, we need to understand moral and military imperatives.

The Military Mind and Military People

According to D.T. Suzuki, the great interpreter of Zen to the West, the samurai "finds a congenial spirit in Zen" because the "military mind . . . is comparatively simple and not at all addicted to philosophizing."[4] And this remarkable index entry may be found in the memoirs of David Lloyd George (1863-1945), British prime minister from 1916 to 1922 and one of Britain's greatest war leaders:

> Military mind, narrowness of, 3051; stubbornness of, not peculiar to America, 3055; does not seem to understand arithmetic, 3077; its attitude in July, 1918, represented by Sir Henry Wilson's fantastic memorandum of 25/7/18, 3109; obsessed with North-West Frontier of India, 3119; impossibility of trusting, 3124; regards thinking as a form of mutiny, 3422.[5]

But if these and similar insults directed toward the "military mind" seem too harsh, it is true that the military tyrant is ubiquitous not only in military literature but in the barracks and on the battlefield as well. A retired U.S. Army two-star general admits that "the authoritarian structure of our profession, even though essential, is the natural breeding ground for the unethical use of authority."[6] If the military endows soldiers with power but fails to inculcate a corresponding sense of responsibility, it may—however unintentionally—create despots with "military minds."

One popular depiction of such a despot is the movie *A Few Good Men* (1993), in which the tyrannical Marine Colonel Nathan Jessup is played by actor Jack Nicholson. The film is at its best, or worst, in depicting Jessup's "military mind," as well as the mind of a young Marine lance corporal to whom the Corps is everything. His loyalty is to unit, Corps, God, and country—in that order. To him, as Lloyd George might have put it, thinking becomes a form of mutiny. The film is hardly an accurate description of the minds of most members of the military. That it does accurately describe the thinking of some, however, is enough to carry us back to the point that every soldier must be thoughtful and moral enough to understand that power and virtue are not always coincidental and that not every order is binding.

Those commissioned into our military forces receive a credential that recognizes their "patriotism, valor, fidelity, and abilities." Thus we return to the loyalty dilemma, discussed in Chapter 2. The officer's fidelity must be a true allegiance, a devotion to principle above purpose, and to purpose above people. "The essence of professionalism," writes Lewis Sorley, "is character. Character may be defined as the commitment to an admirable set of values, and the courage to manifest those values in one's life, no matter the cost in terms of personal success or popularity."[7] Officers cannot know what to do until they first know what to be. Integrity—knowing what to be—is the hallmark of the skilled officer, for character and competence (it bears repeating) are complementary. "Skilled officers, like all other professional men," wrote Army Chief of Staff Douglas MacArthur in May 1932, "are products of continuous and laborious study, training and experience. There is no short cut to the peculiar type of knowledge and ability they must possess. Trained officers constitute the most vitally essential element in modern war, and the only one that under no circumstances can be improvised or extemporized."[8]

To what degree is the "military mind" reflected in the following five situations?

1. Concerned about the enemy's documented buildup of forces and desperate to seize the initiative, Air Force General John Lavelle defied bombing directives for North Vietnam time after time for four months in 1971. To cover his actions, official reports were falsified, describing the bombing sorties as "protective reaction strikes." A young Air Force sergeant wrote to his senator, asking whether his false reports were proper.[9] Was Lavelle wrong to go on the initiative, despite his orders not to bomb the targets he did? Was the sergeant wrong to contact his senator? Did he "betray" the Air Force? (On 1 November 1972 Air Force Chief of Staff Gen. John D. Ryan issued a brief state-

ment condemning lying, saying that "any order to compromise integrity is not a lawful order.")

2. Col. Lucian K. Truscott III tells of weapons missing occasionally from his infantry battalion's armory. After taking vigorous steps to prevent further disappearances, he felt confident that he had solved the problem and concentrated on getting his command ready for combat duty in Vietnam. Suddenly, another pistol was missing. The result might have been a letter of reprimand or even relief from command. Truscott's NCOs, fearful that their colonel might be relieved at the very moment they were about to be shipped overseas, urged him not to report the missing pistol; they would see that it was "lost in combat" when they got to Vietnam. They could take care of it. Truscott's men were paying him a high compliment, and he owed them something—one mere falsehood?[10]

3. An officer assigned to inspect expended rounds on the rifle range (to be certain that primers were detonated before the brass was packed for shipping and salvage) was told by his company commander just to sign the certificates and get into the jeep because he was in a hurry.[11] To insist upon checking before signing such reports is too literal, isn't it? Is there ever a time "to look the other way"? Or would such a signature be a kind of lie?

4. A West Point ethics class question: Captain Jones's company has been trying without success for three days to take an enemy strong point. Company losses are great, with more than 45 percent casualties. Highly agitated, Captain Jones orders Lieutenant Pointer to poison a stream that runs through the enemy area. (According to the "school solution," the lieutenant "is under both a moral and legal duty to confront his commander and advise him that the order is illegal and will not be carried out.")[12]

5. An Army lieutenant colonel, thought to be a rising star, gets an appointment to attend the Army War College but turns it down because he wants his children to finish school where they are at present. After seventeen years of service, he says, "duty, honor, country" must become "duty, honor, family."[13] Is he selfish? wrong? Should his career be over?

What does a "military mind" have to do with these cases? The usual snide remark is that a "military mind" is an oxymoron; but that is hardly helpful. What matters more than instances of the "military mind," then, is "military people" in whose patriotism, valor, fidelity, and abilities all Americans can have confidence.

Professionalism

According to Samuel Huntington's classic definition, a profession is characterized by expertise, responsibility, and corporateness.[14] I define *profession* as a voluntary association of learned people whose primary purpose is to institutionalize standards of accomplishment and behavior worthy of the group. The knowledge and bonding suggested by Professor Huntington find their expression in "responsibility," for without it criminals might fairly be called professional. (I recognize, by the way, that we talk about "professional" football players or about "charismatic" coaches. But here I mean *professional* in its classic sense.) Historically, professions instituted and nurtured a communal sense of honor and shame among their members. Departure from that tradition has cheapened many, if not most, professional organizations, which appear reluctant to stigmatize members guilty of moral turpitude. As pointed out in Chapter 6, modern society, in losing its sense of authority and of mature, settled ethical judgment, is increasingly unable to distinguish between what is and what ought to be. Hence, professional associations are much less likely today to concern themselves with "behavior worthy of the group."

Without a sense of ignominy, disgrace, or shame, professions may exist to sponsor social occasions and to raise dues but cannot reasonably hope to regulate behavior, for they lack understanding of the very values they were originally formed to promote. Without an ethical perspective an association has no responsibility; it has nothing to profess. In 1909 the *Oxford Dictionary* defined the word *profession* as "the declaration, promise, or vow made by one entering a religious order." It is only in that sense that *profession* means something more than "a paid occupation requiring advanced education."

The key element of the military profession, in a word, is *honor*, explained by Morris Janowitz as something involving gentlemanly conduct, loyalty to commander and Constitution, brotherhood, and the pursuit of glory.[15] MacArthur's moving valedictory at West Point in 1962 insisted that honor, duty, and country "build your basic character . . . [and] make you strong enough to know when you are weak, and brave enough to face yourself when you are afraid."[16] Literature is filled with examples of individual heroes faithful to their shining concepts of honor when, all around them, others failed. It is rarely so. Most humans need the counsel and companionship of others to hold them true when challenges mount. "The U.S. military is about the only public institution that is comfortable saying openly that individual rights take second place to the welfare of the whole," said James Fallows.[17] In the novel *Starship Troopers*, Robert Heinlein has a soldier remembering the words of his old teacher: "Citizenship is an attitude, a state of mind, an emotional conviction that the whole is greater than the part . . . and that the part should be humbly proud to sacrifice itself that the whole may live."[18] That novel depicts a governmental system based on the idea that every voter and officeholder demonstrates "through voluntary and difficult service the welfare of the group ahead of personal advantage."

A genuine profession works to accomplish two essentially complementary purposes: to educate its newest members in the way of the group and to inculcate standards and ideals on which the members may rely in time of need. Hortatory and heuristic codes, dogmas, and enduring symbolic rituals imbue members with the ideals of service and with devotion to integrity: that is, both to high morals and to unity of principle, purpose, and people. The Musketeers' familiar chant, "One for all and all for one," catches the spirit of the profession.

At the same time, no profession worthy of the term insists upon devotion to the point of betrayal of conscience. Groups can be, and often have been, wrong. Morality amounts to far more than slavishly following the leader or prostrating one's deepest convictions before the idol of others' opinions. (At the end of this chapter, I suggest some ethical tests which may help us distinguish obedience from obsequiousness.)

Still, it is the communal sense of shame and honor that professions historically existed to instill in their members. In addition to specialized knowledge and the brotherhood of Shake-speare's *Henry V* ("We few, we happy few, we band of broth-ers"), the profession develops trust among its members. That is, after all, what a military commission is: a certificate of trust and a charge of duty. A profession is about discipline, and whoever would learn discipline must first be a disciple and learn well the lessons of the ages. Professional soldiers are secular Jesuits, going forth to represent the ideals they have affirmed in a world much too willing to mock them. As a famous British officer once put it, "the real discipline that a man holds to . . . is a refusal to betray his comrades. The discipline that makes a sentry, whose whole body is tortured for sleep, rest his chin on the point of his bayonet because he knows, if he nods, he risks the lives of the men sleeping behind him."[19]

And if that sentry slept, safe in a foxhole, while the enemy made their way into the encampment, silently slit the throats of his comrades, and he awoke at dawn to see what had been done, what would his reaction be? "You win some, and you lose some"? "I'm glad they didn't get me"? "Their time was up, but mine wasn't"? Or would his sorrow, self-disgust, and shame be beyond all words? Joseph Conrad's powerful novel *Lord Jim* (1900) tells of a character who endures a sense of shame similar to this fictitious sentry's until the chance for redemption or rep-etition presents itself. But Conrad's novel is not widely read these days, and the concept of shame is rarely discussed on MTV.

The idea that one owes a sense of duty and honor to parents, spouse and children, neighbors, and country—indeed, that true faith and allegiance are ultimately the noblest ideals that sustain and uplift the human race—is often regarded as silly and shallow today. The idea that a soldier could be (in fact, must be) a secular Jesuit, that a commission is a religious trust and charge, that the armed forces are above all services in-tended primarily to fight and to prepare to fight—all these seem antiquated, even medieval. But these ideas are so much larger than any words I have that either readers have seen such virtues in others and admired and sought to emulate them, or such a chasm exists in their lives that all the books ever written cannot fill the empty space. People of decency and discretion know, in the end, that they are not worthy of their vows and profession, that their glory is in their attempt to do as they should. Only the most arrogant and the least worthy think themselves fully deserving of titles which, many years ago, at once humbled and honored those who bore them: priest, minister, rabbi, doctor, lawyer, teacher, professor; soldier, sailor, airman, Marine.

What have we done to these noble titles, to these admirable professions? Would they understand and forgive, all those whose standards we have betrayed? Would the soldiers whose throats were slit as the sentry slept forgive their friend?[20]

Would they have that much grace, that much nobility? Can we hear again the call of duty[21] that comes to us from the "snowy heights of honor"? Are the sentiments of 1861 embalmed and buried, never more to concern us as we go about the business of self-advancement, self-enrichment, self-absorption? Or do those sentiments speak to us of what we can be again if we hear well and act wisely.

A week before the battle of Bull Run, Sullivan Ballou, a major in the Second Rhode Island Volunteers, wrote home from Washington, D.C. to his wife in Smithfield. The date was 14 July 1861.

> My very dear Sarah:
> The indications are very strong that we shall move in a few days—perhaps tomorrow. Lest I should not be able to write again, I feel impelled to write a few lines that may fall under your eye when I shall be no more. . . .
> I have no misgivings about, or lack of confidence in the cause in which I am engaged, and my courage does not halt or falter. I know how strongly American Civilization now leans on the triumph of the Government, and how great a debt we owe to those who went before us through the blood and sufferings of the Revolution. And I am willing—perfectly willing—to lay down all my joys in this life to help maintain this Government, and to pay that debt. . . .
> Sarah, my love for you is deathless, [and] it seems to bind me with mighty cables that nothing but Omnipotence could break; and yet my love of Country comes over

me like a strong wind and bears me irresistibly on with all these chains to the battle field.

The memories of the blissful moments I have spent with you come creeping over me, and I feel most gratified to God and you that I have enjoyed them for so long. And hard it is for me to give them up and burn to ashes the hopes of future years, when, God willing, we might still have lived and loved together, and seen our sons grown up to honorable manhood around us. . . . If I do not [return] my dear Sarah, never forget how much I love you, and when my last breath escapes me on the battle field, it will whisper your name. Forgive my many faults, and the many pains I have caused you. How thoughtless and foolish I have often times been! How gladly would I wash out with my tears every little spot upon your happiness. . . . But, O Sarah! if the dead can come back to this earth and flit unseen around those they love, I shall always be near you; in the gladdest days and in the darkest nights . . . *always, always*, and if there be a soft breeze upon your cheek, it shall be my breath, as the cool air fans your throbbing temple, it shall be my spirit passing by. Sarah, do not mourn me dead; think I am gone and wait for me, for we shall meet again.[22]

Major Ballou was killed at the first battle of Bull Run.

Ethical Egoism

Psychological egoism is the claim that people act out of self-interest and that all ultimate motives are selfish. Ethical egoism contends that people *should* act in concert with their own interests. The question is not whether professionals act out of self-interest; of course they do. The question is whether professionals act always or exclusively or even principally out of self-interest. A sense of ambition, healthy self-respect, legitimate concern for one's career—these are desirable traits in any person.[23] But the professional must always bring into balance *I* and *we*. Persons concerned solely with themselves are by definition self-centered, and the very idea of professionalism challenges us to subordinate our personal gratifications to the benefit of the group.[24] Professionals—doctors, lawyers, priests, teachers, soldiers—do what they do, in substantial part, for others; they thereby earn their pay, improve their careers, and save their souls. In a good society, virtuous service to others fulfills the self; virtuous service to self enables one more effectively to serve others. Talents wasted or never developed by the indolent never improve the lot of the lazy, but neither do those latent talents ever benefit the community.[25]

Professionals serve as moral exemplars, and few would be willing to follow those whose sole interest lies in themselves.[26] In a very real sense, ethics is not so much taught as "caught" from those whose standards are high and fair. But if we are to believe our eyes and ears, a rampant solipsism has captured the American spirit, and at long last we recognize Sullivan Ballou as a "fool."[27] All too often, today, one becomes a doctor or lawyer or—perhaps most sadly of all—even a preacher because there is money to be made. In fact, one evening as I was writing this chapter, I watched an NBC news show that described telephone hoaxes in which the elderly would be called and promised bogus prizes once they sent in "registration fees." This sleazy business proved surprisingly lucrative for the criminals involved. One of the crooks explained why: the elderly had grown up in a post-Depression, World War II era when a handshake meant a commitment of honor. The elderly *actually believed you when you gave your word*. But powerful centrifugal forces seem to be propelling us outward, away from the central core values in whose name the republic was established in the eighteenth century.[28]

Speaking to West Pointers, Tom Wolfe has pointed out what the greatest trial of military ethics may be in the years ahead:

> Everyone . . . now has the capability of availing himself or herself of the luxuries of the aristocrat, whether it be a constant string of young sexual partners or whether it be the easy access to anything that stimulates or soothes the mind or the nervous system or simply the easy disregard of rules of various sorts. . . . You will have to deal with it. You are going to find yourselves required to be sentinels at

the bacchanal. You are going to find yourself required to stand guard at the Lucullan feast against the Huns approaching from outside. You will have to be armed monks at the orgy.[29]

It will be no easy thing for future professionals (in any field) to support and to sustain integrity when all around them there is rampant ethical disintegration, a corrosion of the values professionals are expected to foster. Values known so well to Sullivan Ballou.

Professional Egoism

As moral consensus in America breaks down,[30] the professions meet the daily danger of eroded understanding of norms and values. But as serious as are those challenges to military professionalism from moral decay without, moral decay within is an even more pressing danger. The military, to be sure, is not immune to the siren song of egoism. Decent, discreet soldiers who would not for a moment consider lying, cheating, or stealing for reasons of self-enrichment might very well do exactly those things in the name of the good of their service. I offer this as the key threat to professional integrity in the immediate years ahead. As Murray Kempton put it more than three decades ago, "The good soldier will lie under orders as bravely as he will die under them."[31] If there is still agreement that lying is wrong if done solely for purposes of self-promotion, how about lying to advance the "cause" of the Army, Navy, or Air Force?[32]

Professionals, after all, are stewards of the public trust. Without proper stewardship, "professionals," whether enriching themselves or substituting the benefit of their association for the national interest, are mere mountebanks.[33] In an era of "rightsizing" and "drawdowns," military professionals are morally imperiled by the persistent danger of elevating parochial concerns to national ones. That is, military officers who would never otherwise "cheat" may now be tempted to do in the name of their service what they would never do for themselves, such as accepting missions or agreeing to situations which at other times they would professionally reject.

If it is the military's job to fight and to prepare to fight, most other missions they are given may be, at best, diversions. But among the tasks being prepared for the armed forces now are these: noncombatant evacuation, disaster relief, environmental clean-up (other than on military posts and bases), humanitarian intervention, education and training of those who for various reasons are unfit for public schools, infrastructure rebuilding (roads, bridges, canals), nation building in the less developed countries, medical relief, drug wars, border patrol, riot control, prison duty, and arms control verification. If, in order to maintain their size and influence, the military services seize upon such duties, permitting their enduring mission of military readiness to deteriorate and atrophy, they are misfeasant and derelict in their primary duties. Richard Gabriel, although glib at times, is precisely correct in his judgment that "the military represents a threat to the civil order not because it will usurp authority, but because it does not speak out on critical policy decisions. The soldier fails to live up to his oath to serve the country if he does not speak out when he sees his civilian or military superiors executing policies he feels to be wrong."[34]

In 1992, *Parameters* published a remarkable account of a military coup in the United States—in 2012. The author, Charles J. Dunlap, Jr., takes as his premise that because, after the Gulf War of 1991, the United States military was looked up to as a model of efficiency, the government increasingly called upon the armed services to perform a wide variety of missions at best tangential to their primary task of combat training and war fighting. When the U.S. military, its training undone because of its multiple ancillary tasks, was soundly defeated in 2010 by Iranian armies, the backlash was predictable: a military coup! Dunlap has his storyteller ("Prisoner 222305759") explain in this perceptive paragraph:

> In truth militaries ought to "prepare for war" and leave the "peace waging" to those agencies of government whose mission is just that. Nevertheless, such pronouncements—seconded by military leaders—became the fashionable phi-

losophy. The result? People in the military no longer considered themselves warriors. Instead, they perceived themselves as policemen, relief workers, educators, builders, health care providers, politicians—everything but warfighters. When these philanthropists met the Iranian 10th Armored Corps near Daharan during the Second Gulf War, they were brutally slaughtered by a military which had not forgotten what militaries were supposed to do or what war is really all about.[35]

If the military is too ready to seize upon non-traditional roles and missions to preserve its size and influence at the cost of its reason for being, it betrays its fidelity to purpose, its fundamental profession. The armed forces do seem entirely too ready to repeat a Vietnam-era error of using business methods to conduct military operations. Accorded almost biblical respect today are the creeds and canons of "Total Quality Management," which officers resist at their professional peril. Indeed, TQM wields a near-hypnotic effect on certain officers chosen to spread the word among unbelievers. Although preaching against slogans and shibboleths, TQM is in fact a sloganeering nightmare, filled with concepts such as the need to measure everything (honor? justice? love?), the peremptory instruction to adopt the new philosophy (can it be that what works for Toyota may not work in the U.S. infantry?), the notion of "process action teams" and flow charts and a host of other "tools" of management. All of this is an attempt to offer "a total package," which is really a substitute for liberally educated leaders of wisdom and virtue. The entrepreneurial ethic is ever at odds with the professional ethic of the U.S. armed forces.[36] It is the height of professional folly to attempt to use a business technique to do what the military must do: train for and fight wars.[37]

Some military officers, as human beings, seem altogether too eager to be "trendy," and some who see the popularity of TQM in civilian industry are eager to prove their modern attitudes by equipping themselves with TQM techniques. One hopes that alchemy does not gain currency again in the business world; if it did, it would soon be taught at senior service schools. They would be wiser to slow down some and not throw out the baby of military professionalism (proved over the centuries) with the bathwater of those practices that really should be improved upon. The TQM notion of "continuous improvement" is a slogan that is hard to resist. But it should occasionally be resisted. Over the centuries the profession of arms has developed a number of principles, traits, rituals, and codes that have served soldiers, in peace and war, very well. Some concepts (one thinks of the Ten Commandments) do not require "continuous improvement" but only better understanding and application. Though military history is full of examples of soldiers who were reluctant to change when change was necessary, it is equally replete with examples of people who seized the moment to change systems that should never have been toyed with.[38] Knowing when to change and when not to is no easy trick— and TQM manuals do not provide such helpful distinctions.

More than two decades ago Bernard Brodie, a well-known analyst of military affairs said, "I have never observed in any other group besides the military such a tolerance of bragging, especially among senior officers." He also argued that "the profession is more limiting in the personality types it accepts and advances, and—it is much more demanding in conformity and more confining in the kind of character development it furthers."[39] He also wrote, "We see that the whole training of the military is toward a set of values that finds in battle and in victory a vindication. The skills developed in the soldier are those of the fighter, and not of the reflecter on ultimate purposes. Under particular circumstances it may be considered unwise to fight, but it is rarely looked upon as ignoble; and is there any other test of unwisdom except the probability of losing?"[40]

Yes and no. The military's chief task *is* to fight and to win. It does so always and only at civilian bidding, but it can and must advise about the circumstances of any fighting. We know too well the price and penalty of having illiberally educated soldiers, or conceited soldiers whose sole concern amounts to gasconade and self-advancement. To be professional, soldiers must blend competence and character; they must merge wisdom and virtue; they must understand both honor and shame. Soldiers who do not practice their perishable professional skills, contending that they are now businessmen or policemen, will not have those skills when they are needed in combat; soldiers who will not think through moral problems, contending that ethical concerns belong only in churches or classrooms, will fail their profession and their people every time they must determine what should be done, in war or in peace. As a West Point professor, Colonel Charles Larned, put it in 1906: "No education that does not base itself upon ethical actions as its prime motor can have any part or lot in civilization's higher development."[41]

Tests of Ethics

Does God exist? Is there an ultimate truth? How, exactly, does anyone tell right from wrong? If military ethics is the study of honor and shame in the armed forces, what is honor, and what is shame? The reader may well be saying, by now, *"Tell me something!"*

It is possible for a scholar to spend a whole professional life studying ethics and still be a scoundrel. It is also possible to find an illiterate person who is a fine human being. The study of moral philosophy, however, should help us to be a little wiser and a little more virtuous. The central burden of military ethics is that soldiers who are taught to kill are asked to do so carefully; that men who use bayonets, bombs, and bullets are asked to think wisely and well before using them and while using them. This book has repeatedly contended that the soldier can and must be a moral exemplar to the larger society. Although soldiers are not philosophers, they are morally interested human beings. As the philospher C.E.M. Joad (1891-1953) observed three-quarters of a century ago: "Every man has an instinct to call certain things moral. In so far as he does not possess this instinct he is not wholly a man."[42] Good people are not always good soldiers, but good soldiers—in my definition—are almost always good people.

Good people know right from wrong. But how do they know that? What practical prescriptions can we give soldiers about honor and shame? Do we demand that they read dozens of ethics books? Do we send them to universities to take advanced degrees in moral philosophy and theology? Do we conduct seminars for them about synderesis and syneidesis, supererogation and probabilism? No. Graduate-level courses in ethical and methaethical theory are hardly reasonable for most soldiers. But we cannot release them from the responsibility of learning ethics. Since Nuremberg, after all, soldiers *must* know when to disobey. *But how?*

I offer now six tests for determining whether any action is right or wrong, honorable or shameful. These are not tests devised by Aristotle or Kant. They are short and simple ways of trying to decide what is right. To be sure, the tests can overlap; they can even, occasionally, be at odds.[43] But generally there will be substantial agreement among them about the correct action for someone to take in moments of confusion. The tests can be of use to a private as well as to a general, to a student as well as to a professor. The very act of asking the following questions suggests a reasonable attempt to know and to do what ought to be done: In trying to determine whether an action should be done, ask: If people knew about this, would I be ashamed? Will my community approve this action? Is it legal? Do these circumstances warrant special actions? Are its results most likely to be favorable? If I believe in God, would he approve?

1. The *shame test* asks whether this action, if publicized, would embarrass, discredit, or humiliate me.[44] Married people make love and would not want to have their conjugal relations broadcast, but this is a private act and certainly nothing to be ashamed of. Shooting unarmed women and children is deeply shameful; selling drugs to kids is deeply shameful. Do you really want your closest relatives to see you doing this?

2. The *community test* asks whether, in addition to your closest relatives, you would want people in your community—your professional peers—to know about your action. Is this action in keeping with the expectations and traditions of your friends, teachers, neighbors?

3. The *legal test* asks whether, if authorities found out, you would likely be put on trial for the action.

4. The *situation test* asks whether there are peculiar or special circumstances requiring extraordinary action. If time and opportunity presented themselves, would you be able to give a satisfactory response to everyone you care about (as well as to a

jury of professional colleagues) about why you are taking un-usual action now?

5. The *consequences test* asks whether the results of your action are likely to be good. Will the benefits of the action justify the costs?

6. The *God test* asks, if you believe in God, what would his commandment be in this circumstance? Does the Golden Rule apply? Would you want the action done to you? Or, if you do not believe in God, the test asks, is your action universalizable: that is, would you want everyone in the world to be able to do what you are about to do?[45]

We human beings have the responsibility of living with our-selves. In the novel *Once an Eagle* hero Sam Damon says, "A man has to do what he can think well of himself for doing, or he's nothing."[46] But our responsibility is not exclusively to, nor our knowledge primarily from, ourselves. As we owe a debt to ourselves, so do we owe a debt to others. As William Kilpatrick reminds us, "'To thine own self be true' would have seemed utterly foolish advice not only to Augustine but to Cicero and his contemporaries. Even in Shakespeare's play [*Hamlet*], these words are put into the mouth of an old fool."[47]

All professions—including the profession of arms—exist (or *ought to exist*) to serve and to sacrifice for others. Ordinarily, actions are ethical when they legitimately serve the well-being of others without compromising our own cherished ideals. Our ideals are the product of our own reasoned judgment in the context of the communities of which we are a part and to which we own true faith and allegiance. Ethical egoists and those who forget the larger purposes of the professions should be re-minded of what we owe, always, to others' hands:

Each of us lives in and through an immense movement of the hands of other people. The hands of other people lift us from the womb. The hands of other people grow the food we eat, weave the clothes we wear and build the shel-ters we inhabit. The hands of other people give pleasure to our bodies in moments of passion and aid and comfort in times of affliction and distress. It is in and through the hands of other people that the commonwealth of nature is appropriated and accommodated to the needs and pleasures of our separate, individual lives, and, at the end, it is the hands of other people that lower us into the earth.[48]

Conclusions

A profession is a voluntary association of learned people whose main purpose is to institutionalize standards of accomplishment and behavior worthy of the group. The military profession is similar to other professions in seeking to promote the purposes for which it was initially established; it is different from other professions in that its members are pledged to uphold, ultimately, not personal or group interest but the national interest. The chief danger posed to the profession of arms is its continued civilianization. As the military becomes increasingly enmeshed in traditionally exclusive centers of civilian power and influence, its historic codes and competencies will be transmuted or eroded.

Military ethics can help maintain the integrity of the profession of arms by requiring soldiers to distinguish right from wrong—by no means always an easy task. Ethics tests can help. Ask whether something you are about to do might bring shame on you, flout community standards, or be illegal; whether it is appropriate to the situation, likely to have good results, and measures up to divine commands or can be universalized.

8. Excursus
Teaching and Learning about Military Ethics

A juvenile becomes an adult when, and only when,
he acquires a knowledge of duty and embraces it as
dearer than the self-love he was born with.
—Robert Heinlein, *Starship Troopers*

An excursus is a detailed discussion of some point, inserted at
the end of a text. This one is about how to teach and learn moral
philosophy and, more particularly, military ethics.

One professor of ethics, Christina Hoff Sommers, tells an intriguing story. After she pointed out in an article that as important as issues of public morality are (abortion, capital punishment, DNA research), issues of private morality (lying, cheating,
stealing) are also critical, a colleague criticized the piece. The
critic, arguing that moral people will not be common until there
are moral institutions, planned to continue teaching about oppression of women, big business, multinational corporate trans-
gressions in the developing world, and so on. At the end of the
semester this same colleague, visibly upset, came in to see Professor Sommers: "They cheated on their social justice take-
home finals. They plagiarized," she lamented.

To help improve private morality, Sommers suggests that a
three-part program be implemented in the schools: establishing
behavior codes that emphasize "civility, kindness, and honesty"; expecting teachers to emphasize "civility, decency, honesty
and fairness"; and exposing children to "reading, studying and
discussing the moral classics."[1]

That is the concern of this chapter, which is a collection of
notes and notions about the teaching of moral philosophy, which
is the parent of military ethics. To some extent, moral behavior *is*
taught by good teachers and by good readings; to some extent,
it is caught from those same teachers and readings. I do not

want to bemoan the plight of contemporary teaching any more than I wish to bewail some modern teachers, although there is much to mourn on both counts. The notes to this chapter (and to Chapter 1) give sources that discuss the inadequacies of today's secondary and collegiate education. I want rather to stress principally positive and practical ideas about "honor" and "shame." If the definition of military ethics used in this book is at all correct, then there can be no military ethics until students and soldiers have a reasonably clear conception of those two terms, as well as their practical application. The old Chinese proverb "You do not use good men to make a nail or a good man to make a soldier" is, in fact, wholly mistaken. The great burden of military ethics lies in this: if those who control the power to kill and maim are evil or morally unfit, we unleash a torrent of sinister power. Soldiers, no less than doctors and teachers and ministers and lawyers, must be decent and discreet individuals. But we recognize that our professions have failed us as regularly as our schools (witness students who plagiarize in an ethics test) in inculcating private morality. Sir William Francis Butler once observed: "The nation that will insist on drawing a broad line of demarcation between the fighting man and the thinking man is liable to find its fighting done by fools and its thinking done by cowards."[2] We might add a corollary: the nation that will insist on drawing a broad line of demarcation between moral instruction and public schooling is liable to find its educational orders given by the corrupt and its ethical standards set by the illiterate.

Knowing the Difference between "Price" and "Value"

It is sometimes said of mercenary people that they know the price of everything and the value of nothing. All ethics is a debate about comparative value. Unless students and soldiers learn to value wisely and well, they imperil their peers, their mission, their service, and their country. St. Augustine, in *The City of God* (4.4), asks: "Justice being taken away, then, what are kingdoms but great robberies?" Students of military ethics must ask, "Morality being taken away, then, what are armies but great mobs?"

Some twenty years ago Army Chaplain Kermit Johnson declared: "The task of building an ethical environment where leaders and all personnel are instructed, encouraged, and rewarded for ethical behavior is a matter of first importance."[3] Yet, as Manuel Davenport has pointed out, the military seldom encourages or rewards ethical behavior, and all too often soldiers are "allowed to be ethical only when those above them want them to [be]."[4] And after four years at Harvard a recent graduate said in his commencement speech: "Among my classmates— I believe that there is one idea, one sentiment, which we have all acquired at some point in our Harvard careers; and that, ladies and gentlemen, is, in a word, confusion. They tell us that it is heresy to suggest the superiority of some value, fantasy to believe in moral argument, slavery to submit to a judgment sounder than your own. The freedom of our day is the freedom to devote ourselves to any values we please, on the mere condition that we do not believe them to be true."[5] There has been, apparently, very little progress in either the university or the military.

It used to be true in many colleges that professors could be dismissed for "moral turpitude." Not only is that notion apparently obsolete; the very term would be regarded as comical on most campuses. In the military, Article 133 of the Uniform Code of Military Justice still exists, but one must wonder how long it will endure: "Any commissioned officer, cadet, or midshipman who is convicted of conduct unbecoming an officer and a gentleman [sic] shall be punished as a court martial may direct." That might well include such offenses as drunken or reckless driving (Article 111), wrongful use of controlled substances (Article 112a), rape and carnal knowledge (Article 120), larceny and wrongful appropriation (Article 121), writing a bad check (Article 123a), sodomy (Article 125), and perjury (Article 131). But some of these "offenses" appear old fashioned. Will "conduct unbecoming" go the way of "moral turpitude"?

Self-Education

Steven Cahn tells of being asked to give a lecture on the subject "Ethics in the Academic World." When he mentioned the topic to a faculty colleague, the colleague retorted, "It'll be a short

talk." Professor Cahn goes on to quote a history professor at a
state university in the West, who put it bluntly: "I have met few
professors whom I would hire to run a peanut stand, let alone
be the guardian of wisdom and Western civilization."[6] According to a spate of recent books, the American university not only
is not educating its students but is inflicting intellectual and
moral harm upon them.[7] The reasons are easy to enumerate: the
mental laziness of many professors, who sometimes seem not
to read, let alone write, very much or very often; or, alternatively, professors so enraptured by their own research that
they neglect teaching and advising students to the point of
abandonment; the politics of race and sex; grade inflation, easy
course assignments, and lack of intellectual rigor; what often
appears to be lack of interest in teaching. If the university is not
a place to build competence and character, where do we go to
learn the lessons of excellence? Who will teach us value—and
not merely price?

To some degree, we must pursue such lessons ourselves. The
beginning of ethics education consists in choosing one's parents! After that comes wisdom in choosing the right friends,
neighborhood, and school and college. Recently, *National Review*
published its guide to the top fifty liberal arts schools. Though it
clearly favors a conservative curriculum, this list includes a wide
variety of colleges and universities, such as Baylor, Brigham
Young, Chicago, Columbia, Gonzaga, Notre Dame, Wabash,
Washington and Lee, and William and Mary.[8] Among the things
that anyone interested in ethics education can do are these:

1. As far as possible, pick the best teachers available in
the subjects and courses you will take. Good teachers are
highly competent in their fields; their minds bubble with
ideas, and they *want* to teach. They are enthusiastic and
display a sense of humor. They are well organized and
impeccably fair to all students.

2. Read widely in the classics. Suggestions follow in this
chapter.

3. Keep a personal journal, noting your reactions to
classes, readings, national and personal events, and the
like.

4. Think through the ethical dilemmas of your own life in the context of the ethics tests provided in Chapter 7.

5. Use your school, base, post, or public library. Browse in the stacks: some of the best teachers in the world are there for you, whether catalogued by the Dewey Decimal or the Library of Congress system.[9]

Moral philosophy, for example, may be found under 170. Here is a list of other headings in ethics: (171) ethical systems, doctrines, and theories; (172) political ethics; (173) family ethics; (174) professional and occupational ethics; (175) ethics of recreation and leisure; (176) ethics of sex and reproduction; (177) ethics of social relations; (178) ethics of consumption; (179) other topics in ethics.

Other areas of interest to students of military ethics might be these: (201) religious philosophies and theories; (216) good and evil; (241) moral theology; (327) foreign relations; (335) economic ideologies; (341) international law; (344) martial law; (355) military subjects and warfare; (356) infantry; (357) cavalry and mounted services; (358) other arms and services; (359) naval forces; (377) religious and moral education; (399) customs of war; (810) American literature in English; (900) History; (920) Biography.

Each area is broken down in much more detail, of course. For example, under 172.42 you will find the library's holdings on war and peace, conscientious objection, just war theory, pacifism, war prosecution, and so on. The classification 176.8 (obscenity in literature) should be balanced by 179.9, a section dealing with virtues such as modesty and self-control. But just this simple overview enables students to know exactly where to go in most libraries to find books grouped by subject in the ethics field.

As a teacher, I have long concluded my courses with the adjuration to my students, "You must become your own best teacher and your own worst critic." The best education is self-education, and the best teaching establishes a foundation for subsequent learning. As Christina Hoff Sommers has put it, "The best moral teaching inspires students by making them keenly aware that their own character is at stake."[10]

Strong disagreement—sometimes downright hostility—exists among those who discuss the stages of moral growth and methodology for helping to develop moral awareness.[11] Many schemes of moral development directly or indirectly criticize "authorities," dismissing them as cranks or worse.[12] But philosopher William Frankena—after quoting Jim Casey in John Steinbeck's *Grapes of Wrath*: "There ain't no sin and there ain't no virtue, there is just stuff people do"—argues: "I very much doubt that moral education can get off the ground, given the present facts of human life, in a society in which there are no parental or social rules or values, and no praising, blaming, holding responsible, or sanctioning."[13] Certain "Gens," as he terms them (rules, precepts, principles, ideals) are useful in instructing people how to relate to one another. Good people know them. Good people follow them. Such Gens are the stuff of moral philosophy and of military ethics.

The authors of an article on military leadership put it well: "Unlike the operator, who depends solely on the accomplishment of certain goals to maintain his sense of worth, or the team player, who needs to feel accepted or at least respected by his men to maintain his self-esteem, the self-defining leader makes his own judgments about his worthiness."[14] That is the sort of development we must be concerned with in military ethics. In the April 1978 issue of the *Atlantic Monthly*, Admiral James Stockdale has explained in detail why that is true. Stockdale's eight years as a prisoner of war in North Vietnam included four years in solitary confinement and frequent torture. In all his writings, he is clear that the classics prepare us for success and for failure—that is, for life.[15] Good readings and good teachers give us the Gens we need to lead our lives. The teaching of values may be subject to political and pedagogical debate,[16] but the absence of such values leads to moral chaos.

Combatting Moral Chaos

However values are taught, the schools must play a vital role. But schools are under assault morally and, apparently, physically as well: the National Educational Association estimates that every day 100,000 students carry a gun to school, 6,250 teachers are threatened with injury, and 260 are actually assaulted.[17] Moreover, American universities that advocate nihilistic relativism undermine public consensus on values,[18] and the Harvard Business School's teaching of ethics is described by one critic as "a politically correct, cram-down program."[19] All the while the classics sit by in the library. Sidney Axinn has it exactly right: "Military education can teach honor by producing the atmosphere of honor."[20] If a school lacks highly educated teachers and cannot provide an atmosphere of honor in which the Gens of classical morality are imparted, it will erode, not improve, the academic and ethical education of its students.

Former Secretary of Education William Bennett pointed out that students should look for—and expect to find—college professors who can bring to life the subject at hand. But they should also "discover great works that tell us how men and women of our own and other civilizations have grappled with life's relentless questions: What should be loved? What deserves to be defended? What is noble and what is base? As Montaigne wrote, a student should have the chance to learn 'what valor, temperance, and justice are; the differences between ambition and greed, loyalty and servitude, liberty and license; and the marks of true and solid contentment.'"[21] Instead, however, we too often foster bewilderment about enduring principles and precepts. Admiral Stockdale was persuaded that moral philosophy ought to be a key and critical part of the education of senior Navy officers. When he took command at the Naval War College, he initiated a course in which officers read Plato, Epictetus, the Bible, Albert Camus's *Plague*, Joseph Conrad's *Typhoon*, Herman Melville's *Billy Budd*. One observer wrote, "This example should be imitated by the military academies and [by] ROTC programs,"[22] and other educators have urged that a similar program be offered by the schools of America in order to retain those values that gave rise to our country.[23]

Three sources can be suggested as points of departure for a course like the one Stockdale established. The first is a government pamphlet: S.L.A. Marshall, *The Armed Forces Officer* (stock number 008-046-00090-5), published by the Government Printing Office, also published commercially as *The Officer as Leader* (Harrisburg, Pa.: Stackpole Books, 1966). Joseph G. Brennan's *Foundations of Moral Obligation: The Stockdale Course* (Newport, R.I.: Naval War College, 1992) contains the lectures Brennan presented during that course. And Roger Nye's *The Challenge of Command* (Wayne, N.J.: Avery, 1986), offers not only an excellent guide to a reading program in military classics but some incisive commentaries as well. Those who want to teach and learn about military ethics can use this as a good guide to a reading program.

Here, precisely, is the role that the military can play as we seek to find our way out of the moral maelstrom now engulfing us. The way of the soldier, lived right, can, in the words of Charles Van Doren, "force us to think about an ideal way of life. Based on discipline, virtue, especially courage, which many nonsoldiers believe they lack, and dedication to a cause, this way of life seems highly desirable. Although most of us may feel we cannot live up to the high ideal of the good soldier, the ideal nevertheless uplifts us, even inspires us."[24]

Fostering Moral Conviction

The rest of this chapter consists of some long-considered advice about teaching and learning military ethics. In addition to Nye's *Challenge of Command*, those interested in the field should read Peter Stromberg, Malham M. Wakin, and Daniel Callahan, *The Teaching of Ethics in the Military* (Hastings-on-Hudson, N.Y.: Hastings Center, 1982). Although now a bit dated, it is still remarkably valuable and has a useful bibliography (77-85) of additional sources. A companion volume is *The Teaching of Ethics in Higher Education*, also published by the Hastings Center. Daniel Callahan and Sissela Bok edited a book entitled *Ethics Teaching in Higher Education* (New York: Plenum Press, 1980), also contains excellent materials; the short essay "Qualifications for the Teaching of Ethics" (75-80) is useful reading for deans or principals who think virtually anyone can teach such courses.

William Kilpatrick's fine book *Why Johnny Can't Tell Right from Wrong* has an excellent list of recommended readings (268-315), from picture books through much more advanced texts. One of the best short reading lists I know is in Russell Kirk, *Decadence and Renewal in the Higher Learning* (South Bend, Ind.: Gateway, 1978), 275-79. In 1982 the Department of English at the Air Force Academy produced a thoughtful pamphlet, *Literature in the Education of the Military Professional*, edited by Donald Ahern and Robert Shenk. The Air Force Academy also published, from 1980 to 1985 and again in 1988, its *Journal of Professional Military Ethics*. A very good selected bibliography for values education appears in Robert T. Sandin, *The Rehabilitation of Virtue: Foundations of Moral Education*, 267-78.

Kilpatrick tells us why we should think about such readings in studying virtue:

> One of the best ways to teach the virtues is in conjunction with history and literature. In that way, students can see that they are more than abstract concepts. In Robert Bolt's play *A Man for All Seasons*, we see a remarkable combination of all four [cardinal] virtues in one man, Sir Thomas More. The plot of *High Noon* revolves around a tension among justice, courage, and prudence. *To Kill a Mockingbird* shows one kind of courage, *The Old Man and the Sea* another. *Measure for Measure* and *The Merchant of Venice* teach us about justice. *Moby-Dick* depicts a man who has lost all sense of prudence and proportion. In the character of Falstaff, we are treated to a romantic depiction of intemperance; in the story of David and Bathsheba, we are shown a much harsher view of a man who yields to his desires.[25]

All education in ethics is instruction in heroism.[26] In an age when the hero appears to be an absurd anachronism, we need to learn that each of us must truly be the hero of his own life. That is, we must try our best to know and to do what is right. Although we will inevitably fail, at least occasionally, in that quest, we can use a moral compass set on the true north of Gens that endure through the ages to reorient ourselves and continue our lives with wisdom, courage, temperance, and justice. Then the hero in us will know honor and shame, will know value and not merely price.

Moral conviction flows from education, experience, and inspiration. Many of the readings suggested in the sources listed above can help us to find models worthy of emulation. The trials, traumas, and turbulence sometimes found in our lives are not peculiar to us, and we can learn something of patience and endurance from those who have gone before. All readers should be encouraged to build their own libraries graced by those books that hold personal and professional value to them. Reading such books—and reflecting upon them in a personal journal—can ensure that our moral compasses do not get lost. Professions have long encouraged their members to take occasional sabbaticals or retreats as times for contemplation and refreshment. Reading and then reflecting upon a good book is a "mini-retreat."

Here are some suggestions for finding such books (and articles). (1) Ask professors and professional colleagues for their advice. Which books have meant the most to them? (2) Consult standard reading lists. (3) Look through bibliographies, such as the one in this book. (4) Shelf-read in the library in those call number areas in which you may have interest. (5) Read book review sections in the professional journals.

Additional Recommendations

Besides the sources already mentioned, military ethics education can take advantage of such works as James and Sybil Stockdale, *In Love and War* (Annapolis, Md.: Naval Institute Press, 1990), and Elmo Zumwalt, Jr., Elmo Zumwalt III, and John Pekkanen, *My Father, My Son* (New York: Macmillan, 1986), both of which concern human relationships as much as things military. Lewis B. Puller, Jr.'s *Fortunate Son* (New York: Grove Weidenfeld, 1991) is a poignant autobiography by the son of Chesty Puller, the famous Marine general. Terribly wounded in Vietnam, the younger Puller describes his efforts to regain his physical and mental health and raises a number of issues worthy of thoughtful discussion. Pat Conroy's novel *The Great Santini* (1976, rpt. New York: Bantam, 1987) is an intriguing character study of a pilot and father; a good movie followed from that book in 1979.

Malcolm McConnell, *Into the Mouth of the Cat* (New York: Norton, 1985), and Jeremiah Denton with Ed Brandt, *When Hell Was in Session* (Clover, S.C.: Commission Press, 1976), are inspirational. McConnell tells the story of Capt. Lance Sijan, the first Air Force Academy graduate to earn the Medal of Honor, whose efforts at evasion and escape in the jungles of Vietnam were bravery personified. Jeremiah Denton, who returned home and became a U.S. senator, tells the powerful story of his captivity in Vietnam.

An interesting companion volume to "hero literature" is *The Execution of Private Slovik* by William Bradford Huie (New York: Signet, 1954). Slovik was the only American soldier executed for desertion in World War II, and the book raises numerous questions about heroes, discipline, justice, and mercy. James Clavell, *King Rat* (Boston: Little, Brown, 1962), a novel about POWs held by the Japanese in World War II, raises similar questions about selfishness as opposed to group loyalty.

Biographies and autobiographies are useful, especially when read in tandem. That is, reading two or three biographies of people in common situations reinforces their lessons and may reveal points of contention between their authors. Eric Larrabee, *Commander in Chief* (New York: Harper & Row, 1987), tells the story of President Franklin D. Roosevelt and provides short studies of such leaders as George Marshall, Douglas MacArthur, Dwight Eisenhower, Joseph Stilwell, and Curtis Lemay. I think students are well served when they are asked to read biographies with these questions in mind: What would *I* have done in these situations? Can the ethical tests suggested in Chapter 7 be applied to any of the circumstances described or problems encountered in this book? What has this book contributed to *my* education?

Chief among the books I use in teaching courses in military ethics are David Donovan, *Once a Warrior King* (New York: McGraw-Hill, 1985), the remarkable story of an American lieutenant in an advisory role during the Vietnam War;[27] and Robert Heinlein's *Starship Troopers* (1959; New York: Ace, 1987), a science fiction thriller about combat in outer space but, at another level, a work of military philosophy in which perceptive readers will find a mine of materials for discussion.

Although there are numerous good books about platoon leaders and company commanders in combat, there is relatively little about junior officers in peacetime. One attempt to contribute in that regard is my book *The American Military Ethic* (New

York: Praeger, 1992), the first half of which is an autobiographical account of a company-grade U.S. Army officer stationed in Europe during the early 1970s.

The Vietnam literature is extensive.[28] In developing your own reading lists, you will want to browse the section of the library stacks devoted to that war (shelved under 959). One novel that raises particularly troublesome questions about careerism is *The Lionheads* by Josiah Bunting (New York: Braziller, 1972.) An excellent article by Lloyd J. Matthews, "Is Ambition Unprofessional?" *Army*, July 1988, discusses not only that topic but some of the literature dealing with it (see p. 31). Plugging the classic historical novel *Killer Angels* by Michael Shaara (New York: McKay, 1974) into discussions of careerism can be useful to generate debate. The 1994 film *Gettysburg* is also excellent.

The backbone of military ethics courses continues to be the second edition of *War, Morality, and the Military Profession*, edited by Malham Wakin (Boulder: Westview, 1986). Michael Walzer's *Just and Unjust Wars*, 2d ed. (New York: Basic, 1992) is indispensable if the course includes topics in just war.[29] My own book *The Sword and the Cross: Reflections on Command and Conscience* (New York: Praeger, 1992) examines a number of political-moral questions. Anthony E. Hartle, *Moral Issues in Military Decision Making* (Lawrence: Univ. Press of Kansas, 1989), is an excellent basic volume. Finally, Paul Christopher, *The Ethics of War and Peace* (Englewood Cliffs, N.J.: Prentice-Hall, 1994) is a fine short study of these important issues. *Books in Print* can help readers find current editions, many of them in paperback.

One way of determining how "good" a book is, by the way, is to consult *Book Review Digest*. Is Michael Herr's book *Dispatches* a useful volume? From reading the critics in *Book Review Digest*, 1978, one would think that it is (see 599-600). Is James N. Rowe's book *Five Years to Freedom* a useful book to add to your reading program? Consult *Book Review Digest*, 1971, to help in your assessment (1177). Book reviews, by the way, are not always kind—and can be very harsh (sometimes deservedly so).[30]

Classic tales of "military morality" include Herman Wouk, *The Caine Mutiny* (1952); and Neil Sheehan, *The Arnheiter Affair* (New York: Random House, 1971), which tells the parallel story of Navy Commander M.A. Arnheiter. Jeff Stein, *A Murder in War-*

time (New York: St. Martin's, 1992), is a factual account of moral problems in wartime which one reviewer calls "exhaustively researched and highly documented."[31] A Marine officer recommends, with some reservations, Michael Bilton and Kevin Sim, *Four Hours in My Lai* (New York: Viking, 1992), saying that the book "stands as a grim reminder of what can happen when principles and values no longer prevail."[32] Harold Moore and Joseph Galloway tell the moving story of the Vietnam battle of Ia Drang in *We Were Soldiers Once—and Young* (New York: Random House, 1992). Having heard *U.S. News & World Report* writer Joe Galloway speak, I can strongly recommend the book and Mr. Galloway himself.

Throughout this book, in text and notes, I have cited various movies that raise issues in military ethics. Here are three that I particularly recommend. *Twelve O'Clock High*, a World War II story of U.S. flyers in England, made in 1949, is very effective in raising the issue of "men versus mission," leadership styles, and questions of integrity. *Breaker Morant*, a classic Australian film made in 1979, recounts the fate of three soldiers convicted of murder during the Boer War. But was it "murder"? Were two of them executed for reasons merely of political expediency? Were their deaths actually permissible, given the political exigencies of the time? The movie *Glory* (1990) concerns the 54th Massachusetts Volunteers, the first black unit of the Civil War, under the command of Col. Robert Gould Shaw. There are scenes of the training camp and drills in Massachusetts before the men head south into combat; then questions of ethics arise in their burning of a town, corruption among the officers, leadership styles, racial bigotry, and the willingness of their white commander to volunteer his men for hazardous combat—all these issues and more are raised in this extraordinary film. In addition to movies, the PBS television series on the Civil War, produced by Ken Burns, is a treasure; viewers are left horrified by war yet uplifted at the heroism and the true faith and allegiance of so many thousands during that titanic struggle.

Aside from journals (which have footnotes) and magazines, (which generally do not), a number of military publications can also be mined for discussions of military ethics. Good places to start are the bibliography of articles in this book, the extensive notes citing sources for particular episodes (such as the *Pueblo* affair), and the index. Useful military periodicals include *Army, Military Review, Parameters, Naval War College Review, U.S. Naval Institute Proceedings, Air Power Journal,* and *Marine Corps Gazette.* The National Defense University, Ft. Lesley J. McNair, Washington, D.C. 20319, and the Ethics and Public Policy Center (1015 Fifteenth St. N.W., Washington, D.C. 20005; phone 202 682-1200) offer a range of excellent materials on ethics questions.

Because of the extraordinary leadership of Air Force Col. Malham M. Wakin, the Joint Services Conference on Professional Ethics (JSCOPE) has held annual conferences since 1979 on questions of the sort raised in this book. Colonel Wakin is the "Mr. Chips" of teaching in the area of military ethics; all of us who explore these issues do so in the knowledge that he has led the way. As he retires from JSCOPE, he continues to offer advice and counsel when he can. JSCOPE's address is Headquarters, U.S. Air Force Academy, Department of Philosophy and Fine Arts, 2354 Fairchild Drive, Suite 6L37, USAF Academy, Colo. 80840-6256.

Resurrecting the Eagle

In this book my metaphorical use of the "eagle" of course refers to the United States, which in my view is uncomfortably close to becoming the Dis-United States. Our laws, our politics, our daily lives flow from our shared values and our common heroes. When we forget who we are, we neglect to do what we should. Our task is not to achieve perfect agreement but to discover again those values we have in common and to agree to disagree about the values we have in conflict, hopeful that there will be many more of the former than of the latter. Ethics is about honor and shame; about decency, discretion, wisdom, and virtue; about reasoned choice and obligation. I have tried to share my excitement about learning and teaching in this vital field. All of us who study political theory and ethics know that we never know enough, but we know that self-respect comes with our earnest effort to know and to do what is right. The great tragedy of our republic—the sickness of the eagle—is not just that there are the vicious and the criminal among us but that there are the negligent and the apathetic, whose minds and hearts and souls never wrestle with the problems that ethics poses to us daily, personally and professionally.

Military ethics has its special burdens, for it confronts always the task of inspiring the life of virtue against the background of preparing resolutely for combat and death. But we know that we learn through suffering and pain, and I hope that rightful military ethics—with its emphasis always on honor—can help restore the desire in our republic and in our frequently feeble schools "to do the right and to love goodness, and to walk humbly with [our] God."[33]

Conclusions

Without private virtue (such as not lying, cheating, or stealing; keeping promises, working honestly, and treating others fairly)— upon which almost all people of decency and discretion can agree—there is little prospect of public (political, corporate) virtue.

Schools and colleges can inculcate moral virtue by hiring and promoting teachers who are competent, enthusiastic, fair, and organized; by establishing serious curriculums with high standards; and by creating an atmosphere that insists upon reasonable and virtuous behavior.

By "resurrecting the eagle" is meant restoring to the republic the great conversation about honor and shame, virtue and vice, and, insofar as practicable, instilling in all citizens a concern for knowing and doing the right—not just the exigent—thing. When we model such virtues ourselves, we can perhaps then look to our neighbors.

Epilogue

Whatsoever things are true, whatsoever things are
honest, whatsoever things are just, whatsoever things
are pure, whatsoever things are lovely, whatsoever
things are of good report; if there be any virtue and if
there be any praise, think on these things.
            —Paul's Letter to the Philippians, 4:8

There is a wonderful book by Gilbert Highet in which he tells
prospective teachers, among many other things, that they must,
at the end of their courses, firmly "fix the impression."[1] That is,
he suggests that teachers repeat their principal points and review the ground covered, lest the main points of their teaching
be obscured or lost. Thus to fix the impression is the purpose of
this brief epilogue.

Education is different from training in that good education
concerns itself in substantial part with virtue. A course of
schooling that cannot or will not separate right from wrong or
honor from shame may be instruction or training, but it is not
education in its proper, classical sense. One should never merely teach *about* ethics; one must teach ethics. Virtuous conduct is
founded upon a knowledge of certain rules that right reason
has discovered over the centuries; upon social customs and
mores that have so developed; upon the mature recognition of
outcomes and consequences likely to result from our choices;
and upon the circumstances in which one is required to make
ethical judgment. There *may* be times to make exceptions to
rules. Social customs can be wrong. The end does not always
justify the means. And situational ethics can be narrow, selfish,
and wholly mistaken. Wise ethical choice in demanding circumstances is not easy. But men and women of character reflect upon what ought to be done and then do it, learning all
they can from the lessons of the past—as well as from their
own previous faults and flaws.

Military ethics is part of moral philosophy. Because military ethics starts from a judgment about the "terrible swift sword"— that is, there are circumstances in which killing by soldiers is permissible—military ethics *demands* rigorous attention to ethical detail. Soldiers must recognize that they are subject always to the twin responsibilities of obedience to the commands of their own well-formed consciences and to the laws of the civil government. Soldiers must provide their civilian leaders with their best judgment about matters of national security, but the ultimate power of political decision in democratically elected governments resides—and must reside—in the hands of the elected government.

In this book, I modify slightly the traditional military ethic of "duty, honor, and country" to read "principle, purpose, and people." Fidelity to high principle must come first; mission accomplishment normally comes second; and the welfare of one's subordinates and fellow soldiers is third only in the sense that loyalty to people should not supersede commitment to those principles that provide meaning for people in the first place. James Q. Wilson, author of *The Moral Sense*, contends that in the 1993-94 cheating scandal at the Naval Academy (see below) the midshipmen who protected their friends—thereby ignoring the Academy's honor concept—would thus never let their buddies down in war and that we have little to fear in the way of decaying moral fabric among our officers.[2] He is very seriously mistaken. A central, and critical, part of any officer's education is that he or she owes true faith and allegiance to principle before people. The concepts of duty, honor, and country may be seen, by some, as providing cold comfort when they must be chosen ahead of loyalty to buddies. But cadets and midshipmen who cannot and will not make that crucial distinction deserve no commission in our country's armed services, for their oath of office implicitly demands, as the Marine Corps succinctly states it, that "a Marine on guard duty has no friends."[3]

Of course, without good education, one cannot wisely choose, for one does not know virtue. Thus the beginning point for all teaching, military and civilian, lies in ethical education. Because the profession of arms, over the centuries, has taught the virtues of honor, of duty, and of country, the profession of arms can, again, be an exemplar of integrity in a nation increasingly confused about the very existence of integrity itself.

But isn't this all too glib? How is it possible for the military ethic to serve society as a moral paradigm when there is so much corruption in the "venerable" profession of arms itself? In 1993-94, officers at the U.S. Naval Academy discovered that cheating on a massive scale had taken place. As the *Baltimore Sun* put it, the "cheating scandal reveals standards of character and integrity that would be considered abysmal even in our far less exacting civilian society."[4] The response of forty-eight midshipmen was to bring suit in District Court seeking to stop the Navy from expelling them.[5] Congressional investigators contend that sexual harassment of women is "rampant" at the nation's military academies.[6] Reports have come to light that the Army has engaged in biological warfare experiments with unsuspecting civilian populations in such areas as Washington National Airport and the New York City subway. The reports allege that the Army is still conducting such tests at Dugway Proving Ground in Utah, even though winds could carry the diseased agents to Salt Lake City.[7] The Air Command and Staff College of the U.S. Air Force has recently revised its ten-month-long program of instruction into ten subject areas; not one of them deals with ethics.[8] Meanwhile one of the top officers in the Air Force, Lt. Gen. Buster Glosson, is being forced to retire after he "improperly tried to block the promotion of another high-ranking officer." General Glosson denied the allegations against him.[9]

The Navy ended its "Tailhook" investigation in February 1994, but not one of the 140 cases under investigation ended in conviction for any of the men, as *Time* put it, "whose memory—and maybe their consciences—were lost in the fun house."[10] A federal judge accused the Navy's top officer, Admiral Frank B. Kelso II, of "manipulat[ing] the initial investigative process and the subsequent [discipline] process in a manner designed to shield his personal involvement." The judge also ruled that Kelso knew what was going on at Tailhook and was "in error" when he testified he did not go to the third floor of the hotel that night and thus did not see any misconduct.[11] Admiral Kelso said, "I'm an honest man. I didn't lie, and I didn't manipulate."[12] On 15 February 1994, however, the admiral announced that he would retire two months ahead of schedule, saying that he had become a "lightning rod" for criticisms of the Navy's handling of the Tailhook scandal.[13] The Navy officer who brought the Tailhook scandal to light (Lt. Paula Coughlin) finally left the Navy, citing emotional stress from the attack and alluding to adverse treatment from other fliers.[14]

Even the Marine Corps Reserve program known as "Toys for Tots" came under fire, with reports that the Christmas gift drive had collected nearly $10 million in 1992 and 1993 through a direct-mail campaign but that none of the money went to buy toys for needy children.[15] One columnist argued that, as scholars researched more deeply into DESERT STORM, "we learned that U.S. military leaders were incapable of truth-telling" and that General Schwarzkopf's "self-lionization" is "unsupported by fact."[16] In 1986, there were 27,783 reported cases of violence in military families; in 1993, there were 46,287. A recent Army survey concludes that abuse of spouses takes place in one in every three Army families each year, which is double the national rate.[17]

The issue of gays in the military continues to be a matter of controversy.[18] The policy of "Don't ask, don't tell" is hardly wise. As philosopher Sissela Bok points out: "By engaging in this hypocrisy, by saying something matters and then ignoring it, by mandating duplicity, the government will further reduce the public's trust in the honesty of its officials." Law professor Stephen Gillers concurs: "More than any other institution in society . . . , the military insists that its effectiveness demands loyalty to the organization above loyalty to self. If there's something amiss, you're supposed to speak up. If homosexuality or its practice is considered wrong, you're supposed to acknowledge it and others are supposed to expose you. This so-called compromise is dishonorable on its face." Michael Kramer calls the "don't ask, don't tell" policy "reprehensible"; it is, he says, a "first-ever official codification of a policy that encourages concealing a fact deemed material to an institution's smooth functioning. . . . The law prohibits discrimination in part by respecting one's privacy, but in each case the rationale assumes that the 'secret' . . . is immaterial to job performance."[19] As this book was going to press, the Pentagon was agreeing to revise its regulations on homosexuals in the military to make them *more restrictive*.[20] Despite the desire of Secretary of Defense William Perry to see this issue concluded, it is likely to be a matter of emotional debate for many years to come.

The role of women in the military, similarly, will continue to be a matter of debate for many years. Former Defense Secretary Les Aspin overruled the Army and Marine Corps to approve a policy that will expand the role of women even in ground-combat forces. Women still are not to engage in fighting, but Aspin ordered that women be allowed to take dangerous support jobs that have been closed to them.[21] The chief of naval operations, Admiral Jeremy Boorda, said that the Navy may remove the ban on women serving aboard submarines.[22]

Given all these issues, can anyone reasonably hold that the profession of arms can serve society today as an ethical beacon light? The gist of this book is that soldiers (and civilians) of good faith and noble purpose *must* unite legitimate military purpose and high ethical principle and that power and principle, thus united, will be mutually nourishing. A soldier without an understanding of ethical standards can be as dangerous as a political leader without an understanding of military power. When soldiers violate their oaths, they betray their faith and they besmirch their allegiance.

But what, after all, is their faith and their allegiance *to*? I suppose that this whole book boils down to that single question. It is that impression that I want to fix, finally, in place. Soldiers must be loyal to their superiors and to their subordinates. Soldiers must accomplish their assigned missions. In those things, soldiers are no different from the men and women they were as civilians before they donned uniforms, except that their profession can involve them in terrible violence. Soldiers must be loyal to the Constitution. Civilians, too, have the responsibility of reasoned patriotism. But, above all, soldiers must demonstrate integrity, or sound ethical character. Are they, in that regard, any different from civilians? I think not, except that failures of integrity in soldiers can have immediate consequences of life and death. That is one reason why we view lapses in military ethics as particularly sinister. For soldiers still—even in a world of moral nihilism—have a creed to guide them or one which, regrettably, they can break. For too many today, there are no ethical lapses because there are, presumably, no ethical standards.[23] If there are no standards, how can they be broken?

But soldiers are professionals because they *profess* loyalty to things and thoughts beyond themselves. It is only when they twist or distort or misconstrue principle and purpose and people; it is only when they confuse benefit to their own career with the vows of their office; it is only when they lie or cheat or steal—it is only then, *but let it always be then*, that we say, "These soldiers have betrayed the trust given them." That they might sometime betray the trust given them and that they might somehow be perfidious in the performance of their duties should be the fears of all soldiers. But these should be the fears, as well, of all people, soldiers or civilians.

We all fail, perhaps badly, at times, and good ethical conduct cannot be ensured by answering a single question. But if we ask, before acting, "Where does my duty lie?" we may at least improve our chances of knowing and doing the ethical and not just the expedient.[24] As Paul tried to tell us (in the epigraph above), we are likely to do the right if we think constantly about the right. If we educate ourselves and others to think virtuously,[25] then perhaps we can act virtuously. True faith and allegiance to moral precept is a military necessity. In its constant and laudable quest to learn and to teach virtue, despite the lapses we are all heir to, the profession of arms reminds us that worthy human beings, in all times and all places, must seek the wise and the virtuous. From our duty to find the right direction come our conceptions of honor and thus our deepest commitments to country.

Notes

Introduction

1. Irving Kristol, "Ethics, Anyone? Or Morals?" *Wall Street Journal*, 15 Sept. 1987, 32.

2. I do not mean to suggest that there is no place for "big words," but I am not sure that that place is the beginning course in military ethics or in general ethics survey courses. Undergraduate students in ethics, confronted too soon with "act utilitarianism," "deontological ethics," "hedonist calculus," and "universalizability" can become frustrated. At the same time, this is not an appeal for "snap courses" in ethics—quite the reverse.

3. Kristol, "Ethics, Anyone?" 32.

4. "Where NBC Went Wrong," *Time*, 22 Feb. 1993, 59.

5. Barbara Dafoe Whitehead, "Dan Quayle Was Right," *Atlantic Monthly*, April 1993, 77, 58.

6. Sir John Winthrop Hackett, "The Military in the Service of the State," in *War, Morality, and the Military Profession*, 2d ed., ed. Malham M. Wakin (Boulder, Colo.: Westview Press, 1986), 119-20.

7. See John O. Marsh, "Values and the American Soldier," *Military Review*, Nov. 1986, 7.

8. Quoted in Bernard T. Adeney, *Just War, Political Realism, and Faith* (Methuen, N.J.: Scarecrow Press, 1988), 124.

9. See James H. Toner, *The American Military Ethic: A Meditation* (New York: Praeger, 1992).

10. Douglas A. Martz, "Professional Military Ethics," *Marine Corps Gazette*, Aug. 1990, 58.

11. See John Alvis, "Why a Proper Core Curriculum Is Political and Ought Not Be 'Politicized,'" *Intercollegiate Review* 28 (Spring 1993): 24-32.

12. See, e.g., the movie *Presidio* (1988), in which the point is made that soldiers, except in wartime, are not highly prized by the civilian community. For an excellent short summary of the disdain frequently reserved for American soldiers in our society, see Rick Atkinson, *The Long Gray Line* (Boston: Houghton Mifflin, 1989), 377-78; see also Man-

uel M. Davenport, "Professionals or Hired Guns? Loyalties Are the Difference," *Army*, May 1980, 14.

13. Quoted in G. Edward White, *Justice Oliver Wendell Holmes: Law and the Inner Self* (New York: Oxford Univ. Press, 1993), 49.

14. I do not explore here at any appreciable length the issues of "just war," realism, or pacifism, but those topics were treated in an earlier book of mine: James H. Toner, *The Sword and the Cross: Reflections on Command and Conscience* (New York: Praeger, 1992).

15. I would appreciate reader response. Was the book helpful or confusing? Did it clarify or cloud your own thinking? What has it contributed to *your* education? I can be reached at the Department of National Security Studies, Air War College, 325 Chennault Circle, Maxwell AFB, AL 36112-6427.

1. Military Ethics

1. Throughout the book, I use the term *soldier* as generic shorthand for any member of the armed services: Army, Navy, Air Force, Marine Corps, and Coast Guard.

2. Like the word *politics*, the word *ethics* usually takes a singular verb.

3. Quoted in *Time*, 29 June 1981, 48.

4. One response to this, "proving" God's existence, is the idea that because we are finite beings with obviously limited minds, we could not even conceive of the idea of infinity unless he who is infinite suggested his being to us. Therefore, in telling us about his existence, God proved that existence to us.

5. Lucius Garvin, *A Modern Introduction to Ethics* (Boston: Houghton Mifflin, 1953), 2 (original emphasis). Another definition I like is that of J. Elliot Ross, *Christian Ethics* (New York: Devin-Adair, 1948), 29: "the moral rectitude of human acts considered in the light of natural reason."

6. Quoted in Ivan Hill, *Common Sense and Everyday Ethics* (Washington, D.C.: Ethics Resource Center, 1980), 5.

7. Garvin, *A Modern Introduction to Ethics*, 4-5n.

8. *The Teaching of Ethics in Higher Education* (Hastings-on-Hudson, N.Y.: Hastings Center, 1980), 13. See also David Solomon, *Ethics: A Brief Introduction* (New York: McGraw-Hill, 1984), 2: "*Ethics* is that part of philosophy which is concerned with living well, being a good person, doing the right thing, and wanting the right things in life."

9. W.T. Jones et al., eds., *Approaches to Ethics* (New York: McGraw-Hill, 1977), 1.

10. Cal Thomas, syndicated column, *Montgomery Advertiser*, 14 Dec.

1992, 8A. See also Midge Decter, "Homosexuality and the Schools," *Commentary*, March 1993, 19-25.

11. Thomas Sowell, *Inside American Education: The Decline, the Deception, the Dogmas* (New York: Free Press, 1993). See also "Race on Campus," *U.S. News & World Report*, 19 April 1993.

12. William Kilpatrick, *Why Johnny Can't Tell Right from Wrong* (New York: Simon & Schuster, 1992), 100.

13. Alan Wolfe, *Whose Keeper?* (Berkeley: University of California Press, 1989), 19, 5.

14. Kilpatrick, *Why Johnny Can't Tell Right from Wrong*, 116-17.

15. See E.D. Hirsch, *Cultural Literacy: What Every American Needs to Know* (Boston: Houghton Mifflin, 1987).

16. Arthur M. Schlesinger, Jr., in *The Disuniting of America* (New York: Norton, 1992), deplores multicultural studies.

17. Kilpatrick, *Why Johnny Can't Tell Right from Wrong*, 123.

18. James B. Twitchell, *Carnival Culture: The Trashing of Taste in America* (New York: Columbia University Press, 1992), 72-73, 140-41. See also the review of *Carnival Culture* by M.O. Garvey in *Commonweal*, 9 Oct. 1992, 29-30; and Neil Postman, *Amusing Ourselves to Death: Public Discourse in the Age of Show Business* (New York: Viking, 1985).

19. See Brandon S. Centerwall, "Television and Violent Crime," *Public Interest* 111 (Spring 1993): 56-71. See also William J. Bennett, *The Index of Leading Cultural Indicators: Facts and Figures on the State of American Society* (New York: Simon and Schuster, 1994).

20. *Time*, 29 March 1993, 18.

21. Michael Medved, "Hollywood's Poison Factory: Making It the Dream Factory Again," *Imprimis*, Nov. 1992.

22. Wolfe, *Whose Keeper?* 19.

23. Sowell, *Inside American Education*, 68. See also the review by D.G. Myers of Martin Anderson, *Impostors in the Temple: The Decline of the American University*, and of Jaroslav Pelikan, *The Idea of the University: A Reexamination* (*American Spectator*, January 1993, 94-95).

24. I explored these themes in my earlier book, *The Sword and the Cross*.

25. Robert N. Bellah et al., *The Good Society* (New York: Knopf, 1991), 38.

26. Anton Myrer, *Once an Eagle* (New York: Berkley, 1968), 660.

27. Known as deontological ethics, this approach is primarily concerned with acting out of a sense of duty—regardless of consequences—and is associated with Immanuel Kant (1724-1804). See esp. his *Fundamental Principles of the Metaphysic of Ethics*, trans. Otto Manthey-Zorn (New York: Appleton-Century-Crofts, 1938). Kant's concept of the "categorical imperative" was simply this: we should invariably act in

such a way that if our actions were universalized—if everyone did what we did—we would be content. For an excellent discussion, see Donald M. Borchert and David Stewart, *Exploring Ethics* (New York: Macmillan, 1986), chap. 8.

28. Known as teleological, consequentialist, or utilitarian ethics, this approach is associated with John Stuart Mill (1806-73) and with Jeremy Bentham (1748-1832).

29. Known as situation ethics, this approach is usually associated with Joseph Fletcher (1905-91), among others. See, however, the remembrance of Fletcher by Richard J. Neuhaus, "All Too Human," in *National Review*, 2 Dec. 1991, 45: "In his last years, Fletcher deplored the moral sleaze of a culture that acted on the doctrine that he championed: it's right if it's right for you."

30. Carl Wellman, *Morals and Ethics*, 2d ed. (Englewood Cliffs, N.J.: Prentice-Hall, 1988), 29. Wellman's chap. 2, "Right and Wrong," is a clear presentation of many of the ethical themes referred to in passing here. For their application to military ethics, see Samuel D. Maloney, "Ethics Theory for the Military Professional," *Air University Review*, March-April 1981, 63-71.

31. Fulton J. Sheen, *Lift Up Your Heart* (Garden City, N.Y.: Doubleday Image, 1950), 19.

32. For details, see the words *hermeneutics* and *exegesis* in an unabridged dictionary.

33. I am grateful to Col. Malham Wakin of the U.S. Air Force Academy for this example.

34. The movie *Sophie's Choice* (1982), based on the William Styron novel, is worth seeing in this regard.

35. Lewis Sorley, "Doing What's Right: Shaping the Army's Professional Environment," in *The Challenge of Military Leadership*, ed. Lloyd J. Matthews and Dale E. Brown (Washington, D.C.: Pergamon-Brassey's, 1989), 131. See also James Swartz, "Morality: A Leadership Imperative," *Military Review*, Sept. 1992, 77-83.

36. James B. Stockdale, "Moral Leadership," *U.S. Naval Institute Proceedings*, Sept. 1980, 87.

37. See, e.g., the powerful novel *Lord Jim* by Joseph Conrad (1857-1924).

38. Hackett, "The Military in the Service of the State," 119.

2. The U.S. Military

1. Robert A. Heinlein, *Starship Troopers* (1959; New York: Ace Books, 1987), 24.

2. John Silber, *Straight Shooting* (New York: Harper & Row, 1989), 255.

3. Matthew B. Ridgway, *The Korean War* (Garden City, N.Y.: Doubleday, 1967), 212-13.

4. See Edward R. Murphy with Curt Gentry, *Second in Command* (New York: Holt, Rinehart & Winston, 1970), 150. Murphy's account differs in significant ways from that of his skipper: L.M. Bucher, with Mark Rascovich, *Bucher: My Story* (Garden City, N.Y.: Doubleday, 1970). Reading the two accounts together is a case study in itself. Consult also Trevor Armbrister, *A Matter of Accountability* (New York: Coward-McCann, 1970), and Ed Brandt, *The Last Voyage of USS Pueblo* (New York: Norton, 1969).

5. Text in Murphy and Gentry, *Second in Command*, 315.

6. U.S. Navy Rear Admiral Daniel V. Gallery, *The Pueblo Incident* (New York: Doubleday, 1970), 131, argued that the United States will not be protected "if all we ask of our Armed Forces is surrender without a fight when the going gets tough." Bucher was scheduled, in fact, for a general court-martial, but the secretary of the navy refused to permit any disciplinary action against him. In March 1969 the House Armed Services Committee held hearings about the *Pueblo*; the proceedings are available to the public. In *The Pueblo Surrender: A Covert Action by the National Security Agency* (New York: Bantam, 1988), 280, Robert A. Liston has argued the improbable but interesting thesis that the NSA, "through the use of coded information, was able to conceal *Chinese and Soviet* [my emphasis] participation in the *Pueblo* incident from our visible leaders, and that the NSA has thereby assumed awesome power, greatly altering our constitutional form of government."

7. Bucher argued, "I was completely and hopelessly outgunned. And in order for me to man my fifty-caliber machine guns, which would have been the only effective weapon that we had at a range of fifty yards, I knew to send a man up to that gun would have meant certain death for him because he would have been walking to within thirty yards of a mount of machine guns which was already mounted. At that time we would have to have removed the covers to these guns, which were in fact frozen . . . and could not be easily removed. I felt that the minute that I sent people in that general direction they would be immediately shot, and I saw no point in senselessly sending people to their death" (quoted in F. Carl Schumacher, Jr., and George C. Wilson, *Bridge of No Return* [New York: Harcourt Brace Jovanovich, 1971], 220).

8. As a personal note, I was particularly privileged to "commission" my son Chris as an Army second lieutenant after his 1992 graduation from Notre Dame. The oath seemed to mean even more to me then

than in 1969, when I was myself commissioned as an Army second lieutenant.

9. Quoted in John Spanier, *The Truman-MacArthur Controversy and the Korean War* (Cambridge, Mass.: Belknap Press, 1959), 235.

10. For background, see Spanier, *The Truman-MacArthur Controversy*.

11. Hackett, "The Military in the Service of the State," 115.

12. Ridgway, *The Korean War*, 232 (the reference is probably to the anti-fascist 1935 novel *It Can't Happen Here* by Sinclair Lewis [1885-1951], in which America becomes a fascist state).

13. Samuel Eliot Morison, *The Oxford History of the American People* (New York: Oxford University Press, 1965), 1072. For background, see Edward M. Coffman, "The Army Officer and the Constitution," *Parameters*, Sept. 1987, 2-12.

14. *New York Times*, 7 April 1971, 12. For background, see Seymour M. Hersh, *My Lai 4* (New York: Random House, 1970); and Richard Hammer, *The Court-Martial of Lt. Calley* (New York: Coward, McCann & Geoghegan, 1971).

15. *New York Times*, 5 April 1971, 33.

16. Oliver L. North, "Reagan Knew Everything," *Time*, 28 Oct. 1991, 66.

17. Amos A. Jordan, William J. Taylor, Jr., and Lawrence I. Korb, *American National Security*, 3d ed. (Baltimore: Johns Hopkins Univ. Press, 1989), 165.

18. *The Iran-Contra Puzzle* (Washington, D.C.: Congressional Quarterly, 1987), 485. See also Anthony Hartle, "The Ethical Odyssey of Oliver North," *Parameters* 23 (Summer 1993): 28-33.

19. *Time*, 28 Oct. 1991, 66. In September 1991, charges against North were dropped because the prosecutor said he could not show that North's testimony in his trial had not been tainted by the testimony he gave under immunity to the congressional Iran-Contra committee.

20. Quoted in "Loyalty Lets Its Guard Down," *Insight*, 4 May 1987, 9.

21. Ibid., 8.

22. Kermit D. Johnson, "Ethical Issues of Military Leadership," in *The Parameters of Military Ethics*, ed. Lloyd J. Matthews and Dale E. Brown (Washington, D.C.: Pergamon-Brassey's, 1989), 75.

23. Ibid.

24. *New York Times*, 20 June 1993, IV-2; *U.S. News & World Report*, 21 June 1993, 18.

25. Josiah Royce (1855-1916), *The Philosophy of Loyalty* (New York: Macmillan, 1908), 16-17: "A man is loyal when, first, he has some *cause* to which he is loyal; when, secondly, he *willingly* and *thoroughly* de-

votes himself to this cause; and when, thirdly, he expresses his devotion in some *sustained and practical way*, by acting steadily in the service of his cause" (original emphasis).

26. Sidney Axinn, *A Moral Military* (Philadelphia: Temple Univ. Press, 1989), 60-61.

27. Davenport, "Professionals or Hired Guns?" 14.

28. Ibid.

29. Cicero's advice in about 60 B.C. was *Cedant arma togae* (roughly, let the soldier give way to the civilian), which was also the motto on the Wyoming territorial seal.

30. See the classic novel by Fletcher Knebel and Charles W. Bailey II, *Seven Days in May* (New York: Bantam, 1963), about a military takeover plot in the United States. Len Colodny and Robert Gettlin, *Silent Coup: The Removal of a President* (New York: St. Martin's Press, 1991), is an improbable, if fascinating, account of how Nixon "really" fell from power.

31. Quoted in Louis Henkin, "Foreign Affairs and the Constitution," *Foreign Affairs* 66 (Winter 1987-88): 299n. See also Larry N. George, "Tocqueville's Caveat: Centralized Executive Foreign Policy and American Democracy," *Polity* 22 (Spring 1990): 419-41.

32. Congress passed the War Powers Act in 1973 over President Nixon's veto. The law permitted the president to commit U.S. forces to hostilities only under a declaration of war, or with special congressional approval, or during a state of emergency. The president was also required to report to Congress within forty-eight hours about the commitment of U.S. troops to combat, and to withdraw troops within sixty days unless Congress approved their deployment or granted an extension of another thirty days. Congress was empowered to terminate troop commitment by concurrent resolution, and the president was supposed to consult with Congress about committing forces overseas "in every possible instance." See Roger Hilsman, *The Politics of Policy Making in Defense and Foreign Affairs*, 3d ed. (Englewood Cliffs, N.J.: Prentice-Hall, 1993), 139. It is fair to conclude that the act has not worked as its authors intended, and a number of observers have questioned its constitutionality. The Supreme Court, to date, has not explored the issue.

33. Quoted in Edward L. Katzenbach, Jr., "Should Our Military Leaders Speak Up?" *New York Times Magazine*, 15 April 1956, 36. For general information see Martin Shapiro and Rocco Tresolini, *American Constitutional Law*, 6th ed. (New York: Macmillan, 1983), chap. 6.

34. Katzenbach, "Should Our Military Leaders Speak Up?" 17.

35. See *Facts on File* 50 (21 Sept. 1990): 688-89. For comparison with the firing of Army Maj. Gen. John K. Singlaub and Air Force Maj. Gen.

Harold N. Campbell, see *Facts on File* 38 (5 May 1978): 321. Singlaub was relieved in May 1977 as chief of the U.S. command in South Korea after arguing against President Jimmy Carter's troop reduction plans there. On 28 April 1978, he resigned from the Army after publicly calling Carter's plan to postpone production of the neutron weapon "ridiculous" and "militarily unsound." In a public speech on 24 May 1993, Campbell called President Clinton a "dope-smoking," "skirt-chasing," "draft-dodging" commander in chief. By 18 June, he had been fined, reprimanded, and retired. See *Facts on File* (24 June 1993): 466.

36. Katzenbach, "Should Our Military Leaders Speak Up?" 39.

37. In a classic study of American civil-military relations, *The Soldier and the State* (New York: Vintage, 1957), 155, Samuel Huntington asserts that our liberal society invariably seeks either to alter or abolish the American military ethic.

38. Ibid., chap. 4.

39. Kenneth W. Kemp and Charles Hudlin, "Civil Supremacy over the Military: Its Nature and Limits," *Armed Forces and Society* 19 (Fall 1992): 8-9. The "traditionalist approach" suggests that the military will not involve itself in political affairs in any way; the advice it gives the executive and legislative branches will concern military might only. This was a popular civil-military model until World War II. The "fusionist approach" suggests, on the contrary, that professional officers must fuse economic and political considerations when giving military advice. The education of high-ranking officers at senior service schools (such as the war colleges) rests on the notion of the fusionist model, which is typically preferred by civilian leaders.

As Jordan, Taylor, and Korb point out in *American National Security*, 596-97, one opponent of the fusionist model is Samuel Huntington who, in *The Soldier and the State*, 163, contends: "Civilian control has at times existed in the United States, but it has emerged despite rather than because of constitutional provisions"; indeed, "the United States Constitution, despite the widespread belief to the contrary, does *not* provide for civilian control" (163). Technically, Huntington is correct—but only in the sense that the Constitution nowhere provides a guarantee that we will have a democracy; the word *democracy* appears nowhere in the Constitution (the word *republic* does appear, in Article IV, section 4, but the Supreme Court has never satisfactorily defined that noun); thus Huntington's argument about the absence of a provision for civilian control of the military is somewhat specious. I have chosen to address the issue in the notes rather than in the text because the argument can become labyrinthine. To pursue the point, consult Jordan, Taylor, and Korb's notes and Huntington's chap. 7.

40. For good background reading, see Bob Woodward, *The Com-*

manders (New York: Simon & Schuster, 1991). See also Graham Allison, *Essence of Decision* (Boston: Little, Brown, 1971), 130-32, for the interesting exchange in 1962, during the Cuban missile crisis, between Chief of Naval Operations Admiral George Anderson and Secretary of Defense Robert S. McNamara.

41. Recent events have led some to challenge that assertion. See, for example, Edward N. Luttwak, "Washington's Biggest Scandal," *Commentary*, May 1994, 29-33; and Richard H. Kohn, "Out of Control: The Crisis in Civil-Military Relations," *National Interest* 35 (Spring 1994): 3-17.

42. Interservice rivalry continues to plague the military forces today and may well be exacerbated by the 1990s debate over "roles and missions." The Defense Reorganization Act referred to in the text created a "joint specialty," according to which all the services are committed to ensuring that high-ranking officers will have some mutual experience and education. This is occasionally referred to as "wearing a purple suit"—instead of Army green or Navy or Air Force blue.

43. Robert Previdi, *Civilian Control versus Military Rule* (New York: Hippocrene, 1988) argues that "the Goldwater-Nichols Act is a distinct threat to civilian control of the military" (165) and that "creating one military czar . . . can lead . . . to a situation where, at best, the nation is run more by the military and, at worst, the country actually becomes more vulnerable to a military take-over" (9). Edward Luttwak, a supporter of that bill, has recently changed his mind. See "Washington's Biggest Scandal," 30n. For a more balanced view, see Mark Perry, *Four Stars* (Boston: Houghton Mifflin, 1989), 338-44; and Admiral William J. Crowe, with David Chanoff, *The Line of Fire* (New York: Simon & Schuster, 1993), chap. 8.

44. *Schlesinger v. Councilman*, 420 U.S. 738 (1975) at 757. The case was argued on 10 Dec. 1974 and decided on 25 March 1975.

45. *Parker v. Levy*, 417 U.S. 733, 743, 758. Consider also this observation from *In re Grimley*, 137 U.S. 147, 153 (1890): "An army is not a deliberative body. It is the executive arm. Its law is that of obedience. No question can be left open as to the right to command in the officer, or the duty of obedience in the soldier."

46. Huntington, *The Soldier and the State*, 465. By contrast, our society today appears wholly consumed by devotion to "rights." "Where an interest masked as a right is involved, the single-issue proponents can withstand the collapse of the heavens as long as their interest is served," says Fred Siegel in "Nothing in Moderation," *Atlantic Monthly*, May 1990, 110. He quotes Justice Oliver Wendell Holmes, who once warned that "all rights tend to declare themselves absolute to their logical extreme."

3. Military Training

1. Courses in the humanities (such as philosophy and literature) come to mind. But in strengthening our powers of reason and analysis, all *serious* academic courses might well be considered truly educational.

2. Lewis Sorley, "Competence as an Ethical Imperative," *Army*, Aug. 1982, 42.

3. Malham M. Wakin, "The Ethics of Leadership II," in *War, Morality, and the Military Profession*, 2d ed., ed. Malham M. Wakin (Boulder, Colo.: Westview Press, 1986), 211-12.

4. Fred Downs, "To Kill and Take Ground Is the Reality of War," *Hartford Courant*, 23 Aug. 1987, B1, 4.

5. Atkinson, *The Long Gray Line*, e.g., 214.

6. Downs, "To Kill and Take Ground," B4. On the lives of soldiers in the 1980s, see Larry Ingraham, *The Boys in the Barracks* (Philadelphia: Institute for the Study of Human Issues, 1984).

7. Toner, *The American Military Ethic*, chaps. 3-5.

8. *Time*, 18 Jan. 1993, 18-19.

9. "Unspeakable," *Time*, 22 Feb. 1993, 50.

10. Based on Norman Dixon, "Military Incompetence," in *The Oxford Companion to the Mind*, ed. Richard L. Gregory (New York: Oxford Univ. Press, 1987), 484-86; the same list appears in Dixon, *On the Psychology of Military Incompetence* (New York: Basic Books, 1976), 152-53. See also 399-400, for Irving Janis's concept of "groupthink" (Janis's book is *Victims of Groupthink* [Boston: Houghton Mifflin, 1972]). Despite some nonsense in Dixon's book—such as the characterization of ROTC students (279) and chap. 17, "Socialization and the Anal Character"—it is worth reading and pondering. Much better on this general theme is Eliot Cohen and John Gooch, *Military Misfortunes* (New York: Vintage, 1991); for their incisive comments about Dixon, see 8-11. A superb piece of work is that of Richard Neustadt and Ernest May, *Thinking in Time* (New York: Free Press, 1986). On this same theme, see Alistair Horne's remarkable study of Verdun in 1916 in *The Price of Glory* (New York: Harper Colophon, 1962). Richard Gabriel's *Military Incompetence* (New York: Hill & Wang, 1985) is shallow and tendentious—a good example of a bad book; see James H. Kyle with John Eidson, *The Guts to Try* (New York: Orion, 1990), the Iran hostage rescue mission, for a reaction to Gabriel.

11. The movie *An Officer and a Gentleman* (1982) wholly failed to explain adequately what being either an officer or a gentleman is all about.

12. Stephen R. Covey, *Principle-Centered Leadership* (New York: Simon & Schuster, 1991), 184.

13. Kilpatrick, *Why Johnny Can't Tell Right from Wrong*, 25.

14. This applies to civilian education as well. How many thousands of college "students" annually "earn" degrees without ever having done serious, sustained, and substantial academic work? How many of these "graduates" go on to begin teaching careers themselves? When a student is assigned a passing grade—"C"—in a college course, he is being told, supposedly by a competent and serious scholar, that he has achieved satisfactory mastery of the material. If students have not mastered that material, they should be told the truth. But if professors assign passing or higher grades because they want to be liked, or to bolster course enrollments, or to look good at tenure time, or for other ignoble reasons, the professors themselves are liars and incompetent in their fields.

15. The old Army axiom that the commander is responsible for all that the command does or fails to do is profoundly true, provided the commander has adequate authority and powers commensurate with obligations.

16. Hamilton to John Jay, 14 March 1779, in *The Works of Alexander Hamilton*, ed. Henry Cabot Lodge (New York: Putnam, 1904), 9:160-61. Hamilton continues: "I have frequently heard it objected to the scheme of embodying negroes, that they are too stupid to make soldiers. This is so far from appearing to me a valid objection, that I think their want of cultivation (for their natural faculties are as good as ours), joined to that habit of subordination which they acquire from a life of servitude, will enable them sooner to become soldiers than our white inhabitants." There is much to ponder in both his conclusions and his reasons for them—as in the remarkable film *Glory* (1990), which ought to be part of any military ethics or military leadership course.

17. For an extraordinary film treatment of this subject, and others, see the Australian movie *Breaker Morant* (1979).

18. Heinlein, *Starship Troopers*, 46. Heinlein's dedication is instructive: "To 'Sarge' Arthur George Smith—soldier, citizen, scientist—and to all sergeants anywhere who have labored to make men out of boys."

19. Maj. Gen. John M. Schofield explained caring leadership in an address to the West Point Corps of Cadets on 11 August 1879: "The discipline which makes the soldiers of a free country reliable in battle is not to be gained by harsh or tyrannical treatment. On the contrary, such treatment is far more likely to destroy than to make an army. It is possible to impart instruction and to give commands in such manner and such tone of voice [as] to inspire in the soldier no feeling but an intense desire to obey, while the opposite manner and tone of voice cannot fail to excite strong resentment and desire to disobey. The one mode or the other of dealing with subordinates springs from a corre-

sponding spirit in the breast of the commander. He who feels the respect which is due to others cannot fail to inspire in them regard for himself, while he who feels, and hence manifests, disrespect toward others, especially his inferiors, cannot fail to inspire hatred against himself" (quoted in John C. Bahnsen and Robert W. Cone, "Defining the American Warrior," *Parameters*, December 1990, 27). See also Atkinson, *The Long Gray Line*, 524-25.

20. Mark Clark, *From the Danube to the Yalu* (New York: Harper, 1954), 193 (emphasis added).

21. Quoted in Marguerite Higgins, *War in Korea: The Report of a Woman Combat Correspondent* (Garden City, N.Y.: Doubleday, 1951), 221.

22. James A. Van Fleet, "25 Divisions for the Cost of One," *Reader's Digest*, Feb. 1954, 5.

23. I do not mean to lionize the U.S. Army of World War II, and this is not the place to debate its quality. In 1947, S.L.A. Marshall declared that only one in four soldiers ever used a weapon in firefights. Was that claim fabricated? See Philip Gold, "Flak for a Man and His Claim That Few Soldiers Open Fire," *Insight*, 27 March 1989, 18-19; S.L.A. Marshall, *Men against Fire* (1947; New York: Morrow, 1966); Martin Blumenson, "Did 'Slam' Guess at Fire Ratios? Probably: A Legend Remembered," *Army*, June 1989, 16-21.

24. T.R. Fehrenbach, *This Kind of War* (New York: Pocket Books, 1964), 100, 126; see also 92-93 and 152-53. This remarkable book deserves to be at the top of any professional military reading list.

25. Fehrenbach, *This Kind of War*, 126, 100.

26. Higgins, *War in Korea*, 83-92.

27. See Richard Gabriel and Paul Savage, *Crisis in Command* (New York: Hill & Wang, 1978), a tendentious book which, nonetheless, makes some telling points and James W. Gibson, *The Perfect War* (Boston: Atlantic Monthly Press, 1986). David Hackworth with Julie Sherman, *About Face* (New York: Simon & Schuster, 1989), is a self-serving portrait of a very highly courageous soldier—but a man of limited moral vision. Much the same can be said of Hackworth's doppelganger, John Paul Vann; see Neil Sheehan, *A Bright, Shining Lie* (New York: Random House, 1988). Another biography worth reading is John K. Singlaub with Malcolm McConnell, *Hazardous Duty* (New York: Summit, 1991). Army Major General Singlaub is tough on the Marines in Vietnam—"Marines were taking a lot of needless casualties—which seemed to be a point of honor for them" (316)—and on civilian leaders such as the Bundy brothers, McNamara, McNaughton, and others who, he says, "scoffed at the principles of war. They were convinced the ground war could be confined within the borders of South Vietnam, neatly wrapped in the computer spreadsheets. They were also

convinced that if Westmoreland followed their directives faithfully, all the little boxes could be checked, the graph lines would run true, and victory would be inevitable" (290).

28. The chaos extended to the Army in the United States (CONUS) and to the U.S. Army in Europe (USAREUR). See Toner, *The American Military Ethic*, chaps. 3-5; and Atkinson, *The Long Gray Line*, chap. 14.

29. An international officer at the Air War College once remarked to me, "I don't think I'll ever understand the U.S. armed forces. Not only does your Navy have its own army, but your navy's army has its own air force!"

30. Fehrenbach, *This Kind of War*, 246. In *Defeat into Victory* (New York: McKay, 1961), 452, Field Marshal Sir William Slim observes: "We found it a great mistake to belittle the importance of smartness in turn-out, alertness of carriage, cleanliness of person, saluting, or precision of movement, and to dismiss them as naive, unintelligent parade ground stuff. I do not believe that troops can have unshakable battle discipline without showing those outward and formal signs, which mark the pride men take in themselves and their units and the mutual confidence and respect that exist between them and their officers."

31. See, e.g., Atkinson's accounts of the virtual anarchy around Fort Bragg in the early 1970s (*The Long Gray Line*, 310-11).

32. Fehrenbach, *This Kind of War*, 366.

33. For one interesting view, consult Arthur S. Collins, Jr., *Common Sense Training* (San Rafael, Calif.: Presidio Press, 1978). An excellent study of Army basic training is George C. Wilson, *Mud Soldiers* (New York: Scribner, 1989), which suggests, among other recommendations, that young officers undergo basic training with recruits (250-51).

34. Though this might be a sensitive and difficult subject, an IMO curriculum could rely on rules of personal, professional conduct upon which most groups agree: lying, cheating, and stealing are wrong; we should keep promises; we should not do things of which we would be ashamed, and so on—elementary ethical concepts that trainees should know and be encouraged to accept.

35. Ideally, this command would be responsible for all military education and training, from IMO through war college level, to include ROTC, OCS, and the service academies.

36. It seems fair to say that officers of all services should be recruited, educated, and trained according to standards even more rigorous than those for enlisted personnel. Using the Army as an example, I believe that all potential officers (after their graduation from West Point, ROTC, or OCS) should undergo a period of initial officer training (IOT); anyone unable to meet the educational, military, moral, and fitness standards of IOT would not be commissioned. This plan would

help to ensure that all Army officers have a similar rigorous experience before being given the responsibility and privilege of commanding U.S. soldiers. In fact, IOT should be required for all officers in all services, to include chaplains, lawyers, and doctors (they too wear the uniform, accept the pay and benefits, and hold commissions). For background, see Martin Van Crevald, *The Training of Officers* (New York: Free Press, 1990).

37. Donald Abenheim, *Restoring the Iron Cross* (Princeton, N.J.: Princeton Univ. Press, 1988), 13.

38. This is not intended in any way to disparage Operation Desert Storm, which went a long way toward restoring America's military prestige. One hopes that many of the political, ethical, and operational principles that helped make it a success will be preserved in future years, ready for use as needed.

39. One type that may fit either category (or both) is Army Ranger training; see Atkinson, *The Long Gray Line*, chap. 6. In my view, all Army infantry should be ranger- or airborne-qualified. See Toner, *The American Military Ethic*, 58-63.

40. Tim Challans, "Blood-Letting and Goat-Getting," paper presented at the Joint Service Conference on Professional Ethics, National Defense University, Washington, D.C., January 1993. Major Challans teaches in the English Department at West Point.

41. Alfred Vagts, *A History of Militarism* (1937; New York: Meridian Books, 1959), introduction.

42. Challans, "Blood-Letting and Goat-Getting," 9.

43. Scott B. Sonnenberg, "A Philosophical Conflict: A Fighter Pilot's Views on the Ethics of Warfare," *Air University Review*, July-Aug. 1985, 22, 17.

44. James Q. Wilson, *On Character* (Washington, D.C.: AEI Press, 1991), 108.

45. John Vessey, "A Concept of Service," *Naval War College Review* 37 (Nov.-Dec. 1984): 16.

46. Don T. Riley, "Serve Your Soldiers to Win," *Military Review*, Nov. 1986, 11.

4. Military Education

1. Slim, *Defeat Into Victory*, 451.

2. Barbara Tuchman, "Generalship," *Parameters*, Vol. 2, No. 2 (1972): 11.

3. Peter L. Stromberg, Malham M. Wakin, and Daniel Callahan,

The Teaching of Ethics in the Military (Hastings-on-Hudson, N.Y.: Institute of Society, Ethics, and the Life Sciences, 1982), 30.

4. Ibid., 31.

5. Kenneth H. Wenker, "Morality and Military Obedience," *Air University Review*, July-Aug. 1981, 82. He argues that the functional imperative, however, depends upon a decision procedure that is "effective and fair." He also draws interesting distinctions between autonomy, compliance, and obedience.

6. *Facts on File* 51 (15 Aug. 1991): 610D2; *Montgomery Advertiser*, 11 Aug. 1991, 18A.

7. Hale apparently never uttered the famous line attributed to him. See Vincent R. Ruggiero, *The Art of Critical Thinking* (New York: Harper & Row, 1984), 216.

8. Huntington, *The Soldier and the State*, 73.

9. Anthony Hartle, *Moral Issues in Military Decision Making* (Lawrence: Univ. Press of Kansas, 1989), 121, 44.

10. *Trial of the Major War Criminals Before the International Military Tribunal* (Nuremberg: International Military Tribunal, 1947), 2:250. See also A. Frank Reed, *The Case of General Yamashita* (New York: Octagon, 1971); and Lawrence Taylor, *A Trial of Generals* (South Bend, Ind.: Icarus, 1981). See *In re Yamashita*, 327 U.S. 1 (1948) for the case itself. For the "first trial of a war criminal," see John McElroy, *This Was Andersonville* (New York: McDowell, Obolensky, 1957), chap. 24, which relates the story of Confederate Captain Henri Wirz, executed on 10 November 1865. A good fictional account is MacKinlay Kantor, *Andersonville* (Cleveland: World, 1955).

11. *The Law of Land Warfare*, Field Manual 27-10 (Washington, D.C.: Department of the Army, 1956), para 509a. The paragraph concludes by saying that if a soldier acts pursuant to orders in committing a possible war crime, such a fact may be submitted in mitigation. An important philosophical distinction exists between "invincible" and "vincible" ignorance. The former is unlikely to be overcome: e.g., mental retardation may lead to invincible ignorance, and immoral acts committed by a retarded person are not normally imputed to him. Vincible ignorance can and should be overcome. Professional people have a responsibility to be informed, and "ignorance is no excuse."

12. Ibid., para. 509b.

13. Eric Sevareid, *Not So Wild a Dream* (New York: Knopf, 1946), 388-89.

14. See Lewis Sorley, "On Knowing When to Disobey Orders: Creighton Abrams and the Relief of Bastogne," *Armor*, Sept.-Oct. 1992, 8.

15. Sevareid, *Not So Wild a Dream*, 390-91.

16. Philip Lewis, Karl Kuhnert, and Robert Maginnis, "Defining Military Character," *Parameters* 16 (Summer 1987): 34-35.

17. *Time*, 3 Feb. 1992; and the *Montgomery Advertiser*, 21 Jan. 1992.

18. Quoted in *Time*, 23 Sept. 1991, 27.

19. Myrer, *Once an Eagle*, 292-305.

20. Atkinson, *The Long Gray Line*, 271. The lieutenant was Tom Carhart, whose own book about Vietnam is *The Offering* (New York: Morrow, 1987).

21. J. Glenn Gray, *The Warriors: Reflections on Men in Battle* (New York: Harper Colophon, 1970), 185-86.

22. For another series of excellent cases, see Hartle, *Moral Issues in Military Decision Making*, 78-84, 129-51.

23. Jeane Kirkpatrick, "Virtue Not Prerequisite of Leadership," *Montgomery Advertiser*, 5 Feb. 1992, 8A. Among those who would consider virtue irrelevant to leadership is Richard M. Nixon. See Stephen E. Ambrose, *Nixon*, vol. 3, *Ruin and Recovery, 1973-1990* (New York: Simon & Schuster, 1991), 581-97.

24. Hartle, *Moral Issues in Military Decision Making*, 84.

25. This is not to say that public officials' lives will be spotless and pure; to expect perfection of our leaders is to set impossible standards. What matters, generally, is that sins and errors not be repeated. Contrition, the Christian tradition tells us, must be fulfilled not only by suitable penance but through a firm purpose of amendment.

26. John Adams, "Dissertation on the Canon and the Feudal Law," in *The Selected Writings of John and John Quincy Adams*, ed. Adrienne Koch and William Peden (New York: Knopf, 1946), 18.

27. Perry M. Smith, *Taking Charge: A Practical Guide for Leaders* (Washington, D.C.: National Defense University Press, 1986), 15.

28. Morgan W. McCall, Jr., and Michael M. Lombardo, "What Makes a Top Executive?" *Psychology Today*, Feb. 1983, 30-31.

29. Hans Morgenthau, "Epistle to the Columbians," *New Republic*, 21 Dec. 1959, 9. This article grew out of episodes of cheating on TV quiz shows by a Columbia University professor, some of whose students thought that such cheating was "all right" when the teacher was "off duty."

30. Myrer, *Once an Eagle*, 913.

31. Kilpatrick, *Why Johnny Can't Tell Right from Wrong*, 85.

32. Perry Smith explains what he means by the "cowardice of silence" in his useful article "Leadership at the Top—Insights for Aspiring Leaders," *Marine Corps Gazette*, Nov. 1990, 33-39.

33. See Stromberg, Wakin, and Callahan, *The Teaching of Ethics in the Military*, pp. 32-33.

34. Heinlein, *Starship Troopers*, 96.

35. On the theme of publicity, see Axinn, *A Moral Military*, 177-79. Kenneth Blanchard and Norman Vincent Peale, *The Power of Ethical Management* (New York: Fawcett Crest, 1988), 20, makes a similar point: How will doing this make me feel about myself? Will it make me proud? What if my decision were in the newspaper? What if my family knew about my decision?

36. "I am an American. I serve in the forces which guard my country and its way of life. I am prepared to give my life in their defense."

37. See Articles 133 and 134 of the Uniform Code of Military Justice.

38. General John D. Ryan, quoted in Wakin, *War, Morality, and the Military Profession*, 189.

39. Wakin, "The Ethics of Leadership II," 204.

40. See Kermit D. Johnson, "Ethical Issues of Military Leadership," in Matthews and Brown, *The Parameters of Military Ethics*, 73-78.

41. We would be going too far afield here to get into the difficulties surrounding the question of agreement about universals. John F. Fitzgibbon, in his pamphlet *Ethics: Fundamental Principles of Moral Philosophy* (Lanham, Md.: University Press of America, 1983), xi, contends that "there is no incontestable evidence that there exists [sic] any real, fundamental moral differences between societies or cultures." Although I am inclined to agree, Fitzgibbon is a little too cavalier in this respect. Still, in international law the idea of *jus cogens* (a peremptory norm upon which states agree and by which they are bound) is coming back into favor. Are there international norms binding upon all states, regardless of whether they are legally accepted by those states?

42. E.g., false claim for lodging, advance travel pay not reported on settlement voucher, inflated costs of reimbursable expenses, travel claimed but not performed by a service member or dependent; claim of POV (private car) but travel by other means; false information presented on household goods claim, inflated weight tickets; excess amount for taxi fare; annual sick leave taken but not recorded, charging sick leave when a charge to annual leave is appropriate, living in government quarters and receiving BAQ (basic allowance for quarters); receiving BAQ but not supporting a dependent. All these examples are taken from a "Fraud, Waste and Abuse" memorandum produced by the U.S. Air Force.

43. See Clay T. Buckingham, "Ethics and the Senior Officer: Institutional Tensions," *Parameters*, Autumn 1985, 71.

44. "A Thousand Points of Blight," *Time*, 9 Nov. 1992, 68-69.

45. Silber, *Straight Shooting*, 258.

46. See the *Minneapolis Star Tribune*, 13 Feb. 1993, 15. For an interesting exchange of views on this principle, see *Washington Post* 4 April 1993. Two Marines, D.S. Jonas and H.W. Frank, argued (I believe correctly)

that as military officers [we] are not issued 'gag orders' with our uni-forms. . . . Our duty is one of thinking obedience, not blind submission. In fact, we are duty-bound to disobey unlawful orders" (C7). The *Post* editorialized: "If military leaders oppose Mr. Clinton's position on gays, they have a right to say so. What they cannot do is act publicly in ways that even appear to deny the president's legitimate authority" (C6)—a valid, important point. But on 8 April a Navy Supply Corps officer, D.C. Orr, argued that officers "express [themselves] at [their] own risk" and that the military system "is geared to ruthlessly suppress all dissent and to efficiently weed out those who cannot or will not conform" (18). Orr's judgment is extreme but has enough merit to cause discomfort among all considerate soldiers and, indeed, all reflective people in all professions. When, where, and to what extend to tolerate—or encourage—discussion, debate, and dissent is truly a perennial question.

47. Douglas Southall Freeman, "Leadership," in *Concepts for Air Force Leadership*, ed. Richard I. Lester and A. Glenn Morton (Maxwell AFB, Ala.: Center for Aerospace Doctrine, Research, and Education, 1990), 418.

48. See, for example, Matthew 4:19, 8:22, 9:9, 10:38; Mark 1:17, 2:14, 8:34, 10:21; Luke 5:27, 9:23 and 59. Colonel Wakin put it this way: "Our advice to those who aspire to become worthy military leaders can be none other than that of the ancient Chinese sage: 'The way to do is to be'" ("The Ethics of Leadership I," in Wakin, *War, Morality, and the Military Profession*, 197).

5. Military Codes

1. The four cardinal virtues cited in the last chapter may be under-stood as remedies for corresponding defects: Wisdom overcomes igno-rance; justice overcomes dishonesty; temperance overcomes concupisc-ible urges; and fortitude overcomes irascible instincts. These concepts and others, such as the seven capital vices (arrogance, greed, gluttony, lust, anger, envy, and sloth), are not much in vogue at present. See Henry Fairlie, *The Seven Deadly Sins Today* (New York: Simon & Schus-ter, 1978).

2. Douglas MacArthur, "The Unbreakable Spirit Code," *Vital Speeches of the Day*, 15 April 1942, 397.

3. George Roche, *A World without Heroes: The Modern Tragedy* (Hills-dale, Mich.: Hillsdale College Press, 1987), 30. Robert Payne, *The Cor-rupt Society* (New York: Praeger, 1975), is worth reading. (Its dedication is to Richard M. Nixon.)

4. See Toner, *The Sword and the Cross*.

5. Joseph Brennan, *Foundations of Moral Obligation* (Newport, R.I.: Naval War College, 1992).

6. Ibid., 206.

7. This is not to argue that teachers—any more than political leaders—must always be paragons of virtue; all humans make mistakes. But, again, what matters is our "fundamental option" (as it is sometimes referred to in theology): do we, despite our occasional failings, try our best to lead lives of decency and compassion, endeavoring to know and do what is ethical rather than just what is expedient?

8. Carl Becker, *The Heavenly City of the Eighteenth-Century Philosophers* (New Haven: Yale University Press, 1932), 102-3.

9. Real horror stories explore the tragedies of human existence: e.g., William Golding's *Lord of the Flies*, Joseph Conrad's *Heart of Darkness*, and William Styron's *Sophie's Choice* (and the movie made from it).

10. See Howard G. Chua-Eoan, "The Uses of Monsters," *Time*, 19 Aug. 1991, 66.

11. A useful short study of William Peter Blatty's novel *The Exorcist*, Golding's *Lord of the Flies*, J.D. Salinger's *Catcher in the Rye*, and J.R.R. Tolkien's *Lord of the Rings* is William J. O'Malley, "Evil, Ordinary & Extraordinary," *New Oxford Review*, April 1992, 18-23. See also Lance Morrow, "Evil," *Time*, 10 June 1991, 48-53.

12. According to Roche, "You will never hear [television newscasters] say the one straightforward thing: that today's horror was *wrong*, an evil act. Every other conceivable explanation will be trundled out, lest we admit evil. Society was to blame. The terrorists were trying to dramatize their protest. The criminal came from a bad neighborhood. Only a psychotic would hack his mother into small pieces to collect the insurance" (*A World without Heroes*, 43).

13. See Karl A. Menninger, *Whatever Became of Sin?* (New York: Hawthorn, 1973).

14. Russell Kirk, "Libertarians: The Chirping Sectaries," *Modern Age* 25 (Fall 1981): 349.

15. Alasdair MacIntyre, *After Virtue*, 2d ed. (Notre Dame, Ind.: Univ. of Notre Dame Press, 1984), 11-12 (original emphasis).

16. Hannah Arendt, *Between Past and Future* (New York: Viking, 1961), 91, 106.

17. Morgenthau, "Epistle to the Columbians," 10.

18. See Robert Maginnis, "A Chasm of Values," *Military Review*, Feb. 1993, 8-9.

19. Ross, *Christian Ethics*, 103. "Under the head of superstition come idolatry, divination, magic, and many forms of occultism. . . . The mere enumeration of various forms—astrology, aeromancy, palmistry, capnomancy, alomancy, cartomancy, anthropomancy, beloman-

cy, geomancy, necromancy, oneiromancy, philters, charms, amulets, lucky and unlucky numbers and days, evil eye, incantations, ordeals, etc.—makes quite an imposing array" (102-3).

20. Maginnis, "Chasm of Values," 8-9.

21. See chaps. 8-9 in Toner, *American Military Ethic*.

22. Quoted in Edward C. Meyer, "Professional Ethics Is Key to Well-Led, Trained Army," *Army*, Oct. 1980, 12.

23. Donald Atwell Zoll, "The Moral Dimension of War and the Military Ethic," in Matthews and Brown, *The Parameters of Military Ethics*, 124.

24. Cecil V. Crabb, Jr., *American Foreign Policy in the Nuclear Age*, 3d ed. (New York: Harper & Row, 1972), 31.

25. In domestic politics, our safeguards are separation of powers and its corollary of checks and balances. In international affairs our safeguard is concern for the balance of power.

26. Stephen K. Bailey, "Ethics and the Public Service," in *Public Administration and Democracy*, ed. Roscoe C. Martin (Syracuse, N.Y.: Syracuse University Press, 1965), 287. The U.S. Constitution has endured since 1787 because it is based upon a realistic understanding of human nature. The same holds true, in my view, for the *Federalist*, the eighty-five essays written by James Madison, Alexander Hamilton, and John Jay urging acceptance of the Constitution; Numbers 10 and 51 complement the text above.

27. Bailey, "Ethics and the Public Service," 287.

28. Wakin, "The Ethics of Leadership II," 208.

29. See William F. Buckley, Jr., *Gratitude: Reflections on What We Owe to Our Country* (New York: Random House, 1990).

30. See J.L.A. Garcia, "Moral Reasoning and the Catholic Church," *New Oxford Review*, June 1992, 13.

31. Crimes are frequently unforgivable among professionals and usually deserve severe punishment. Mistakes are not only forgivable but generally should not be punished. The distinction generally is one of intention. If a professional does everything the reasonable and prudent person can be expected to do but there is still an error, he or she very probably deserves no censure—but perhaps more training. On the other hand, a deliberate breach of integrity is a "crime." A briefing officer who unintentionally gives mistaken information (and admits and corrects it when the error is discovered) is generally not to be punished (and may even be praised). But one who attempts to "fudge" information, knowing that he does not know, commits a "crime." (I appreciate the counsel of Colonel Larry Carter, USAF, on these matters.)

32. James E. Swartz, "Morality: A Leadership Imperative," *Military Review*, Sept. 1992, 79-80.

33. Bellah et al., *The Good Society*, 40.

34. Ibid., 12

35. Russell Kirk, "The Necessity of Dogmas in Schooling," *Modern Age* 22 (Winter 1978): 4.

36. *O'Callahan v. Parker*, 395 U.S. 258, 281 (1969).

37. Kenneth H. Wenker, "Professional Military Ethics: An Attempt at Definition," *USAFA Journal of Professional Military Ethics* 1 (April 1980): 28.

38. Atkinson, *The Long Gray Line*, 400, 516, 508.

39. Anthony Hartle, "Do Good People Make Better Warriors?" *Army*, Aug. 1992, 23. Cf. John Leo, "The Professors of Dogmatism," *U.S. News & World Report*, 18 Jan. 1993, 25 (Leo and Kirk do not use the word *dogmatism* in the same way). See also the comments of Stephen Danckert about learning from heroes and the "Hanoi Hilton" experience, in *Military Review*, May 1990, 83-84.

40. Nicholas Fotion and G. Elfstrom, *Military Ethics* (Boston: Routledge & Kegan Paul, 1986), 67.

41. Kirk, "The Necessity of Dogmas in Schooling," 2.

42. Fotion and Elfstrom, *Military Ethics*, 76-79.

43. See Maxwell D. Taylor's two articles: "A Do-It-Yourself Professional Code for the Military," *Parameters*, Dec. 1980, 10-15; and "A Professional Ethic for the Military?" *Army*, May 1978, 18-21. Also useful is Lewis Sorley, "Beyond Duty, Honor, Country," *Military Review*, April 1987, 2-13.

44. *Contrails: Air Force Academy Handbook*, vol. 38 (1992-93), 8.

45. William F. Diehl, "Ethics and Leadership: The Pursuit Continues," *Military Review*, April 1985, 41.

46. Richard Gabriel, *To Serve with Honor* (New York: Praeger, 1987), 140.

47. Hartle, *Moral Issues in Military Decision Making*, 121.

48. See Joseph G. Brennan, "Ethics Instruction in the Military: Teach Them Plato or Hammer It into Their Heads," *Naval War College Review* 42 (Autumn 1989): 63-64. See also Richard T. De George, "The Need for a Military Code of Ethics," *Army*, Dec. 1984, 22-30; Martz, "Professional Military Ethics," 57-58; and Patrick Tower, "A Creedal Code of Ethics," *USAFA Journal of Professional Military Ethics* 4 (Feb. 1984): 17-25.

49. Brennan, "Ethics Instruction," 64-65.

50. John H. Napier III, *Air Force Officer's Guide*, 29th ed. (Harrisburg, Penn.: Stackpole, 1992), 123-24. Executive Order 10631 was signed 7 Aug. 1955 by President Eisenhower; it was amended in May 1988.

51. William H. Stayton, "Ethics and the Military Profession," in

Studies in Defense, comp. Eston T. White (Washington, D.C.: National Defense University, 1983), 12.

52. Wakin, "The Ethics of Leadership I," 186. L.M. Ewing expressed similar reservations about codes in "Teach It, Live It, Don't Write It," *Army*, May 1984, 16.

53. Roy Clark, lyrics for "Yesterday, When I Was Young" (DOT Records).

54. Viktor Frankl, *Man's Search for Meaning*, 3d ed. (New York: Simon & Schuster, 1984). Originally published in 1963 by Beacon Press.

55. James M. Rowe, *Five Years to Freedom* (Boston: Little, Brown, 1971).

6. Active Duty

1. "Women in the Military," *CQ Researcher*, 25 Sept. 1992, 836-39. See also Charles Moskos, "Army Women," *Atlantic Monthly*, Aug. 1990, 72-73.

2. On the difficulties the first women cadets experienced at West Point, see Atkinson, *The Long Gray Line*, 410-14. Among them was Captain Carol Barkalow, who says that by the time she returned for her ten-year reunion, "my male classmates had changed tremendously. They recognized us [women] as peers" (*Newsweek*, 5 Aug. 1991, 30). In Barkalow with Andrea Rabb, *In the Men's House* (New York: Poseidon, 1990), 21-140, she tells of her experiences at West Point.

3. "Women in the Military," 843.

4. Annette Fuentes, "Equality, Yes—Militarism, No," *The Nation* 253 (28 Oct. 1991): 516-19.

5. Brian Mitchell, *Weak Link: The Feminization of the American Military* (Washington, D.C.: Regnery Gateway, 1989), 170.

6. A.F.C. Webster, review of *Weak Link* by Brian Mitchell, *American Spectator*, Dec. 1989, 54.

7. A.F.C. Webster, "Paradigms of the Contemporary American Soldier and Women in the Military," *Strategic Review*, Summer 1991, 29.

8. David Horowitz, "The Feminist Assault on the Military," *National Review*, 5 Oct. 1992, 47.

9. For background, see *Congressional Quarterly Weekly Report* 48 (10 March 1990): 762-63.

10. *Time*, 12 Aug. 1991, 31. See also Jeanne Holm, *Women in the Military*, rev. ed. (Novato, Calif.: Presidio, 1992), chap. 27.

11. Rhonda Cornum with Peter Copeland, *She Went to War* (Novato, Calif.: Presidio, 1992). Samuel Francis's view of women in captivity is

different from that of Major Cornum; see his article in *Washington Times*, 10 July 1992, F3.

12. *Newsweek*, 5 Aug. 1991, 30.

13. Barkalow and Rabb, *In the Men's House*, 200-266.

14. See the "DoD Risk Rule," explained in Barkalow, *In the Men's House*, 281, and in Moskos, "Army Women," 73.

15. Charles Moskos, in *Air Force Times*, 2 Nov. 1992, 8.

16. "Women in the Military," 846.

17. Horowitz, "The Feminist Assault," 48.

18. Moskos, "Army Women," 78.

19. Quoted from the *New York Times*, 28 Nov. 1992, 18. The contention that other nations often use women in combat is largely mistaken. The Israelis, for example, use women in many military roles but rarely in combat. See *National Review*, 5 Feb. 1990, 18-19; and Martin van Crevald, "Why Israel Doesn't Send Women into Combat," *Parameters* 23 (Spring 1993): 5-19.

20. *New York Times*, 28 Nov. 1992, 18.

21. Quoted in *Newsweek*, 5 Aug. 1991, 30.

22. Cornum and Copeland, *She Went to War*, 197-98. Moskos reports in "Army Women," 77, that of seventy-nine women recruited into infantry training in Canada, one completed the course, and she subsequently requested a transfer. Major Cornum would not likely take exception to that: the standards were set; they were applied fairly and uniformly; everyone had an equal chance at making the grade.

23. Quoted in Moskos, "Army Women," 77.

24. A basic question that must continually be asked and answered is whether women can perform a particular combat mission under battlefield conditions. The rule of fundamental equality can have legitimate exceptions, depending upon professional assessment of the impact of having women routinely and regularly assigned to the hazards of infantry duty. Marine Corps Major Kathleen G. Bergeron contends that "there should be valid sex-based assignment exclusions based on clear differences between the sexes" ("Nobody Asked Me Either, But . . . ," *U.S. Naval Institute Proceedings* 119 [Jan. 1993]: 96). The only Canadian military job still closed to women is in submarine service.

25. Of 868 women soldiers surveyed, 73 percent of the officers and 79 percent of enlisted personnel supported voluntary combat for women; only 13 percent, however, said they would volunteer for such duty (*Facts on File* 52 [1 Oct. 1992]: 730).

26. Quoted in Moskos, "Army Women," 76. General Foote contends that female officers were never consulted on the changes that allowed pregnant women and single parents to remain in the Army, something she generally opposes.

27. See "Annie Get Your Gun," *Time*, 10 May 1993; and "Pentagon Plans to Allow Combat Flights by Women," *New York Times*, 28 April 1993, 1, 4; *Facts on File* 53 (29 April 1993): 304. Aspin indicated, however, that he would not recommend ending restrictions on women in such areas as infantry and armor.

28. For general background, see Chandler Burr, "Homosexuality and Biology," *Atlantic Monthly*, March 1993, 47-65; "Gay Rights," *CQ Researcher* 3 (5 March 1993); and Ronald D. Ray, *Military Necessity and Homosexuality* (Louisville: First Principles, 1993), which contains a useful bibliography. Paul Kahn, "Love Field," *New Republic*, 8 March 1993, 19-20, asks "Will military service be so changed by modern technology and modern ideas of the liberal state in a world community that it will simply become another form of employment . . . ?"

29. *New York Times*, 20 July 1993, 1, 12.

30. Comdr. Eugene Gomulka, USMC, in his "Position Paper on the DOD Policy on Homosexuality," is very clear that *behavior*, not *orientation*, is the basis for separation of homosexuals from the military.

31. John A. Eidsmoe, *Gays and Guns: The Case against Homosexuals in the Military* (Lafayette, La.: Huntington House, 1993). I am grateful to Dean Charles H. Davis IV of the Air War College for calling to my attention an earlier version of this well-done volume.

32. A point well made by Mark E. Cantrell in "No Place for Homosexuals," *Marine Corps Gazette*, April 1993, 67.

33. Alan L. Gropman, "Homosexuals in the Military—Not a Civil Right," *Air Force Times*, 11 Jan. 1993, 31. I thank Col. Bryant Shaw, USAF, for calling this article to my attention. A good short piece is "Shape Up or Ship Out," *U.S. News & World Report*, 5 April 1993, 24-33.

34. There can be no doubt that homosexuals "in the closet" (that is, unannounced) have served and served well over the years. See, e.g., Mary Ann Humphrey, *My Country, My Right to Serve* (New York: Harper Collins, 1990). See also "Sex, Lies, and the Military," *Time*, 6 July 1992, 29-30; and "I Just Don't Want to Go," *Time*, 6 July 1992, an interview with Col. Margarethe Cammermeyer, a lesbian. If the military is compelled to recognize homosexuality as legitimate and acceptable behavior, however, the consequences—military, moral, and social—are what properly concern armed forces authorities. If certain members of the military forces were to practice religious rituals offensive to many others —such as animal sacrifice—and the military were to recognize those practices as normal and acceptable, it would bestow on them a status at odds with national cultural norms. The military cannot and should not control every element of personal and private behavior, but the very act of recognizing an announced and trumpeted behavior as acceptable personal and professional conduct would give it tacit legit-

imacy. In *Conduct Unbecoming: Gays and Lesbians in the U.S. Military* (New York: St. Martin's, 1993), Randy Shilts argues that there is a "vast" gay subculture within the military and that "at least one gay man has served on the Joint Chiefs of Staff" (quoted in *Time*, 1 March 1993, 9). How "vast" that subculture may be is open to debate, and I do not see how extended conclusions can be drawn from the fact, even if true, of a homosexual general or admiral.

35. Quoted in *Crisis*, July-August 1992, 46.

36. Mickey Kaus, "Unusual Suspects," *New Republic* 22 (Feb. 1993): 4.

37. *Parker v. Levy*, 417 U.S. 733 (1974). For details of legal cases relevant to the homosexual issue, see Eidsmoe, *Gays and Guns*.

38. *Washington Times*, 8 Feb. 1993, 5.

39. *Facts on File* 52 (22 Oct. 1992): 793. Interestingly, the *Army Times* and the *Air Force Times* have called for an end to the ban; the *Navy Times* called for the ban to stay in place but not be enforced.

40. *U.S. News & World Report*, 15 March 1993, 23.

41. *Army Times*, 22 Feb. 1993, 6.

42. *Chicago Tribune*, 20 Oct. 1992, 25.

43. William P. Snyder and Kenneth L. Nyberg, "Gays and the Military: An Emerging Policy Issue," *Journal of Political and Military Sociology* 8 (1980): 73.

44. Quoted in *Montgomery Advertiser*, 30 Jan. 1993, 3B.

45. See R.D. Adair and Joseph C. Myers, "Admission of Gays to the Military: A Singularly Intolerant Act," *Parameters* 23 (Spring 1993): 15. Numerous other considerations (such as AIDS) are well beyond the confines of this book; Adair and Myers provide details.

46. Mike McManus, syndicated column, *Montgomery Advertiser*, 30 Jan. 1993, 3B. Among countries that do allow homosexuals in the armed forces (e.g., Denmark and Sweden), few have the extended and rigorous service requirements of the U.S. services. When Australia ended its ban in November 1992, no uniformed homosexuals declared themselves. For a full report, see *Air Force Times*, 11 Jan. 1993, "A Special Report: Gays in the Ranks." Also see *Time*, 6 Feb. 1993, 16.

47. *Navy Times*, 30 March 1992, 27. The suggestion that homosexuals could be admitted to the service but strictly separated from heterosexuals is extremely ill advised, for it would create contending camps within each military service.

48. The 19 July 1993 policy letter issued by Secretary of Defense Aspin stipulated: "Applicants for militiary [*sic*] service will not be asked or required to reveal their sexual orientation. . . . Servicemembers will be separated for homosexual conduct."

49. Mark D. Mensack, "The Homosexual and the Military," paper

presented to the Joint Services Conference on Professional Military Ethics, National Defense University, Washington, D.C., Feb. 1993.

50. Charges that West Point graduates are "ring-knockers" have been made for years. But for every allegation that one West Pointer favors another because they have similar class rings, there is the countercharge that West Pointers are *tougher* on their fellows because they expect more. The same charges, pro and con, could be made about alumni of VMI, the Citadel, Texas A & M, Notre Dame, or any institution noted for camaraderie among alumni.

51. Useful studies of frat appear in the *USAF Journal of Professional Military Ethics* for 1985. See also William Reed, Jr., "In Search of Moral Leadership," *Marine Corps Gazette*, Jan. 1990, 27-28.

52. *Time*, 11 May 1992, 16.

53. "Women in the Military," 844. See "Navy Harassment Probe Stymied," *Washington Post*, 1 May 1992.

54. More than 140 people will be referred to the military's legal system for possible disciplinary action, Pentagon officials have indicated (*Montgomery Advertiser*, 20 April 1993, 6A).

55. *Facts on File* 53 (10 June 1993): 427.

56. *Washington Times*, 8 March 1993, 1.

57. *Montgomery Advertiser*, 6 June 1992, 5A.

58. Quoted in James Webb, "Witch Hunt in the Navy," *New York Times*, 6 Oct. 1992, 23.

59. See *U.S. News & World Report*, 13 July 1992; and *Time*, 13 July 1992.

60. Syndicated column of 26 July 1992, *Montgomery Advertiser*.

61. *San Diego Union-Tribune*, 17 Feb. 1993, 1.

62. *Facts on File* 53 (10 June 1993): 427.

63. Webb, "Witch Hunt in the Navy."

64. Quoted in *Time*, 13 July 1992, 36; *U.S. News & World Report*, 13 July 1992, 25.

65. Sexual harassment is intolerable. If "everyone" in the military is not responsible, some people, chiefly men, are. Problems with sexual harassment are not occurring just "in the ranks." The service academies, for exaple, are still encountering difficulties, as Lt. Gen. Bradley Hosmer, superintendent of the Air Force Academy, recently acknowledged (*Chicago Tribune*, 7 March 1993, 6; see also "Shrinking the Military," *Newsweek*, 30 Aug. 1993, 30).

66. Gabriel, *To Serve with Honor*, 184.

67. Lloyd Matthews, "Resignation in Protest," *Army*, Jan. 1990, 20. Matthews, in my view, leaves ample room for principled resignation, in either war or peace, but points out that matters worthy of such a step are rare. Resignation ought never to be taken as lightly as it sometimes

is—as it would be if, for instance, I were gallantly to offer another's resignation in an affair of my conscience. See also Edward Weisband and Thomas M. Franck, *Resignation in Protest* (New York: Grossman, 1975). In August 1993 four State Department officials resigned over U.S. policy toward the Balkans; see *New York Times*, 26 Aug. 1993, A5.

68. Matthews, "Resignation in Protest," 18.

69. A "mutiny" supposedly took place at the British army camp of Curragh in 1914 when officers there resigned their commissions rather than coerce Ulster. A "revolt"—including the angry resignation of Navy Secretary John Sullivan—took place in the United States in 1949 with regard to unification; see K.D. McFarland, "The 1949 Revolt of the Admirals," *Parameters* 11 (June 1981): 53-63. Another useful consideration of resignation is Mel G. Chaloupka, "Ethical Responses: How to Organize One's Organization," *Naval War College Review* 40 (Winter 1987): 80-90, esp. 85.

70. Ibid., 21.

7. The Profession of Arms

1. Deuteronomy 8:3; Matthew 4:4.

2. Charles de Gaulle, *The Edge of the Sword*, trans. Gerard Hopkins (New York: Criterion, 1960), 9.

3. Gen. Sir John Hackett, *The Profession of Arms* (New York: Macmillan, 1983), 9.

4. Rick Fields, *The Code of the Warrior* (New York: HarperCollins, 1991), 175.

5. David Lloyd George, *War Memoirs* (London: Ivor Nicholson & Watson, 1936), 6:3497.

6. Buckingham, "Ethics and the Senior Officer," 23.

7. Sorley, "Doing What's Right," 12.

8. Quoted in D. Clayton James, *The Years of MacArthur*, vol. 1, 1880-1941 (Boston: Houghton Mifflin, 1970), 360.

9. *Time*, 26 June 1972, 14.

10. *Army*, Aug. 1970, 57.

11. Sorley, "Beyond Duty, Honor, Country," 9.

12. Atkinson, *The Long Gray Line*, 523; see also 399. At Infantry OCS in 1969, I learned this bit of doggerel: "Here lie the bones of Lt. Jones, the pride of the institution. He died one night, in his first fire fight, by applying the school solution."

13. Porcher L. Taylor III, "Professional Values versus Personal Values," *Military Review*, Nov. 1986, 33-34.

14. Huntington, *The Soldier and the State*, 7-10. See also Arthur J.

Dyck, "Ethical Bases of the Military Profession," in Matthews and Brown, *The Parameters of Military Ethics*, 106.

15. Janowitz, *The Professional Soldier*, 217-25.

16. Douglas MacArthur, "Duty, Honor, and Country," *Vital Speeches of the Day* 28 (1 June 1962): 519.

17. James Fallows, "Military Efficiency," *Atlantic Monthly*, Aug. 1991, 21.

18. Heinlein, *Starship Troopers*, 144-45, 129. The concept, of course, can be taken too far. Numerous heroes, real and fictional, have known when to uphold and when to disobey their groups.

19. Slim, *Defeat into Victory*, 451-52.

20. One thinks of the fictional character Adam Trask, forever willing to forgive his wife, the evil Kate, in John Steinbeck's powerful *East of Eden* (1952).

21. One of Heinlein's characters says, "The basis of all morality is duty" (*Starship Troopers*, 95).

22. Quoted in Geoffrey C. Ward, Ric Burns, and Ken Burns, *The Civil War: An Illustrated History* (New York: Knopf, 1990), 82-83; also appearing, with some differences in text, in Department of the Army, Second Infantry Division, "The Reasons Why" (mimeographed), 1 July 1992, 13. I thank Col. Dan Vannatter, U.S.A., for giving me this volume.

23. See Matthews, "Is Ambition Unprofessional?" 28-37. His answer is no.

24. The argument can become convoluted. If I give blood, am I doing so because I want to help others or because I will thus think more highly of myself—and hope that others will, too? Did Jesus die as an act of selflessness, or egotistically, to immortalize himself? Isn't it possible to do the "egotistical" thing and the "right" thing at the same time? When good people and good laws work together, isn't personal fulfillment the same as social improvement, and private conscience the same as public duty?

25. This is the sense of Luke 12:48. Gabriel puts it well: "As long as the focus of military ethics remains tied to notions of individual self-interest and as long as ethics are viewed as only descriptive devices instead of prescriptive and proscriptive rules requiring observance, it will be impossible to develop a sense of community obligation for the individual" (*To Serve with Honor*, 19).

26. See Sorley, "Doing What's Right," 14-15; William P. Boyd, "Men of Character, Principles of Honor?" *Army*, Sept. 1985, 22-29; and Joseph G. Brennan, "Ambition and Careerism," *Naval War College Review* 44 (Winter 1991): 76-82.

27. A "fool" too would have been Col. Robert Gould Shaw of the

54th Massachusetts Volunteers, whose story is brilliantly told in the moving film *Glory* (1990).

28. See Robert Hughes, "The Fraying of America," *Time*, 3 Feb. 1992, 44-49.

29. Tom Wolfe, "The Meaning of Freedom," *Parameters*, March 1988, 14.

30. See Richard John Neuhaus, *America against Itself* (Notre Dame, Ind.: University of Notre Dame Press, 1992), for one readable account.

31. *New Republic*, 30 Nov. 1963, 14. I thank Col. Malham Wakin for referring to this book review in a lecture he gave at the Air War College.

32. See "Sea of Lies," *Newsweek*, 13 July 1992, 29-39, concerning the Navy's attack on an Iranian airbus in July 1988. Murat Williams once deplored the fact that it seems that few any longer know the story of the liar Ananias (Acts 5): See "The Faded Specter of Ananias," *Chronicle of Higher Education*, 13 Feb. 1978, 40. See also Kenneth S. Kantzer, "The Pinocchio Syndrome," *Christianity Today*, 6 Oct. 1989, 13.

33. See Terence R. Mitchell and William G. Scott, "Leadership Failures, the Distrusting Public, and Prospects of the Administrative State," *Public Administration Review* 47 (Nov.-Dec. 1987): 445-52.

34. Gabriel, *To Serve with Honor*, 178.

35. Charles J. Dunlap, Jr., "The Origins of the American Military Coup of 2012," *Parameters*, Winter 1992-93, 12.

36. See Richard Gabriel and Paul Savage, *Crisis in Command* (New York: Hill & Wang, 1978), pp. 23, 30. I have long argued against business techniques in the military; see James H. Toner, "The Military Ethic: On the Virtue of an Anachronism," *Military Review*, Dec. 1974, 9-18.

37. Of course, the "management" of goods and services—logistics—is critical to war fighting, and some TQM techniques may well have value for logisticians. But too many military officers apparently regard TQM as an amulet that will resolve virtually all military problems. It is not the responsibility of the U.S. armed forces to prove themselves to TQM apostles; quite the reverse is true.

38. One thinks of the quantification techniques instituted by Secretary Robert S. McNamara when he became Secretary of Defense in 1961. Quantification can be useful, but McNamara might have been better served by improving his knowledge of the history, politics, religions, and geography of Southeast Asia.

39. Bernard Brodie, *War and Politics* (New York: Macmillan, 1973), 485n, 479.

40. Ibid., 492.

41. Quoted in Dyck, "Ethical Bases of the Military Profession," 112.

42. C.E.M. Joad, *Common-Sense Ethics* (New York: Dutton, 1921), 81. For most of his life (he died in 1953) Joad was a pacifist and an agnostic.

But his last work, *Recovery of Belief* (1952), explains his new-found faith in a theistic system. At the very last, he may have had more in common with C.S. Lewis than with H.G. Wells and G.B. Shaw.

43. Hard cases, said Justice Oliver Wendell Holmes, make bad law (*Northern Securities Co. v. U.S.*, 193 U.S. 197, 400 [1904]). Imagine trying to devise a general legal code for society based upon what may happen, say, to survivors of an airplane crash who are stranded in icy mountains. One might discover that the "ethical suggestions" of one test conflict with those of another. Fortunately, such cases are rare.

44. As Richard Halloran puts it: "For all senior officers, I suggest a check: before you sign off on a decision, ask yourself what it will look like on the front page of tomorrow's newspaper" ("Soldiers and Scribblers Revisited: Working With the Media," *Parameters*, Spring 1991, 16).

45. The idea of acting according to duty, not consequences, is the deontological approach to ethics. It is properly associated with Immanuel Kant (1724-1804), whose "categorical imperative" held essentially that if we cannot correctly and comfortably universalize our actions and principles, they are likely to be immoral. I am indebted to Ivan Hill for his discussion of this issue in "What Is Ethical?" *Rotarian*, May 1981, 12.

46. Myrer, *Once an Eagle*, 313.

47. Kilpatrick, *Why Johnny Can't Tell Right from Wrong*, 105.

48. James Stockinger, quoted in Bellah et al., *The Good Society*, 104.

8. Excursus

1. Christina Hoff Sommers, "Teaching the Virtues," *Imprimis* 20 (November 1991).

2. Quoted in Peter G. Tsouras, *Warrior's Words: A Quotation Book* (New York: Cassell Arms and Armour, 1992), 333.

3. Johnson, "Ethical Issues of Military Leadership," 38-39.

4. Quoted in *Washington Times*, 30 Nov. 1989, 8.

5. Quoted in Bellah et al., *The Good Society*, 43-44.

6. Steven M. Cahn, *Saints and Scamps: Ethics in Academia* (Totowa, N.J.: Rowman & Littlefield, 1986), preface, 1. The book he quotes is *This Beats Working for a Living: The Dark Secrets of a College Professor*, by "Professor X."

7. See Martin Anderson, *Impostors in the Temple* (New York: Simon & Schuster, 1992); Dinesh D'Souza, *Illiberal Education* (New York: Random House, 1992); Roger Kimball, *Tenured Radicals* (New York: Harper & Row, 1990); Jaroslav Pelikan, *The Idea of the University: A Reexamination* (New Haven: Yale University Press, 1992); Sowell, *Inside American Edu-*

cation; and Charles J. Sykes, *ProfScam* (Washington, D.C.: Regnery Gateway, 1988).

8. See Charles Sykes and Brad Miner, eds. *The National Review College Guide* (New York: National Review, 1991).

9. Most large research and university libraries use the Library of Congress classification scheme, in which the first letter in the book's call number indicates one of twenty-one major areas of knowledge. For example, B indicates philosophy and religion; J is political science; K is for law; L, education; U, military science; and V, naval science. The following letters and numbers in the book's code classify it in more detail.

10. Christina Hoff Sommers, "Teaching the Virtues," *Public Interest* 111 (Spring 1993): 13.

11. Carl Rogers, *Freedom to Learn for the 80's* (Columbus, Ohio: Merrill, 1983), is sharply and, I think, correctly challenged by Sowell, *Inside American Education*. Louis Raths, Merrill Harmin, and Sidney Simon, *Values and Teaching: Working with Values in the Classroom* (Columbus, Ohio: Merrill, 1966) developed this scheme of values clarification: "Choosing: (1) freely (2) from alternatives (3) after thoughtful consideration of the consequences of each alternative; prizing: (4) cherishing, being happy with the choice, (5) willing to affirm the choice publicly; acting: (6) doing something with the choice (7) repeatedly, in some pattern of life" (30). But Robert T. Sandin maintains, again quite properly, that this concept's "strong opposition to authoritative, indoctrinative approaches to moral education leaves it inattentive to the simple requirements of disciplinary rigor in moral thinking" (*The Rehabilitation of Virtue* [New York: Praeger, 1992], 60). Other important references in the area of development are Robert Coles, *The Moral Life of Children* (Boston: Atlantic Monthly Press, 1986); James W. Fowler, *The Stages of Faith* (New York: Harper & Row, 1981); and Lawrence Kohlberg, *Essays on Moral Development*, vol. 1: *The Philosophy of Moral Development* (New York: Harper & Row, 1981), esp. 117-20; and Jean Piaget, *Judgment and Reasoning in the Child* (1928), trans. Marjorie Warden (London: Routledge & Kegan Paul, 1969). As innocuous as Kohlberg's "stages" appear to be—from (1) acting in fear of punishment [stage 1] to (6) acting in accordance with "universal principles of justice" [stage 6]), Carol Gilligan calls both Piaget and Kohlberg to task because, she says, in the work of the former, "girls are an aside," and in the work of the latter, "females simply do not exist" (*In a Different Voice* [Cambridge, Mass.: Harvard Univ. Press, 1982], 18).

12. William G. Perry, Jr., "Cognitive and Ethical Growth: The Making of Meaning," in Arthur W. Chickering and Associates, *The Modern American College* (San Francisco: Jossey-Bass, 1981), starts his scheme of development with this first "position": "Authorities know, and if we

work hard, read every word, and learn Right Answers, all will be well." One "grows" into the ninth position: "I must be wholehearted while tentative. . . . I see that I shall be retracing this whole journey over and over" (79). Perry calls this "Commitments in Relativism developed." I would call it confusion.

13. William K. Frankena, *Thinking about Morality* (Ann Arbor: Univ. of Michigan Press, 1980), 75-76, 37.

14. Lewis, Kuhnert, and Maginnis, "Defining Character in Military Leaders," 126.

15. See James B. Stockdale, "The World of Epictetus," *Atlantic Monthly* 241, no. 4 (April 1978): 98-106, reprinted as "In War, in Prison, in Antiquity," in Matthews and Brown, *The Parameters of Military Ethics*, 168-74.

16. See Frederick H. Borsch, "It's Often Difficult Helping Students Learn More about Values and Ethics," *Chronicle of Higher Education*, 5 Sept. 1984, 104.

17. *Time*, 8 Feb. 1993, 37.

18. See J. Brian Benestad, "Catholicism and American Public Philosophy," *Review of Politics* 53 (Fall 1991): 698. Benestad discusses John Courtney Murray (1904-1967), a Jesuit theologian who is credited with writing much of the religious liberty decree passed by the Vatican II Ecumenical Council, 1965.

19. *Business Week*, 6 April 1992, 34. See also Michael Levin, "Ethics Courses: Useless," *New York Times*, 25 Nov. 1989, 23: "Moral character does not require any particular stance on any public issue, be it pollution or apartheid. Honesty, industry, and respect for others form the gyroscope that stabilizes an individual on his journey through life, not an itinerary of policy positions." Father William J. Byron, S.J., president of Catholic University, soon challenged Levin, branding the view that moral character does not require any particular stance on any public issue that of "a moral nomad," and saying that "whether we think our way into just actions, or act our way into an understanding of justice" was a question not answered by Levin (*New York Times*, 9 Dec. 1989, 24). I think they were talking past each other. Levin, as I understand him, was saying that carving ethics up into different "kinds" (business, medical, agricultural) is mistaken and misleading—a good point. Father Byron contends, I think correctly, that students can indeed be well served by serious ethics courses. There is room for principled negotiation.

20. Axinn, *A Moral Military*, 63.

21. William J. Bennett, "The Lure of Learning," *U.S. News & World Report*, 25 Nov. 1985, 55.

22. Neil L. Golightly, "Classical Approach to Leadership," *U.S. Naval Institute Proceedings* 107 (June 1981): 77.

23. In the 1980s, Mortimer Adler developed such an approach to learning. See his *Paideia Proposal* (New York: Macmillan, 1982); *Paideia Problems and Possibilities* (New York: Macmillan, 1983); and an earlier work, *Reforming Education* (Boulder: Westview, 1977). But teachers trained in running true seminars and highly educated in the classics are very rare—in part because of the vacuous nature of most college majors in "education."

24. Charles Van Doren, *A History of Knowledge* (New York: Ballantine, 1991), 286.

25. Kilpatrick, *Why Johnny Can't Tell Right from Wrong*, 242.

26. For one account of how heroism can inspire soldiers—and the rest of us—to do even mundane tasks with a little more pride, see the story of SP4 David K. Stoddard in Mark Hertling, "Whence Values Come," *Military Review*, Dec. 1987, 18.

27. "David Donovan" is a pseudonym. The author is Terry Turner, a biologist who teaches at the University of Virginia's medical school. The accounts in the book are true.

28. For one review of much of that literature, see Edward Eckert, "The Vietnam War: A Selective Bibliography," *Choice* 24 (Sept. 1986): 51-71.

29. The Gulf War of 1991 is just starting to generate material, not all of it valuable (I reviewed some of the worst in *Choice* 29 [July-August 1992]: 1752-53). Ramsey Clark, *The Fire This Time: U.S. War Crimes in the Gulf* (New York: Thunder's Mouth Press, 1992), which summarizes Clark's tendentious position, is nevertheless a good corrective for the mistaken notion that the United States wages morally pure war. See also David E. DeCosse, ed., *But Was It Just?* trans. Peter Heinegg (New York: Doubleday, 1992). More useful is the exchange between Nicholas Fotion and George Lopez, "The Gulf War: Cleanly Fought," *Bulletin of the Atomic Scientists* 47 (Sept. 1991): 24-35. Louis Manzo offers a good background piece, "Morality in War Fighting and Strategic Bombing in World War II," in *Air Power History* 39 (Fall 1992): 35-50. John Langan, "An Imperfectly Just War," *Commonweal* 118 (1 June 1991): 361-72 is a balanced treatment. Michael J. Glennon offers a political-legal perspective in "The Gulf War and the Constitution," *Foreign Affairs* 70 (Spring 1991): 84-101. And James Turner Johnson and George Weigel offer analysis and key documents in *Just War and the Gulf War.* (Washington, D.C.: Ethics and Public Policy Center, 1991).

30. A recent work by Richard Gabriel and Karen Metz, for example, concerned the history of medicine in the military. One reviewer, in his criticism, wrote: "It is an unpleasant and disheartening task to so thoroughly condemn [this work]. . . . [E]rrors of fact, failures of documentation and attribution, and overclose paraphrasing strike at the very

heart of scholarly work." Robert J.T. Joy, review in *Naval Institute Proceedings*, Jan. 1993, 101.

31. Bruce Van Voorst, *Time*, 19 Oct. 1992, 78.

32. Quang X. Pham, *Marine Corps Gazette*, March 1993, 80-81.

33. Micah 6:8.

Epilogue

1. Gilbert Highet, *The Art of Teaching* (New York: Vintage, 1950), 146-53.

2. "The State of Military Honor," *U.S. News & World Report*, 7 Feb. 1994, 12.

3. Sir Thomas More (1478-1535) knew this when he accepted death rather than stay with his family. See Robert Bolt's play *A Man for All Seasons* (New York: Random House, 1962).

4. *Baltimore Sun*, 30 Jan. 1994, 2E.

5. *Washington Post*, 11 Feb. 1994, D6.

6. *Washington Post*, 4 Feb. 1994, D3. The report said that 97 percent of female students felt some harassment in 1991.

7. *Christian Science Monitor*, 8 Feb. 1994, 18.

8. P. Carpenter and G.T. McClain, "Air Command and Staff College Air Campaign Course: The Air Corps Tactical School Reborn?" *Airpower Journal* 7 (Fall 1993): 72-83.

9. *Air Force Times*, 31 Jan. 1994, 3.

10. "Lost in the Fun House," *Time*, 21 Feb. 1994, 45.

11. *Montgomery Advertiser*, 9 Feb. 1994, 3A; *Washington Post*, 9 Feb. 1994, 1.

12. *New York Times*, 12 Feb. 1994, 1.

13. *Washington Post*, 16 Feb. 1994, 1.

14. *Washington Times*, 11 Feb. 1994, 10. For background, see "Many Officers, Not Many Gentlemen," *U.S. News & World Report*, 3 May 1993, 44, 49.

15. *Washington Post*, 10 Feb. 1994, 1; 12 Feb. 1994, 18; *New York Times*, 11 Feb. 1994, B1.

16. Colman McCarthy in the *Washington Post*, 3 Aug. 1993, C10. See also James G. Burton, "Pushing Them out the Back Door," *U.S. Naval Institute Proceedings* 119 (June 1993): 37-42.

17. "The Living Room War," *Time*, 23 May 1994, 48. See also Robyn Chumley, "Life at Leavenworth," *Airman*, May 1994, 209.

18. For the Clinton administration's revised position (revised from his campaign) on the issue, see the *New York Times*, 20 July 1993.

19. See *Time*, 26 July 1993, 41. For background, see *USA Today*, 23-26

Dec. 1993, 3A. For different views, see John Boswell, "Battle-Worn," *New Republic*, 10 May 1993, 15-18; and Robert L. Maginnis, "A Case against Lifting the Ban on Homosexuals," *Army*, Jan. 1993, 37-39.

20. *Army Times*, 14 Feb. 1994, 9; *Washington Times*, 10 Feb. 1994, 1. For the reasons I outline in Chapter 6, I strongly agree with a policy that is more restrictive.

21. *Time*, 24 Jan. 1994, 22. For background, see "Annie Get Your Gun," *Time*, 10 May 1993, and the *New York Times*, 28 April 1993, 1.

22. *Washington Times*, 4 May 1994, 1; *New York Times*, 4 May 1994, 20.

23. For example, read the Hippocratic oath.

24. Someone with a warped sense of duty—or someone whose concept of duty amounts solely to self-advancement—is likely to provide a much different answer to the question than we might like.

25. See William J. Bennett, ed., *The Book of Virtues* (New York: Simon & Schuster, 1993). Also excellent is James Q. Wilson, *The Moral Sense* (New York: Macmillan, 1993). A useful review of Wilson is that of Alasdair MacIntyre in the *New York Times Book Review*, 29 Aug. 1993. Also worth noting is Stephen L. Carter, *The Culture of Disbelief* (New York: Basic Books, 1993). For one review of both Carter and Wilson, consult Robert Marquand in the *Christian Science Monitor*, 15 Oct. 1993, 15.

Selected Bibliography

Articles

Adair, R.D., and Joseph C. Myers. "Admission of Gays to the Military: A Singularly Intolerant Act." *Parameters* 23 (Spring 1993): 10-19.

Bahnsen, John C., and Robert W. Cone. "Defining the American Warrior Leader." *Parameters*, Dec. 1990, 24-28.

Bailey, Stephen K. "Ethics and the Public Service." In *Public Administration and Democracy*, ed. Roscoe C. Martin, 283-98. Syracuse, N.Y.: Syracuse Univ. Press, 1965.

Boyd, William P. "Men of Character, Principles of Honor?" *Army*, Sept. 1985, 22-29.

Brennan, Joseph G. "Ambition and Careerism." *Naval War College Review* 44 (Winter 1991): 76-82.

———. "Ethics Instruction in the Military: Teach Them Plato or Hammer It into Their Heads." *Naval War College Review* 42 (Autumn 1989): 55-65.

Buckingham, Clay T. "Ethics and the Senior Officer: Institutional Tensions." *Parameters*, Autumn 1985, 23-32.

Bunting, Josiah. "The Conscience of a Soldier," *Worldview*, Dec. 1973, 6-11.

Burr, Chandler. "Homosexuality and Biology." *Atlantic Monthly*, March 1993, 47-65.

Cahn, Stephen M. "Tangled Ivy." *New Republic*, 18 April 1981, 18-20.

Cantrell, Mark E. "No Place for Homosexuals," *Marine Corps Gazette*, April 1993, 65-73.

Challans, Tim. "Blood-Letting and Goat-Getting." Paper presented to the Joint Service Conference on Professional Ethics, National Defense University, Washington, D.C., 28-29 Jan. 1993.

"Chiefs Back Clinton on Gay-Troop Plan." *New York Times*, 20 July 1993, 1, 12.

Davenport, Manuel M. "Professionals or Hired Guns? Loyalties Are the Difference." *Army*, May 1980, 13-14.

De George, Richard T. "The Need for a Military Code of Ethics." *Army*, Dec. 1984, 22-30.

Diehl, William F. "Ethics and Leadership: The Pursuit Continues." *Military Review*, April 1985, 35-43.

Downs, Fred. "To Kill and Take Ground Is the Reality of War." *Hartford Courant*, 23 Aug. 1987, B1, 4.

Dunlap, Charles J., Jr., "The Origins of the American Military Coup of 2012." *Parameters* 22 (Winter 1992-93): 2-20.

Dyck, Arthur J. "Ethical Bases of the Military Profession." *Parameters* 10 (March 1980): 39-46.

Eidsmoe, John A. "Gays and Guns: The Homosexual and the Armed Forces." Paper presented to the Dean of the Air War College, Maxwell AFB, Ala., Jan. 1993.

Fallows, James. "Military Efficiency." *Atlantic Monthly*, Aug. 1991, 18-21.

Fuentes, Annette. "Equality, Yes—Militarism, No." *The Nation* 253 (28 Oct. 1991): 516-19.

Garvey, Michael. Review of *Carnival Culture*, by James B. Twitchell. *Commonweal*, 9 Oct. 1992, 29-30.

Gold, Philip. "Flak for a Man and His Claim That Few Soldiers Open Fire." *Insight*, 27 March 1989, 18-19.

Gomulka, Eugene T. "Position Paper on the DOD Policy on Homosexuality." Paper presented to the Joint Service Conference on Professional Ethics, National Defense University, Washington, D.C., 28-29 Jan. 1993.

Grace, John J. "The Need to Be More Professional—Whatever That Means." *Naval War College Review* 27 (May-June 1975): 9-23.

Guttman, Allen. "Political Ideals and the Military Ethic." *American Scholar* 34 (1965): 221-37.

Hartle, Anthony E. "Do Good People Make Better Warriors?" *Army*, Aug. 1992, 20-23.

———. "The Ethical Odyssey of Oliver North." *Parameters* 23 (Summer 1993): 28-33.

Helprin, Mark. "At Rest between the Wars," *Assembly*, March 1993, 18-22.

Hertling, Mark P. "Whence Values Come." *Military Review*, Dec. 1987, 16-23.

Hill, Ivan. "What Is Ethical?" *Rotarian*, May 1981, 12.

Horowitz, David. "The Feminist Assault on the Military." *National Review*, 5 Oct. 1992, 46-49.

Hughes, Robert. "The Fraying of America." *Time*, 3 Feb. 1992, 44-49.

Johnson, Kermit D. "Ethical Issues of Military Leadership." *Parameters* 4, no. 2 (1974): 35-39.

"A Just Corner of the Bronx: A Moral Curriculum for the Inner City." *Newsweek*, 1 July 1991, 59.

Kantzer, Kenneth S. "The Pinocchio Syndrome." *Christianity Today*, 6 Oct. 1989, 13.

Karen, Robert. "Shame." *Atlantic Monthly*, Feb. 1992, 40-70.

Katzenbach, Edward L. "Should Our Military Leaders Speak Up?" *New York Times Magazine*, 15 April 1956, 17-39.

Kirk, Russell. "The Necessity of Dogmas in Schooling." *Modern Age* 22 (Winter 1978): 2-7.

"The Knife in the Book Bag." *Time*, 8 Feb. 1993, 37.

Kohn, Richard H. "Women in Combat, Homosexuals in Uniform: The Challenge of Military Leadership." *Parameters* 23 (Spring 1993): 2-4.

Kristol, Irving. "Ethics, Anyone? Or Morals?" *Wall Street Journal*, 15 Sept. 1987, 32.

Lewis, Philip, Karl Kuhnert, and Robert Maginnis. "Defining Character in Military Leaders." In *The Challenge of Military Leadership*, ed. Lloyd J. Matthews and Dale E. Brown, 121-29. (Washington, D.C.: Pergamon-Brassey's, 1989).

Locke, Charles E., Jr. "Leadership Ethics: A Time for Reckoning." *Marine Corps Gazette*, Nov. 1990, 61-62.

MacArthur, Douglas. "Duty, Honor, and Country." *Vital Speeches of the Day* 28 (1 June 1962): 519-21.

Maginnis, Robert L. "A Chasm of Values." *Military Review*, Feb. 1993, 2-11.

Maloney, Samuel D. "Ethics Theory for the Military Professional." *Air University Review*, March-April 1981, 63-71.

"Many Officers, Not Many Gentlemen." *U.S. News & World Report*, 3 May 1993.

Manzo, Louis A. "Morality in War Fighting and Strategic Bombing in World War II." *Air Power History*, Fall 1992, 35-50.

Marsh, John O. "Values and the American Soldier." *Military Review*, Nov. 1986, 4-9.

Martz, Douglas A. "Professional Military Ethics." *Marine Corps Gazette*, Aug. 1990, 57-58.

Matthews, Lloyd J. "Is Ambition Unprofessional?" *Army*, July 1988, 28-37.

———. "Resignation in Protest." *Army*, Jan. 1990, 12-21.

Medved, Michael. "Hollywood's Poison Factory: Making It the Dream Factory Again." *Imprimis*, Nov. 1992.

Mensack, Mark D. "The Homosexual and the Military." Paper presented to the Joint Service Conference on Professional Ethics, National Defense University, Washington, D.C., 28-29 January 1993.

Meyer, Edward C. "Leadership: A Return to Basics." *Military Review*, July 1980, 4-9.

————. "Professional Ethics Is Key to Well-Led, Trained Army." *Army*, Oct. 1980, 11-14.

Mitchell, Terence R., and William G. Scott. "Leadership Failures, the Distrusting Public, and Prospects of the Administrative State." *Public Administration Review* 47 (Nov.-Dec. 1987): 445-52.

"Morality." *U.S. News & World Report*, 9 Dec. 1985, 52-62.

Morgenthau, Hans J. "Epistle to the Columbians." *New Republic*, 21 Dec. 1959, 8-10.

Moskos, Charles. "Army Women." *Atlantic Monthly*, Aug. 1990, 70-78.

Myers, D.G. Review of *Impostors in the Temple* by Martin Anderson, and of *The Idea of the University: A Reexamination*, by Jaroslav Pelikan. *American Spectator*, Jan. 1993, 94-95.

Neuhaus, Richard John. "All Too Human." *National Review*, 2 Dec. 1991, 45.

"The New Top Guns." *Time*, 12 Aug. 1991, 31.

"Pentagon Plans to Allow Combat Flights by Women; Seeks to Drop Warship Ban." *New York Times*, 28 April 1993.

Riley, Don T. "Serve Your Soldiers to Win." *Military Review*, Nov. 1986, 10-19.

Rivers, Julian Pitt. "Honor." In *International Encyclopedia of the Social Sciences*. New York: Macmillan and Free Press, 1968.

Ryan, Alan. Review of *Systems of Survival* by Jane Jacobs. In *New York Review of Books*, 24 June 1993, 3-4.

Sagan, Carl. "A New Way to Think about Rules to Live By." *Parade Magazine*, 28 Nov. 1993, 12-14.

Salkever, Stephen G. "Virtue, Obligation and Politics." *American Political Science Review* 68 (March 1974): 78-92.

"Sea of Lies." *Newsweek*, 13 July 1992, 29-39.

"Secrets of the Cold War." *U.S. News & World Report*, 15 March 1993, 30-55.

"See You in Court." *Time*, 2 Aug. 1993, 29-30.

"Shape Up or Ship Out." *U.S. News & World Report*, 5 April 1993, 24-33.

Smith, Everard H. "Chambersburg: Anatomy of a Confederate Reprisal." *American Historical Review* 96 (April 1991): 432-55.

Smith, Perry M. "Leadership at the Top—Insights for Aspiring Leaders." *Marine Corps Gazette*, Nov. 1990, 33-39.

Snyder, William P., and Kenneth L. Nyberg. "Gays and the Military: An Emerging Policy Issue." *Journal of Political and Military Sociology* 8 (Spring 1980): 71-84.

Sommers, Christina Hoff. "Teaching the Virtues." *Imprimis* 20 (Nov. 1991).

————. "Teaching the Virtues." *Public Interest* 111 (Spring 1993), 3-13.

Sonnenberg, Scott B. "A Philosophical Conflict: A Fighter Pilot's Views on the Ethics of Warfare." *Air University Review*, July-Aug. 1985, 14-23.

Sorley, Lewis. "Beyond Duty, Honor, Country." *Military Review*, April 1987, 2-13.

———. "Competence as an Ethical Imperative." *Army*, Aug. 1982, 42-48.

———. "Doing What's Right: Shaping the Army's Professional Environment." *Parameters*, March 1989, 11-15.

Stockdale, James B. "Moral Leadership." *U.S. Naval Institute Proceedings*, Sept. 1980, 86-89.

———. "The World of Epictetus." *Atlantic Monthly*, April 1978, 98-106.

Swartz, James E. "Morality: A Leadership Imperative." *Military Review* Sept. 1992, 77-83.

Taylor, Maxwell D. "A Do-It-Yourself Professional Code for the Military." *Parameters*, Dec. 1984, 10-15.

———. "A Professional Ethic for the Military?" *Army*, May 1978, 18-21.

Taylor, Porcher L., III. "Professional versus Personal Values." *Military Review*, Nov. 1986, 32-36.

Toner, James H. "Basic Training: No 'Free Lunch'" *Army*, Feb. 1975, 39-41.

———. "Teaching Military Ethics." *Military Review*, May 1993, 33-40.

Truscott, Lucian K., III. "Honor Travels in a Strait So Narrow." *Army*, Aug. 1970, 57.

"Unspeakable." *Time*, 22 Feb. 1993, 48-50.

Van Creveld, Martin. "Why Israel Doesn't Send Women into Combat." *Parameters* 23 (Spring 1993): 5-9.

Vessey, John W., Jr. "A Concept of Service." *Naval War College Review* 37 (Nov.-Dec. 1984): 13-18.

Webb, James. "Witch Hunt in the Navy." *New York Times*, 6 Oct. 1992, 23.

Webster, Alexander F.C. "Paradigms of the Contemporary American Soldier and Women in the Military." *Strategic Review*, Summer 1991, 22-30.

Wenker, Kenneth H. "Morality and Military Obedience." *Air University Review*, July-August 1981, 76-83.

———. "Professional Military Ethics: An Attempt at Definition." *USAFA Journal of Professional Military Ethics* 1 (April 1980) 23-28.

"What Price Honor?" *Time*, 7 June 1976, 18-30.

Whitehead, Barbara Dafoe. "Dan Quayle Was Right." *Atlantic Monthly*, April 1993, 47-84.

Williams, Murat W. "The Faded Specter of Ananias." *Chronicle of Higher Education*, 13 Feb. 1978, 40.

Wolfe, Tom. "The Meaning of Freedom." *Parameters*, March 1988, 2-14.

"Women in Battle." *National Review*, 5 Feb. 1990, 18-19.

"Women in Combat: Maybe? Yes?" *New York Times*, 28 Nov. 1992, 18.
"Women Have What It Takes." *Newsweek*, 5 Aug. 1991, 30.
"Women in the Military." *CQ Researcher* 2 (25 Sept. 1992): 833-55.

Books

Abenheim, Donald. *Reforging the Iron Cross: The Search for Tradition in the West German Armed Forces*. Princeton, N.J.: Princeton Univ. Press, 1988.

Adeney, Bernard T. *Just War, Political Realism, and Faith*. Methuen, N.J.: Scarecrow Press, 1988.

Adler, Mortimer J. *A Guidebook to Learning: For a Lifelong Pursuit of Wisdom*. New York: Macmillan, 1986.

———. *Paideia Problems and Possibilities*. New York: Macmillan, 1983.

Atkinson, Rick. *The Long Gray Line*. Boston: Houghton Mifflin, 1989.

Axinn, Sidney. *A Moral Military*. Philadelphia: Temple Univ. Press, 1989.

Barkalow, Carol, with Andrea Rabb. *In the Men's House*. New York: Poseidon, 1990.

Bellah, Robert N., Richard Madsen, William M. Sullivan, Ann Swidler, and Steven M. Tipton. *The Good Society*. New York: Knopf, 1991.

Bennett, William J., ed. *The Book of Virtues*. New York: Simon and Schuster, 1993.

Bloom, Allan. *The Closing of the American Mind*. New York: Simon & Schuster, 1987.

Bok, Sissela. *Lying: Moral Choice in Public and Private Life*. New York: Pantheon, 1978.

Borchert, Donald M., and David Stewart. *Exploring Ethics*. New York: Macmillan, 1986.

Brennan, Joseph G. *Foundations of Moral Obligation: The Stockdale Course*. Newport, R.I.: Naval War College Press, 1992.

Brodie, Bernard. *War and Politics*. New York: Macmillan, 1973.

Bunting, Josiah. *The Lionheads*. New York: Braziller, 1972.

Cahn, Steven M. *The Eclipse of Excellence*. Washington, D.C.: Public Affairs Press, 1973.

———. *Education and the Democratic Ideal*. Chicago: Nelson-Hall, 1979.

———. *Saints and Scamps: Ethics in Academia*. Totawa, N.J.: Rowman & Littlefield, 1986.

Callahan, Daniel, and Sissela Bok, eds. *Ethics Teaching in Higher Education*. New York: Plenum Press, 1980.

Carhart, Tom. *The Offering*. New York: Morrow, 1987.

Carter, Stephen L. *The Culture of Disbelief*. New York: Basic Books, 1993.

Christopher, Paul. *The Ethics of War and Peace*. Englewood Cliffs, N.J.: Prentice-Hall, 1994.

Cohen, Eliot A., and John Gooch. *Military Misfortunes*. New York: Vintage, 1991.

Cornum, Rhonda, with Peter Copeland. *She Went to War*. Novato, Calif.: Presidio, 1992.

De Gaulle, Charles. *The Edge of the Sword*. Trans. Gerard Hopkins. New York: Criterion, 1960.

Del Vecchio, John M. *The 13th Valley*. New York: Bantam, 1983.

Dyer, Kate, ed. *Gays in Uniform*. Boston: Alyson, 1990.

Fehrenbach, T.R. *This Kind of War*. New York: Pocket Books, 1964.

Fitzgibbon, John F. *Ethics: Fundamental Principles of Moral Philosophy*. Washington, D.C.: University Press of America, 1983.

Flanagan, Edward M. *Before the Battle*. Novato, Calif.: Presidio, 1985.

Ford, Daniel. *Incident at Muc Wa*. Garden City, N.Y.: Doubleday, 1967.

Fotion, Nicholas. *Military Ethics: Looking toward the Future*. Stanford, Calif.: Hoover Press, 1990.

Fotion, Nicholas, and G. Elfstrom. *Military Ethics: Guidelines for Peace and War*. Boston: Routledge & Kegan Paul, 1986.

Frankena, William K. *Ethics*. 2d ed. Englewood Cliffs, N.J.: Prentice-Hall, 1973.

————. *Thinking about Morality*. Ann Arbor: University of Michigan Press, 1980.

Frankl, Viktor E. *Man's Search for Meaning*. 3d ed. New York: Simon & Schuster, 1984.

Gabriel, Richard A. *To Serve with Honor*. New York: Praeger, 1987.

Gabriel, Richard A., and Paul L. Savage. *Crisis in Command*. New York: Hill & Wang, 1978.

Garvin, Lucius. *A Modern Introduction to Ethics*. Boston: Houghton Mifflin, 1953.

Gibson, James W. *The Perfect War*. Boston: Atlantic Monthly Press, 1986.

Hackett, Sir John. *I Was a Stranger*. New York: Berkley, 1987.

————. *The Profession of Arms*. New York: Macmillan, 1983.

Hackworth, David H., and Julie Sherman. *About Face*. New York: Simon & Schuster, 1989.

Hadley, Arthur. *The Straw Giant*. New York: Random House, 1986.

Harman, Gilbert. *The Nature of Morality*. New York: Oxford Univ. Press, 1977.

Hartle, Anthony. *Moral Issues in Military Decision Making*. Lawrence: Univ. Press of Kansas, 1989.

Heinlein, Robert A. *Starship Troopers* New York: Ace, 1987.

Herbert, Anthony B., and James T. Wooten. *Soldier*. New York: Dell, 1973.

Heslep, Robert D. *Education in Democracy: Education's Moral Role in the Democratic State*. Ames: Iowa State University Press, 1989.

Highet, Gilbert. *The Art of Teaching*. New York: Vintage, 1950.

Hirsch, E.D., Jr. *Cultural Literacy*. Boston: Houghton Mifflin, 1987.

Holm, Jeanne. *Women in the Military*. Rev. ed. Novato, Calif.: Presidio, 1992.

Huie, William B. *The Execution of Private Slovik*. New York: Signet, 1954.

Humphrey, Mary Ann. *My Country, My Right to Serve*. New York: HarperCollins, 1990.

Huntington, Samuel P. *The Soldier and the State*. New York: Vintage, 1957.

Janowitz, Morris. *The Professional Soldier*. New York: Free Press, 1971.

Joad, Cyril E.M. *Common-Sense Ethics*. New York: Dutton, 1921.

Jones, Bruce E. *War without Windows*. New York: Berkley, 1987.

Jones, W.T., Frederick Sontag, Morton Beckner, and Robert Fogelin, eds. *Approaches to Ethics*. 3d ed. New York: McGraw-Hill, 1977.

Kilpatrick, William K. *Why Johnny Can't Tell Right from Wrong*. New York: Simon & Schuster, 1992.

Kirk, Russell. *Decadence and Renewal in the Higher Learning*. South Bend, Ind.: Gateway, 1978.

Larrabee, Eric. *Commander in Chief*. New York: Harper & Row, 1987.

Lerner, Max. *Values in Education*. Bloomington, Ind.: Phi Delta Kappa Educational Foundation, 1976.

Lewis, C.S. *The Abolition of Man*. New York: Macmillan, 1947.

Lippmann, Walter. *Essays in the Public Philosophy*. New York: New American Library, 1955.

———. *A Preface to Morals*. New York: Macmillan, 1929.

MacIntyre, Alasdair. *After Virtue*, 2d ed. Notre Dame, Ind.: Univ. of Notre Dame Press, 1984.

———. *Whose Justice? Which Rationality?* Notre Dame, Ind.: Univ. of Notre Dame Press, 1988.

Marshall, S.L.A. *The Officer as a Leader*. Harrisburg, Pa.: Stackpole, 1966.

Matthews, Lloyd J., and Dale E. Brown, eds. *The Challenge of Military Leadership*. Washington, D.C.: Pergamon-Brassey's, 1989.

Matthews, Lloyd J., and Dale E. Brown, eds. *The Parameters of Military Ethics*. Washington, D.C.: Pergamon-Brassey's, 1989.

Military Ethics. Washington, D.C.: National Defense University Press, 1987.

Mitchell, Brian. *Weak Link: The Feminization of the American Military*. Washington, D.C.: Regnery Gateway, 1989.

Moore, Harold G., and Joseph L. Galloway. *We Were Soldiers Once—and Young*. New York: Random House, 1992.

Moral Obligation and the Military: Collected Essays. Washington, D.C.: National Defense University Press, 1988.

Myrer, Anton. *Once an Eagle*. New York: Berkley, 1968.

Neuhaus, Richard John. *America against Itself*. Notre Dame, Ind.: Univ. of Notre Dame Press, 1992.

Neuhaus, Richard John, and George Weigel, eds. *Being Christian Today*. Washington, D.C.: Ethics and Public Policy Center, 1992.

Perry, Mark. *Four Stars*. Boston: Houghton Mifflin, 1989.

Raymond, George L. *Ethics and Natural Law*. 2d ed. New York: Putnam, 1920.

Roche, George. *A World without Heroes*. Hillsdale, Mich.: Hillsdale College Press, 1987.

Ross, J. Elliott. *Christian Ethics*. New York: Devin-Adair, 1948.

Rowe, James N. *Five Years to Freedom*. Boston: Little, Brown, 1971.

Royce, Josiah. *The Philosophy of Loyalty*. New York: Macmillan, 1908.

Sandin, Robert T. *The Rehabilitation of Virtue: Foundations of Moral Education*. New York: Praeger, 1992.

Sarkesian, Sam C. *Beyond the Battlefield: The New Military Professionalism*. New York: Pergamon, 1981.

Schwarzkopf, H. Norman, and Peter Petre. *It Doesn't Take a Hero*. New York: Linda Grey Bantam, 1992.

Sheehan, Neil. *A Bright Shining Lie*. New York: Random House, 1988.

Sheen, Fulton J. *Lift Up Your Heart*. Garden City, N.Y.: Doubleday Image, 1950.

———. *Peace of Soul*. Garden City, N.Y.: Doubleday, 1954.

Silber, John. *Straight Shooting*. New York: Harper & Row, 1989.

Singlaub, John K., and Malcolm McConnell. *Hazardous Duty*. New York: Summit, 1991.

Solomon, Robert C. *Ethics*. New York: McGraw-Hill, 1984.

Sowell, Thomas. *Inside American Education: The Decline, the Deception, the Dogmas*. New York: Free Press, 1993.

Stevens, Richard, and Thomas J. Musial. *Reading Discussing, and Writing about the Great Books*. Boston: Houghton Mifflin, 1970.

Stromberg, Peter L., Malham M. Wakin, and Daniel Callahan. *The Teaching of Ethics in the Military*. Hastings-on-Hudson, N.Y.: Hastings Center, 1982.

Taylor, Robert L., and William E. Rosenbach, eds. *Military Leadership*. 2d ed. Boulder: Westview, 1992.

The Teaching of Ethics in Higher Education. Hastings-on-Hudson, N.Y.: Hastings Center, 1980.

Toner, James H. *The American Military Ethic: A Meditation*. New York: Praeger, 1992.

———. *The Sword and the Cross: Reflections on Command and Conscience.*
    New York: Praeger, 1992.
Twitchell, James B. *Carnival Culture: The Trashing of Taste in America.*
    New York: Columbia Univ. Press, 1992.
Urban, Wilbur M. *Fundamentals of Ethics.* New York: Holt, 1930.
Wakin, Malham M., ed. *War, Morality, and the Military Profession.* 2d ed.
    Boulder: Westview, 1986.
Wellman, Carl. *Moral & Ethics.* 2d ed. Englewood Cliffs, N.J.: Prentice-
    Hall, 1988.
Westmoreland, William C. *A Soldier Reports.* Garden City, N.Y.: Double-
    day, 1976.
Wilson, George C. *Mud Soldiers.* New York: Scribner, 1989.
Wilson, James Q. *On Character.* Washington, D.C.: AEI Press, 1991.
———. *The Moral Sense.* New York: Free Press, 1993.
Wolfe, Alan. *Whose Keeper? Social Science and Moral Obligation.* Berkeley:
    Univ. of California Press, 1989.
Wyatt, Thomas C., and Reuven Gal, eds. *Legitimacy and Commitment in
    the Military.* Westport, Conn.: Greenwood, 1990.

Index